The Choice Principle

The Biblical Case for Legal Toleration

Andy G. Olree

UNIVERSITY PRESS OF AMERICA,® INC.
Lanham • Boulder • New York • Toronto • Oxford

University Press of America,® Inc.
4501 Forbes Boulevard
Suite 200
Lanham, Maryland 20706
UPA Acquisitions Department (301) 459-3366

PO Box 317
Oxford
OX2 9RU, UK

Printed in the United States of America
British Library Cataloging in Publication Information Available

Library of Congress Control Number: 2006921599
ISBN-13: 978-0-7618-3453-2 (paperback : alk. paper)
ISBN-10: 0-7618-3453-3 (paperback : alk. paper)

∞™ The paper used in this publication meets the minimum
requirements of American National Standard for Information
Sciences—Permanence of Paper for Printed Library Materials,
ANSI Z39.48—1992

To Kelley

My wife and confidante,
And an expert on toleration

Contents

Introduction

This is a book about evangelical Christians living in a democratically controlled country called the United States. It is a book about what these Christians have done, and will do, with their political influence in that democracy. It is about a group of Christians who believe in absolute truth that can be known from Scripture; who believe in an all-powerful and all-loving God; who believe that certain miraculous, earth-shattering events actually occurred in history; and who believe in obligatory standards of personal morality that do not change according to culture, time, or convenience. And it is about whether all that truth must somehow be written into our laws.

If one central premise undergirds the evangelical Christian movement, it might be this: an insistence on unchanging, knowable truth. Evangelicals believe in a God who not only speaks truth, but is truth. They believe in a God who does not change, who made himself known through a son who does not change, who ultimately revealed his will to mankind through Scriptures that do not change. Having made himself known to men, he is knowable by men. He longs to be known, demands to be known, as he is—not as we would have him to be. And once he is known, by knowledge of his son through the Scriptures, he changes us. Truth changes us, and we become born again. We spread the truth to others because truth matters. Evangelicals are evangelical because they believe they know the unalterable, eternal, life-changing truth.

Growing numbers of evangelicals are frustrated these days by a surrounding culture that seems increasingly to disagree with them. The disagreement is not just about the content of the truth. Rather, evangelicals are frustrated—in fact, shocked—that the culture around them, including many who wear the name Christian, seem to doubt the very existence of "truth," at least as evangelicals understand that word. Seemingly, every moral principle has become relative, everything we thought we agreed on is up for grabs, and toleration of competing visions of the good is the order of the day. Scripture, and even Jesus himself, now serve as (at most) signposts cryptically suggesting optional paths on one's spiritual journey, rather than historical models of perfection or the revealed mind of God.

In the arena of American politics and public policy, evangelical frustration has sometimes manifested itself in calls to political action. Viewpoints on the political Right have until recently dominated popular evangelical discourse in the United States. But the evangelical Left, too, is frustrated by moral relativism and has begun gaining attention in its appeals for political action to combat poverty, racial and gender discrimination, and the squandering of natural resources, for example. More often than not, all these evangelical appeals have taken the form of diatribes against sinful popular culture, coupled with calls to political activism of a sort that will "lead this nation back to God." Gone are the days when the bulk of American evangelicals thought of politics as dirty and unworthy of Christian attention. Instead, the clarion call among today's evangelical spokesmen, Right and Left, as well as a great number of the rank and file, is a militaristic appeal to use the machinery of democracy to "take the government by storm."

But evangelicals are struggling to conceive of a truly evangelical, consistent, unifying understanding of Scripture that supports these appeals. Evangelicals and fundamentalists on the political Right, in particular, have failed to use their advantages of grass roots organization and media attention to articulate a consistent theology. Their appeals are rife with examples of the cultural problems evangelicals see around them—abortion on demand, legalized euthanasia, homosexual marriages, legalized pornography, publicly funded teen pregnancy, and the like—but have offered little in the way of a thorough and consistent plan for godly political action, and even less in the way of biblical justifications for their own particular preferences for legislation or tolerance. This is certainly curious coming from a group making such strong claims about the supreme authority of the Bible in all human affairs. Although some evangelicals have brightened this picture a bit during the last twenty or thirty years by their diligent work toward an evangelical public philosophy, their work appears to be unknown or unheeded by the most popular politically conservative evangelical spokespeople, who continue to call for particular legislation and other political action *ad hoc*, without any deeper supporting analysis than an identification of the various moral precepts our culture has forsaken. In fact, evangelicals as a group have yet to widely accept even the rudiments of a consistent, thorough theology that makes sense of their particular policy preferences in light of their insistence on biblical authority.

Instead, many evangelicals seem to assume that such a theological framework is unnecessary. Once the societal problems are demonstrated and accepted, the political solutions will be self-evident to any true Christian. If the problem is pornography, then obviously pornography must be outlawed. If the problem is alcohol abuse, outlaw alcohol (or severely limit its availability). If the problem is homosexuality, then make homosexual acts illegal, or deny homosexuals' monogamous pairings the legal status of "marriage." If the problem is that children are never told about God, then require public school teachers to teach creation science. If the problem is poverty, then tax the rich and force them to support the poor. And so on. Those Christians reluctant to follow our particular political prescriptions are said to be hypocritical—claiming a new birth but unwilling to submit to Christ in the voting booth. They are denying the truth in political matters. Or perhaps they have been deceived by the secular humanists and moral relativists into believing that there is no absolute truth at all.

These seem to be the assumptions of a great many popular evangelical leaders today. And yet the fact is that one can logically endorse the moral absolutes revealed in Scripture without also believing that God wants Christians to impose them on other people through the law. And there's the rub. Evangelicals are fighting so hard against moral relativism that they have neglected to provide a biblical justification for the particular set of laws they support. Current evangelical political discussions spend lots of time and ink endorsing lists of particular moral standards regarded as "absolute" and marshaling biblical support for these, and then comparing these lists to secular culture. The analyses may then include calls to specific political action. But they are virtually silent on the *separate* question of *what God's will is*—not regarding the moral standards, but regarding the *political action*—and how we know. Perhaps they are silent because they have never understood this to be a logically separate question.

What emerges from within the mainstream of evangelicalism, then, is a sometimes subtle, sometimes explicit political orthodoxy. It is assumed that Christians who believe in absolute truth, who take the lordship of Christ seriously, will of course vote to change the sinful culture—by outlawing it. Those who understand the evil that's going on in the world but are unwilling to vote to outlaw it are obviously unwilling to accept Christ as lord of their political lives. They have loved the world too much. They have bought into its godless philosophies. They must wear the label of moral relativist—or worse. Perhaps some, having found themselves unable conscientiously to support the legislative agenda of some evangelical spokesperson, have been led to doubt whether they are really evangelicals after all. Could it be that an understood evangelical political orthodoxy has even caused some to abandon faith in Christ altogether, or never to take it up in the first place?

This state of affairs saddens me. I myself am an evangelical. I believe that evangelicals have much of value to say to a morally untethered world. I believe the personal sacrifice and piety of countless evangelicals has greatly improved the human condition over the centuries, to God's glory. But I believe evangelicals have been widely dismissed from dominant political conversation in the United States because some of their most visible leaders have insisted, erroneously and unnecessarily, on an intolerant political and legislative agenda that is not to be found in the pages of God's word.

This book is my humble attempt to suggest the possibility of a different, and still thoroughly evangelical, theology. I hope to demonstrate, first and foremost, that there is no place for a political litmus test in the Lord's church. Christians need not be Republicans, or Democrats, in order to be Christians. Most evangelicals would probably agree with this assertion in principle, but when it comes to certain political issues we deem to be crucial (abortion laws, laws defining marriage, laws about racism, or whatever the issue might be), we (individually and sometimes collectively) act as if all true Christians must think and vote alike. But sincere Christians, indeed sincere and thoughtful evangelicals, may have differing public policy preferences without sacrificing faith commitments along the way. For example, I hope to show how one could conclude that it is wrong to outlaw prostitution, while remaining a sincere evangelical Christian—that is, insisting on unchanging, knowable truth exactly as revealed in the Scriptures, believing in spiritual rebirth through the saving power of the cross, and feeling assured of eternal life and responsible for sharing this good news with others.

Secondly, I hope to provide a further tentative step toward the development of a consistent, rational, biblically sound theology of political involvement. The understanding I propose is organized around a theme I call the Choice Principle. The Choice Principle is not intended to become the new political orthodoxy, excluding as Non-Christians (or non-evangelicals) those who disagree with us politically. We don't need more political orthodoxy. What *is* urgently needed among evangelicals is a political *theology*, by which I mean both an orderly exposition of God's will and a legitimate method of inquiry for determining God's will. If we believe we should be politically active, we need to know why we believe this, and we need an organized and internally consistent theory explaining how we should go about it. We need a biblically derived and consistent set of political preferences, and we need a legitimate, evangelical way of discovering these. At its best, theology of this sort does not draw boundary lines of fellowship, but rather opens the floor for debate, for the proposal of contrary theologies.

The Choice Principle posits that Christians are called to influence law and government in ways that maximize opportunities for human freedom of choice—that is, for individual autonomy. This book offers the Choice Principle as a possible alternative to the current evangelical political orthodoxies of the Right and Left. And yet the understanding I propose is not purely passive; the theology of the Choice Principle provides support for evangelicals who feel called to be politically active, who believe that part of Christian duty is civic duty. This is a message evangelicals need to hear. Many outside evangelicalism need to hear it as well, though, because too often evangelicals acting in the political sphere are assumed to be little more than theocrats. Observers often criticize evangelical politicians (like former presidential candidate Pat Robertson) for reading the Bible too literally, or for being too intolerant of sin, when the real problem with Robertson and his ilk is their unsupported and largely unstated background assumption that God for some reason wants most overt sins to be penalized or corrected by human governments, unless there are really good reasons not to do so. One need not become tolerant of sin or view the Bible as fable in order to dispute that unexamined supposition. Christians, even evangelical Christians, may conscientiously, consistently, and rationally oppose any efforts to force God's moral code upon mankind at gunpoint, without embracing moral relativism in any form.

The secularism pervading our culture presents Christians with many challenges and opportunities, but evangelicals have often responded to it unproductively, with mere astonishment and perhaps defensiveness. Chapter 1 documents that response by some notable evangelical leaders and attempts, in a limited way, to explain it, and also to warn of its dangers. Before the Scriptures are analyzed in detail, Chapter 2 introduces some of the competing theological possibilities through a study of selected influential Christians and their political theologies. Turning then to the Scriptures for guidance in the realm of politics and law, the first question one confronts is whether God prefers that Christians remain altogether uninvolved politically. Chapters 3 and 4 examine that question in light of the biblical text, concluding that it is plausible that God wants Christians to view political involvement in a democracy as a stewardship opportunity. The next question is whether God prefers any certain type of public policy over any other. This question is taken up in Chapters 5 and 6, which make the biblical case for the Choice Principle as a possible foundation for a consistent, rational, and biblical political theology. Chapter 7 examines some of the most common objections to proposals like the Choice Principle. One of the most powerful objections, in my view, has been raised by Robert George in his book *Making Men Moral*, and in Chapter 8 I address his particular arguments. Chapter 9 suggests some real-world applications of the Choice Principle in deciding amongst competing public policies. In Chapter 10, I apply the Choice Principle in one especially controversial context: the ongoing religious and political debate in America about abortion and abortion rights. In Chapter 11, I offer a few brief concluding observations.

I propose the Choice Principle as a possibility, not a certainty. If nothing else, I hope to illustrate a coherent alternative to the narrow streams now carrying evangelical political discourse—not to establish a watertight argument that ends political discussion, but to provide a starting point for expanding political discussion. If this book causes more evangelicals to think through the issues, I will be pleased. I believe this sort of theology—this healthy contemplation of the will of God in all areas of politics, derived from core evangelical assumptions about absolute truth—is too rare among us. But it is urgently needed as more and more evangelicals consider their role as citizens in a democracy.

Part I

OUR PLACE IN HISTORY

Chapter One

A Land of Confusion

It's hard to live like Jesus, these days. Sometimes it seems as if each new day brings with it a new cost of discipleship, imposed by the godless culture around us. Anyone with a television set is reminded daily of our culture's emphasis on the material and the base, on physical beauty, wealth, and unlimited sexual titillation. How simple life would be, we are inclined to believe, if only the world around us shared our basic values! If only MTV specialized in prompting questions like "What happens after I die?" instead of "How can I get rid of pimples?" or "How can I have sex with someone who looks like that?"

In fact, a whole cottage industry has developed, supported largely by Christian consumers, whose stock in trade is criticizing "today's culture" and blaming it for a host of our social problems. The charges are familiar: Crime rates are skyrocketing. Divorce has obsoleted the "traditional family." Abortions are performed casually. Illegitimate births are a national epidemic. School children are gunning down their teachers and classmates. Illicit drugs are everywhere. Violence and sex flood the airwaves and cables. All mention of God is being systematically removed from our public life. Homosexuality is publicly celebrated. With all the forces of secularism and immorality arrayed against Christians in our culture, it certainly is hard to live like Jesus these days.

But before taking our cultural criticism too far, maybe we should ask whether these assertions are true. The evidence does not always back up our claims that things are getting worse all the time. Sometimes crime rates drop. Sometimes our public officials do pray or otherwise recognize God, and in any event such recognition is probably much more common in America today than in most cultures and times in human history. In fact, the current U.S. President is an outspoken evangelical Christian. Sometimes Christians control the radio and television programs; sometimes the Christian perspective dominates the broadcasts, particularly in the many small rural markets across the country. In an increasingly tolerant and diverse society in which over 80 percent of us profess to be "Christian,"[1] the penalty for wearing Christ's name is probably no more severe in American culture today than in other cultures and times.

So while it certainly is hard to live like Jesus these days, the truth is, it's hard to live like Jesus, *any* days. It was fairly challenging in the first century, too. Jesus himself tried living like Jesus, and look what happened to him. Later in the first century, a similar fate awaited many others who tried living like Jesus. It would seem that "secularism" was not unknown even in the culture of the first century. Of course, the Christians of the first century knew nothing of the "trials" of living in a society in which their neighbors could access pornography at will over the internet, or where their children might be forced to read Darwin's *The Origin of Species* in school without concurrently being taught the account of creation found in the book of Genesis. But they did live in a culture that practiced infanticide, winked at notorious homosexuality, glorified torture and violence for public entertainment, and cruelly abused the poor and weak. It has a familiar sound. Add to this a heap of compulsory patriotic sacrifices in pagan temples, and a legal regime that occasionally imposed the death penalty for the crime of professing Christianity, and you have a recipe for a fairly immoral society. Maybe twenty-first century American culture is not so uniquely depraved after all.

In *any* culture, the main difficulty with living like Jesus is that to do it right, one must be prepared to die like Jesus. And that means, first, dying to self. There are no short cuts. Two thousand years have come and gone, cultures have risen, thrived, and disappeared; but the challenge of Christianity remains the same. Jesus said:

> A disciple is not above the teacher, nor a slave above the master; it is enough for the disciple to be like the teacher, and the slave like the master. If they have called the master of the house Beelzebul, how much more will they malign those of his household! (Matt. 10:24–25)

We Christians are disciples of Jesus of Nazareth. Our "teacher" and "master" was a wandering rabbi who was crucified for stirring up trouble in Jerusalem at Passover. Whatever culture surrounds us, we must surely expect persecution and trials. "Living like Jesus" has never been a good strategy even for laying low, much less for receiving heartfelt acceptance into the dominant culture. It is somewhat puzzling, then, why we should be so shocked that our culture makes it difficult for us to follow Jesus Christ—or why we should long to be accepted by the sinful, complacent American culture in the first place. Nevertheless, a stroll through almost any Christian bookstore will confirm that many Christian authors in the United States are actually surprised by the sinfulness, not just of individual Americans, but of "American culture." The September 11 attacks have reminded us that these authors are not alone in their shock, or their assessment of our culture.

EVANGELICAL BEWILDERMENT

If it is tough to be a Christian in America today, it is even tougher to be an evangelical Christian. Evangelicals feel particularly persecuted, in fact positively bewildered, by American culture. To fully understand why this is so, it is necessary to understand something of the evangelical world view.

In a 2001 survey of 2,041 American adults, each respondent who claimed to be "Christian" was asked whether he considered himself either "evangelical" or "born again." Those who answered yes were termed "evangelical" for purposes of the survey. Using this measure, the survey showed that 36 percent of the American population are evangelicals.[2] Self-identified "evangelicals," then, comprise something like one-third of the population of our country—a huge group. Some self-identified "evangelicals" are found in what are conventionally thought of as "mainline Protestant denominations," such as the Episcopal Church and the United Methodist Church. But far higher concentrations of evangelicals are found in more religiously conservative fellowships, including Baptist, Pentecostal, and nondenominational and independent fellowships such as "community churches."[3] What do these people think they have in common with one another? Why might they see themselves as having more in common with other "evangelicals" than with other members of their own denominations? In short, what does the term "evangelical" mean?

Answering these questions requires a definition of "evangelical" that delineates based on core beliefs rather than denominational affiliations or self-identification. Mark Noll, one of today's foremost authorities on American evangelicalism, has adopted a useful definition of evangelicalism originally propounded by the British historian David W. Bebbington. Using this definition, let us assume that evangelical Christians are those Christians, from whatever denominational affiliation, who: (1) rely on a common sense interpretation of the Bible as their ultimate religious authority; (2) stress the literal death and resurrection of Christ as the key to human well-being; (3) seek a life-changing "new birth" conversion for salvation; and (4) practice their faith actively in obedience to God, especially by seeking converts to Christianity.[4]

This definition of "evangelical" gives us some important clues about the evangelical world view. Evangelicals assume that the best way to know God and his will for man is by reading the Bible for oneself, without human mediation or interpretation. This implies a certain emphasis on basic education—at least to obtain rudimentary English reading skills (and sometimes even skills in reading ancient Greek or Hebrew)—coupled with an innate trust in each person's common sense intuition. It simultaneously betrays a certain mistrust of higher education, theology, intellectualism, religious hierarchies, and clergy who claim to have special spiritual insight. Evangelicals also assume Jesus was an actual person who did real miracles, including rising from the dead. This perhaps implies faith in a powerful God, a God worth praying to, who sometimes supernaturally intervenes in human affairs even today. Evangelicals' stress on the new birth conversion is indicative of their conviction that human beings can and must radically change their sinful habits through the power of God. And the evangelical emphasis on activism and evangelism tells us that they believe good works are important—if not for salvation itself, then at least as an aid to others and as the outward sign of a saved soul.

But arguably these beliefs are premised upon an even more fundamental assumption, an assumption about the nature of truth. In order for evangelicals to believe what they believe, they must begin with an assumption that there is such a thing as "truth," that it does not vary for different people or times or according to human preferences, and that it is significantly knowable. For evangelicals, God is truth, and he possesses all these characteristics in full measure. He manifested himself in the form of his son Jesus, who was the personification of truth. Evangelicals also believe their most reliable source of truth is the Bible, the meaning of which is unchanging over the centuries and significantly ascertainable by ordinary people. All this means that most evangelicals could also be classified as moral absolutists, by which I mean those Christians and Non-Christians who believe in an absolute and unchanging moral code that is binding on everyone in every time and culture.[5] Evangelicals believe that God, like truth, does not change. They believe his unchanging nature demanded an atonement for sin, which Jesus provided on the cross. They believe that knowledge of the truth is life-changing, and because no one should live in ignorance, they feel compelled to spread the gospel.

Hence, assumptions about absolute truth arguably provide the foundation for the entire evangelical world view in each of its distinctive features. This is certainly not to say that evangelicals are the only ones who believe in absolute truth, or even that all evangelicals do.[6] It is merely to say that as a general rule, a belief in absolute truth, including moral absolutes, characterizes *evangelicals* as a group but may *not* characterize *non-evangelicals* as a group, at least in the United States today. For example, in a recent survey, when asked whether "morals should be based on an absolute, unchanging standard," 68 percent of self-identified evangelicals said yes, compared to only 31 percent of other respondents.[7] Data like this suggest that the evangelicals' dedication to the idea of absolute truth, including the idea of moral absolutes, may set them apart from others. At any rate, many evangelicals clearly believe this to be the case, as we will soon see.

The number of evangelicals in the United States is growing. Between 1990 and 2001, while membership was declining among many non-evangelical fellowships nationwide, evangelicals have seen their numbers increase by 42 percent.[8] And the number of people identifying themselves as "nondenominational Christians"—a key identifier for many U.S. evangelicals—increased by a whopping 1,120 percent.[9] Statistics like these astound many observers outside evangelicalism. As I write this in October of 2005, NBC has just aired a one hour prime time program called *Tom Brokaw Reports: In God They Trust*, in which Brokaw examines the rising prominence of American evangelicals. When evangelicals begin talking about changing the culture, when they preach about how Christianity ought to affect their political choices, when they in fact exert a decisive influence as a voting block in the name of Jesus, some outsiders clearly feel more than just an intellectual curiosity; they feel threatened. They wonder: Do evangelicals want to take over American government? Do they want to remake American culture? What would that look like?

Evangelicals may be quite patriotic, praising what they see as traditional American values and the "American way of life," but as a group they are clearly not very happy with today's American culture. Evangelical literature is replete with critiques of postmodernist moral relativism and calls for a cultural acknowledgment of absolute truth, especially regarding matters of morality, even as the surrounding American culture seems (to them) less and less inclined to admit any absolutes whatever.[10] In fact, some research suggests that most American evangelicals feel persecuted or disrespected by their culture precisely because of a perceived increase in moral relativism and secularism in the dominant culture.[11] They may have some reason to feel this way. Robert Wuthnow reports that during the 1980s, at least, surveys showed a substantial decrease in tolerance of evangelicals and fundamentalists by the nation as a whole.[12] Moreover, national Gallup surveys

> in 1981 and again in 1987 showed, respectively, that 11 percent and 13 percent of the public would not like to have fundamentalists as neighbors; the proportions expressing similar attitudes toward Catholics and Jews, respectively, were 1 percent and 2 percent in 1981, and 1 percent and 3 percent in 1987.[13]

But regardless of how "secular" American culture really is or how the dominant culture views evangelicals, it is at least clear that many evangelicals, perhaps most, believe American culture discounts their values and upholds values of moral toleration and diversity in place of the notion of absolute moral truth. Researchers in a national telephone survey in 1996, for example, found that 77 percent of self-identified evangelicals believed that the mass media is hostile to their own moral and spiritual values. Less than half of all other respondents reported feeling such persecution.[14] And 93 percent of evangelicals agreed that "Christian values are under serious attack in the United States today."[15] In a more recent survey conducted in 2004, the numbers had not changed much, at least among white evangelicals: 75 percent of white evangelicals (but only 52 percent of the general population including evangelicals) agreed that "the mass media is hostile toward my moral and spiritual values," and fully 47 percent of white evangelicals said they believe that "evangelical Christians are looked down upon by most Americans."[16]

For purposes of my argument here, it is not so important to document whether there is *actually* a phenomenon presently occurring in American society that could properly be called a "culture war."[17] The important point is that large numbers of American evangelicals *believe* that such is the case. Not only this, but they believe they are called to participate in that war, on the side of the moral absolutists, fighting against the forces of creeping moral relativism and toleration in our culture. And they believe they are the underdogs.

CHRISTIANS AGAINST CULTURE

If many Christians at large, and evangelicals in particular, feel themselves persecuted or marginalized by mainstream American culture, it is understandable that they would want to talk about it. Few would suggest that Christians should court persecution at the hands of their surrounding culture, or blithely acquiesce in it. Paul certainly didn't. When cultural or governmental persecution was *avoidable*, at any rate, Paul seems to have insisted on his legal rights, calling for an end to the discrimination and immorality in the culture around him.[18] Perhaps Christians should follow his example.

In America today, if we don't agree with something, we generally have the legal right to speak against it publicly. Many Christians who disagree with certain values, values they believe are being praised and propped up by the dominant culture, have been busy doing just that. By now a number of vocal Christians—including such popular authors as William Bennett, Stephen Carter, Os Guinness, and many others—have produced quite a volume of work criticizing American secular culture and its immoral values.

In general, Christians should probably recognize this social criticism as a positive development. Authentic Christianity will always be countercultural, so it should come as no surprise that conscientious Christians, following the lead of their master, would more often criticize than praise the surrounding culture. Jesus' ministry was characterized by discomfort, nonconformity, and intense criticism of the ungodliness and hypocrisy he saw in the world around him. He was, quite simply, divisive. Recall his own words from Matt. 10:34–36:

> Do not think that I have come to bring peace to the earth; I have not come to bring peace, but a sword.
> For I have come to set a man against his father,
> and a daughter against her mother,
> and a daughter-in-law against her mother-in-law;
> and one's foes will be members of one's own household.

This is not the language of a member of the hegemonic power structure, a defender of the status quo. This is the language of a rebel, a fly in the ointment; and it is, in large measure, the language of the "Christians against culture" movement. Our Lord was in fact a rebel against the cultural establishment of his day, and for this he was executed. To the extent today's critics echo the concerns Jesus voiced, we should celebrate their discipleship, rather than chiding them for appearing radical, judgmental, or looney.

Another reason to celebrate this movement is that it is saying something people need to hear. Some of the societal criticism voiced by these vocal Christians rings true. In the first place, several Christians have recently been decrying a secularism in our society that often results in prejudice against religious people and viewpoints, especially in discussions of public policy or social welfare.[19] Secularists ought to admit that policy arguments founded on religious values are no more *per se* illegitimate than policy arguments based on their own deeply-held moral values, values such as "genocide is wrong" or "diversity is good." Everyone who values open discourse and pluralism owes the Christian critics a debt of gratitude for shining light on the anti-religious bigotry that sometimes infects our culture and our public discourse. In the second place, some statistical measures show that America really does have some stubborn social problems that are getting worse instead of better.[20] It does not seem so farfetched to claim, as some Christian critics have, that many of these may be related to a general moral decline in our culture that can be documented by attitudinal survey data. For two and a half millennia respected philosophers have told us that societies without virtue are destined to crumble, to implode upon themselves.[21] The Bible makes the same point.[22] Noted historians also attest to the importance of virtue spread through society.[23] And certainly intuition confirms this truth. It does not take a great genius, for example, to figure out that: (1) unwed teen pregnancies create more societal problems than they solve; (2) a great number of these pregnancies would be prevented if more unwed teens abstained from premarital sex; and (3) more unwed teens would abstain from premarital sex if they were reared in an environment that frowned on premarital sex as immoral.

Christians, of all people, should be emphasizing the importance of virtue and purity in society. Of course, it is a separate question what Christians should do to encourage virtue among others; but it should be indisputable that a society characterized by a high level of individual virtue is desirable, and that American culture today stands a long way from that noble goal. The best Christian social criticism reminds us of the need for a virtue-rich society and provides suggestions for measuring our progress toward it.

THE FEARMONGERS

But Christian criticism of the sinful culture becomes counterproductive when it turns into sensationalist fearmongering. Sadly, a significant amount of what passes for Christian social commentary these days, especially the most popular politically conservative social commentary in fundamentalist quarters, is little more than that. Failing to present current American culture in historical perspective, these vitriols often portray American society as if nothing so blatantly immoral had ever before been seen on the face of the earth. Of course this is demonstrably false, as even a cursory familiarity with ancient Rome or medieval Europe will confirm. The Fearmongers typically refer us to an idyllic American moral past which supposedly began in the colonial or founding era and continued until about the 1950s, when America lost her Christian moral footing and began the slide to depravity. They make a number of tenuous claims about the "Christian values" upon which our government institutions were supposedly "founded" and the common morality that Americans supposedly "shared" throughout the nineteenth and early twentieth centuries. In the process they fail to mention, or gloss over, the many documented instances of public and private immorality and heterodoxy in American history: rampant prostitution and alcoholism, severe social and legal restrictions on women, institutionalized slavery, imperialism and wars of aggression, religious bigotry and persecutions, the unchecked greed and corruption of powerful leaders of government and industry, and the deep dissenting convictions of many persecuted minority groups. They also tend to exaggerate the dangers secularism poses to Christianity in the United States today, sometimes implying that Christians themselves are a persecuted minority in danger of extinction—even as they claim membership in a "moral majority." At the same time these Fearmongers simplistically reduce complex societal problems to a contest between moral absolutes and moral relativism, which they in turn equate with the age-old struggle of good versus evil (implying in some cases, for example, that school violence is attributable to certain U.S. Supreme Court decisions forbidding government sponsored prayer in schools).

Such appeals are packed with emotional power, certainly, but they lack analytical rigor. At their worst, they are sensationalist, paranoid, and intemperate. They divide the world into two camps—Us and Them—and demonize all who disagree with their political agenda as either hypocrites or Non-Christians. One wishes to be charitable, but these sorts of claims must proceed from either a self-conscious attempt to deceive or a woefully insufficient attention to history and our place in it.

Roy Moore

One of the most famous Fearmongers of recent days is Alabama's former Chief Justice Roy S. Moore. Moore made a national reputation for himself in the mid-nineties, during his days as a state trial court judge, by posting a homemade plaque of the Ten Commandments in his courtroom and refusing to remove it even after being sued, claiming that the legal systems of the United States were all founded upon a belief in God and that he must obey God rather than men. Widely known as the "Ten Commandments judge" ever after, he received awards from a number of Christian organizations, including Samford University, the American Family Association, the Family Research Council, Vision America, and the D. James Kennedy Center for Christian Statesmanship. He began to make appearances on Jerry Falwell's "Old Time Gospel Hour," Pat Robertson's "The 700 Club," James Dobson's "Focus on the Family" radio program, and other national platforms. His rising popularity helped him win statewide election in 2000 as Chief Justice of the Alabama Supreme Court.[24] Within a year he had erected a 5,300-pound granite monument to the Ten Commandments in the Supreme Court building rotunda, which he again refused to remove even after he was sued. In August of 2003 a federal court ordered Moore to remove the monument, finding its display to be a violation of the First Amendment to the U.S. Constitution; upon his refusal to comply with the court order his eight colleagues on the Alabama Supreme Court ordered it removed and put into storage. Chief Justice Moore was himself removed from the bench three months later by unanimous decision of the nine-member Court of the Judiciary of Alabama. The Court of the Judiciary found that Moore's refusal to comply with the nation's highest law, as interpreted by the federal courts, had violated the Alabama Canons of Judicial Ethics. As of this writing, Moore has just announced his candidacy for the office of Alabama governor.[25]

Roy Moore's drive to display the Ten Commandments was based on his belief that the state and national governments of the United States were founded upon Christianity and cannot survive without acknowledging their divine source of authority. Undeterred by the failure of the U.S. Constitution to mention God, Divine Providence, the Creator, Christianity, true religion, or anything of the sort, Moore claims that "God's law was the source of our law and the basis of our Constitution."[26] Within the First Amendment's statement that "Congress shall make no law respecting an establishment of religion, or prohibiting the free exercise thereof"—or perhaps despite this statement—Moore finds "that the First Amendment to the U.S. Constitution is founded on a belief that we have a duty to worship God."[27]

In fact, to Moore, history is crystal clear on this point, and all the evidence points the same way:

> [The] Ten Commandments acknowledged a particular God. Many Christian theologians . . . have been misled to believe that our government must be neutral toward God for others to have freedom of conscience. But our founding fathers believed it was a particular God—the God of the Holy Scriptures—who gave man freedom of conscience with which the government could not interfere. . . .
>
> [The] God of the Bible is the basis for America's religious and civil liberty. It is a historic and legal fact that America was founded by Christians on the God of the Holy Scriptures who gave the Ten Commandments to Moses on Mt. Sinai.[28]

But Moore believes those Founding Era ideals have recently been betrayed:

> America was founded on a belief in God and God's law. . . .
>
> The men who drafted the Declaration of Independence and the U.S. Constitution were godly men who consciously, respectfully, and overtly acknowledged the providence of God. . . .
>
> But during the past one hundred years there has been a lapse in instruction on these basic concepts. Today, the ACLU, Freethought Association, Americans United for Separation of Church and State, and other such groups are seeking to remove the knowledge of God from our land. It is our right, indeed our duty, to resist.[29]

Groups like the American Civil Liberties Union, then, are trying to change First Amendment law, not enforce it. Moore is sure such groups are opposed to governmental endorsements of God because the groups are filled with libertines who do not believe in any higher moral code:

> The acknowledgment of God by the state [is] an obstacle to [the ACLU's philosophy] because it implied a higher law by which all people are bound and

> within which freedom exists. Those who wish to be free of God's law are "offended" by the recognition of a higher moral code that restricts their behavior.[30]

Moore believes America is allowing secularist groups like the ACLU to rewrite our history and our laws, and we are denying God in the process. Forsaking our godly heritage as we have, Moore warns, endangers our nation's very survival:

> As citizens, we must be aware of attempts to subvert our law and government. An understanding of our history is crucial to a vision of our future. No longer can we afford to ignore attempts to destroy our culture and our heritage by efforts to create a new world by divorcing ourselves from God. . . .
>
> [America] is fighting a long battle against a cancer that has sapped our strength, restricted our freedom, and confined us as a people. The removal of our right to publicly acknowledge God is a cancer that will slowly take the life of our nation, and it must be stopped! . . .
>
> There is a spiritual battle raging across our land—a battle between good and evil, right and wrong, light and darkness. This is a struggle between those who acknowledge Almighty God and those who deny His sovereignty.[31]

According to Moore, the battle is simple to understand. It is a struggle between the good guys and the bad guys. No one in the fight has mixed motives or a morally ambiguous character, and there is no possible neutrality. Those who would keep the government silent about God are the bad guys. They are not only denying our history, but denying God, and this is clearly because they don't want to be bound by his laws in their own lives. The solution is clear. Our governments must return to their roots and become godly again. And apparently, godly governments are those that make laws explicitly endorsing "the God of the Holy Scriptures" while for some reason remaining scrupulously silent about the resurrected Christ, the Holy Spirit, salvation by grace, heaven and hell, and most other matters of eternal significance.

Jerry Falwell

Roy Moore is not the only Christian who predicts doom for America unless we repent. Moore's vision of America's past and future, from the pious Founding to the current list of villains who would deny our godly heritage, is very reminiscent of an exchange between Jerry Falwell and Pat Robertson on an episode of *The 700 Club* airing shortly after the September 11 terrorist attacks:

> FALWELL: The abortionists have got to bear some burden for this because God will not be mocked. And when we destroy 40 million little innocent babies, we

> make God mad. I really believe that the pagans, and the abortionists, and the feminists, and the gays and the lesbians who are actively trying to make that an alternative lifestyle, the ACLU, People for the American Way—all of them who have tried to secularize America—I point the finger in their face and say, 'You helped this happen.'
>
> ROBERTSON: Well, I totally concur, and the problem is we have adopted that agenda at the highest levels of our government. . . . And, the top people, of course, is the court system.[32]

Hence those "who have tried to secularize America" are aiding and abetting the terrorists. And the courts, by protecting the rights of homosexuals and abortionists and the ACLU, have promoted sin in our culture, thereby causing God to allow terrorists to kill our people.

Jerry Falwell, of course, is a longtime advocate of the Fearmongers' pristine-founding-to-current-depravity myth of American history. Sometimes credited with creating the Religious Right as a moving force in politics, Falwell is the founder of the now-defunct Moral Majority and the founder and Chancellor of Liberty University, and frequently appears on national news talk shows. The following passage is typical of his social commentary:

> Today our widespread rejection of the historic faith of our fathers, however, and because of a loss of commitment to the family, we are seeing an erosion which can result in our decline as a great country. [sic] Never before has the American family been in so much trouble. . . .
>
> No single institution in our society has done more to undermine time-honored traditional American moral and spiritual values than the Hollywood motion picture industry. . . .
>
> We [Christians] must rise up in the cause of biblical and traditional righteousness. There is still "a moral majority" out there, but unless there is a revival in America and a return to moral and ethical values, there will soon be an "immoral majority."[33]

Falwell's critique is rooted in his views of American history. To him, governmental silence about God is a denial of our godly American heritage. Falwell has written a foreword for a book by Gene Wolfenbarger, a Baptist pastor from Texas; this book provides an extended description of America's heritage and our wrong turn away from it:

> Splendid and desired by all nations, America took a wrong turn in 1962. Now she must return to that crossroad and turn right.
>
> God married America as surely as He married ancient Israel. In centuries past, He greatly desired a new country to love. He sought a nation that would love Him and honor His Word. So—"in 1492, Columbus sailed the ocean blue." . . .

> [But shortly after World War II], America was ready for a change. . . . [She] became more relaxed. Less restrained. . . . Before long, she began listening to authorities other than God. She dutifully held the Supreme Court's hand and listened as they doubted the historical significance of her relationship with her God. . . . She sensed no danger. Why should she? These were *her* judges. Supreme. Sovereign. Absolute. . . . She forgot that only her God was to be Supreme, Sovereign, and Absolute. . . . So she offered no struggle in 1962 when they told her she could no longer pray in her public school.
>
> [Never] before had she so obviously contaminated her national and public relationship with God. In her past, she had always purely and publicly acknowledged her love for Him and her dependence upon Him. Now she polluted her relationship by agreeing with her judges that she would not support her children praying to her God in public places anymore. She consented to removing her young children's dependence upon her God. It was America's first act of spiritual adultery.
>
> [Within] only a few decades, America changed dramatically. . . . Some of her own children no longer recognize her as the mother they once knew. Some are so young that, from birth, they have only known her only [sic] as being violent and wanton and promiscuous. Yes, America is different now.[34]

Wolfenbarger's book has attracted the strong endorsement of several evangelical leaders besides Falwell, including Beverly LaHaye (founder and Chairman of Concerned Women for America and wife of former Moral Majority leader and bestselling author Tim LaHaye) and Don Wildmon (founder and President of the American Family Association), among others.

James Dobson

It is probably fair to say that no evangelical has wider influence today than Dr. James Dobson, best-selling author, radio commentator, and founder/president of Focus on the Family. A recent article in *U.S. News & World Report* declared him "unrivaled as an evangelical leader"[35] and "the best-known leader among America's 50 million-strong evangelical Christians."[36] Tapes of Dobson's worldwide radio broadcasts reach an estimated 200 million listeners in over 24 languages, and his active mailing list includes more than 2.5 million names.[37]

Unfortunately, he has also become a Fearmonger in the political sphere, echoing almost all of the Fearmongers' familiar historical and cultural arguments. His enormous popularity among evangelicals has provided an ample platform from which to spread the "Christian America" version of history, so much so that one suspects it would be challenging to find an adult among American evangelicals today who has not heard the story (despite, we are told, the silence of public schools and history textbooks). The many publications of Focus on the Family, providing not only advice about marriage and child rearing but also lessons in American history and politics, have included a number of broad historical claims like the following:

> The concept of a secular state was virtually non-existent in 1776 as well as in 1787, when the Constitution was written . . . . The Constitution was designed to perpetuate a Christian order.[38]

And Dobson, like the other Fearmongers, is convinced that since World War II, America has abandoned her moral roots—not just in private life, but in our governments:

> This really was a Christian nation and, as far as its founders were concerned, to try separating Christianity from government is virtually impossible and would result in unthinkable damage to the nation and its people. Much of the damage we see around us must be attributed to this separation.[39]

To Dobson, our laws are not only the reflection of our culture's immorality, but also a contributing *cause* of our immorality. In fact, "separation of church and state," a political preference smuggled into our laws by godless judges, poses a danger to our very souls. Immoral people make immoral laws, or reinterpret good laws in immoral ways, which causes more and more people to become immoral. The righteous, in Dobson's view, must fight to break this cycle. The situation in America during the past twenty or thirty years is nothing short of a war—a war of values, a war for the soul of our nation. And the enemy has been winning, at least until the 2004 elections. In 1990, he put it this way:

> Nothing short of a great Civil War of Values rages today throughout North America. Two sides with vastly differing and incompatible world-views are locked in a bitter conflict that permeates every level of society. . . .
>
> On one side of this Continental Divide are the traditionalists whose values begin with the basic assumption that "God *is*." . . . Their beliefs are deeply rooted in Scripture, beginning with the Ten Commandments and continuing through the New Testament teachings and the gospel of Jesus Christ.
>
> Until approximately thirty years ago, these biblically based concepts were the dominant values and beliefs in Western society. . . .
>
> Then, slowly at first, another way of looking at the world began to emerge. It evolved from the basic assumption that "God isn't. . . ." Everything emanating from the Creator was jettisoned, including reverence for Scripture or any of the transcendent, universal truths. "Right" was determined by what *seemed* right at a particular time. . . .
>
> [The] hottest battles in this civil war are being fought on educational turf, and that is where eventual victory or defeat will occur. At this moment, the traditionalists are being mauled, but they're not yet down for the count.[40]

The rhetoric is important. The battle, we are told, is a contest between good and evil, between right and wrong. The problems we see around us are all attributable to, and part of, this one big battle. The struggle of good versus evil becomes the struggle of "good family people" against the impulses in our society that wreck marital stability and the emotional health of children; and as we finally unmask the veiled threat, our struggle turns out to be, in part, a political struggle to oust godless, activist judges and reintroduce prayer recitations into public school classrooms. The battle to return to (or create) a "Christian America" is just one facet of the age-old battle for virtue in individual hearts. The battle for a virtuous culture is the same as the battle for criminalizing abortion, and assisted suicide, and the publication of *Playboy* magazine. The battle against homosexual conduct in individual lives is the same as the battle to keep homosexual candidates from being elected to public office—a battle Dobson fought unsuccessfully in 2004 against an openly gay candidate for a seat on the state supreme court in Oregon (during the contest, Dobson labeled Oregon "the Gettysburg" in an ongoing values war).[41] Those who oppose Dobson's political agenda are the immoral, those whose beliefs are *not*, in his words, "deeply rooted in Scripture." Christians on that side are, quite simply, selling out to the devil.

Dobson now foresees impending disaster for America which can only be averted if the remnant of the faithful stand up politically, for Christ—by which he clearly means, among other things, enacting a number of intolerant laws derived from Christian teachings about proper behavior. But is this "remnant" a persecuted minority, or a moral majority? In a speech in 1998, Dobson claimed:

> There are millions and millions and millions and millions of people in this country who do honor the Holy One of Israel and have not bowed at the feet of Baal. There are millions of them out there. . . . They're good people. They love their kids. They love their spouses, their families. They love their God and they are very, very concerned about what's happening today. They see this moral freefall. They see this moral relativism and they're very concerned about it. It contradicts everything they stand for and they also feel under attack. They feel under assault by Hollywood . . . and by the rock music industry . . . and MTV . . . and the "Ellen"-type programs . . . and cable TV and all those sorts of things. They see it and they're very alarmed about it and they can't do anything about it. They feel the culture has got their families. . . . These people out there are worried about what they see and they're in contradiction with the elite and with the cultural trend setters and it is very difficult for any of us to get anyone in government to understand those people or to treat them like they had a legitimate point of view, and that is my concern. . . . Why don't [Republican government officials take action on these cultural issues]? I don't know. It's a lack of conviction that there is a boss to the universe, and yet there are moral standards that we are held to, and we need officials who will stand up and represent them.[42]

Judging by this speech, government officials who will "stand up" for moral standards are apparently those who will vote to censor movies, rock music, MTV, and any sitcom that includes a favorable depiction of a major character who is homosexual. However, Dobson, in characteristic Fearmonger fashion, never puts it exactly that way. He never uses the C-word—"censorship"—and never even gives the broad outlines of acceptable legislation. Yet if he is not advocating censorship, what public policy proposal is he standing for? And if he *is* advocating censorship, upon what basis will the lines be drawn between acceptable entertainment and unacceptable entertainment? And who will enforce the lines? And what will we do with the troublesome First Amendment, and the troublesome judges who misread it?

Standing up for moral standards in government also seems to mean standing up for a government that overtly praises God (but not Jesus Christ, perhaps) and encourages its citizens to worship him. Along these lines, Dobson has recently linked arms with Roy Moore. When the evangelical political group Vision America hosted a rally in support of Moore in Montgomery, Alabama, on August 16, 2003, Dobson, who could not attend in person, endorsed Moore in writing as:

> a hero to me, as he should be to any Christian who longs for God to be recognized as the ultimate giver of laws. Judge Moore's commitment to this cause is an example of what one godly man can accomplish when he takes a courageous stand in a righteous manner.[43]

But what, exactly, did this "one godly man" accomplish for God? What is "this cause," the holy fight for which Moore sacrificed so much? The "courageous," "righteous" stand every Christian should support, apparently, is the prominent display of passages of Scripture on government property—albeit passages that never once mention Jesus, the only begotten son of God, the fulfillment of all Scripture and the only hope of mankind.[44]

But even if our governments are silent about Jesus, they simply must advocate belief in God, according to the Fearmongers. To be silent about Jesus is merely political pragmatism or religious toleration, perhaps, but to be silent about God would be the same as advocating atheism. There is no possible neutrality. This is why the Fearmongers constantly tell us that anyone who advocates governmental neutrality is deceiving himself or others. This is why Pat Robertson's recent book argues that the federal court order requiring Roy Moore to remove his Ten Commandments monument from display in a state government building proves that the federal court views the Ten Commandments as "The Ten Offenses."[45] There can be no neutrality.

As of this writing, Dobson continues to use his huge influence to urge evangelicals to take political action. Most recently, he was enlisted by President George W. Bush to help with Harriet Miers's abortive bid for a seat on the U.S. Supreme Court. When Bush announced that he had nominated Miers, the response even among Republicans was unenthusiastic; Bush then took steps to encourage support for her among evangelicals and other social conservatives. Early in the process, Bush advisor Karl Rove privately passed information about Miers's religion (and her denomination's views on abortion) along to Dobson. Rove told Dobson that Miers is an evangelical and a member of a denomination that views abortion negatively. Bush defended what was essentially a public statement about Miers's religion, on the grounds that people want to know as much as they possibly can about Miers's background, and "part of Harriet Miers's life is her religion." Dobson, declaring himself to be acting on the basis of Rove's disclosure, publicly declared his support for Miers, although Miers ultimately withdrew herself from consideration.[46]

Pat Robertson

Robertson, the founder of Christian Coalition and host of *The 700 Club*, is of course another longtime Fearmonger. The story Robertson tells has not changed in many years and is typical Fearmonger fare. In 1990 he put it this way:

> Today [in 1990] we are witnessing the disintegration of all the values we once considered "American virtues." The traditional family is in shambles; our culture is in a nosedive of moral decline; government is raping the American taxpayer through its own arrogant and self-absorbed greed; and the courts have legislated Judeo-Christian values out of American public life and, in effect, turned the nation over to the godless.
>
> After a period of head-scratching and regrouping, conservative and religious Americans are beginning to realize that they are under assault. What is happening in America is not a debate, it is not a friendly disagreement between enlightened people. It is a vicious one-sided attack on our most cherished institutions.
>
> Suddenly the confrontation is growing hotter and it just may become all out civil war. It is a war against the family and against conservative and Christian values.
>
> Even as we are witnessing an ongoing crisis in the Middle East, we are engaged in a war in our midst of profound spiritual dimensions . . . .[47]

By 2004, his opinions had not changed:

> History shows that those who founded the United States consciously intended America to be a Christian nation, guided above all else by the truths of the Bible.

The fundamental principles for the laws and liberties of this new nation were found in the Ten Commandments of the Old Testament and the Sermon on the Mount of the New Testament. . . .

For decades, certain "elites" in America have been hard at work to banish the God of the Bible from all discussion and debate concerning our most important national issues—issues that are, in fact, matters of life and death. Because this war between the spiritual and secular vision for America is long and slow, and the battles are fought in distant courtrooms, most Americans are only vaguely aware of the alarmingly serious threat to our nation's foundation and Christian heritage. We have failed to recognize the relentless, ongoing war for America's soul. . . .[48]

Robertson believes that the stakes in this war are huge, and he is not optimistic. If the secular humanists win the day—and it looks like they will—not only will Christianity lose its place as the dominant force in Western society, but America's survival as a Great Power will be in jeopardy. As of 1990:

In 1990 we see family disintegration, unrestrained sex, a holocaust of abortion, an epidemic of drugs and alcohol, deteriorating educational standards, growing poverty amidst unrestrained opulence, business greed and fraud, and a runaway federal budget.

We have these things because we have allowed Christian and biblical standards to be removed from our national life. It has taken the left some 70 years to reduce us to this level. . . .

The United States of America today is the last great expression of the triumph of Christendom. America has been the strongest of all the nations that came out of the Christian tradition extending from Charlemagne to the present.

But as we look back upon the vast sweep of history, it now appears that the end of this millennium will signal the end of a long and colorful cycle of history in which the Christian tradition had been the dominant moral and social force.[49]

And in 2004:

The incident in Alabama [in which a federal court required the removal from government display of Roy Moore's monument to the Ten Commandments] is just one small piece of the greater erosion of Judeo-Christian morality that is occurring all around us. As those who oppose God's standards continue to win ground in both courts and culture, none of us is safe from the devastating consequences. And what we are about to see, if we do not stand against the erosion of our spiritual foundation, is a virtual earthquake of violence, immorality, and untold suffering.[50]

Little wonder that many evangelical readers and listeners, after feeding on a steady diet of this stuff, feel attacked by culture, unfairly lampooned and ostracized by various popular media and other opinion shapers. Some even feel like an oppressed religious minority group. Although over 80 percent of Americans claim to be Christians,[51] a number of evangelicals seem to believe American culture today makes it tough to be a Christian. If they mean "a faithful Christian," they are probably right—although this fact alone does not make their suffering unique in human history, nor does it prove that most Americans are not true Christians. But it is surely true that moral relativism and postmodernism have become more widespread in our culture during the past fifty or so years. And the faith commitments of evangelicals by and large preclude moral relativism. Hence the "Us versus Them" understanding of American culture today. The cultural rift some evangelicals are sensing is the divide they perceive between themselves and others, Christian and Non-Christian, who prioritize tolerance over moral absolutes. And it is that rift which is incessantly showcased, exaggerated, and exploited by the Fearmongers.

Tim LaHaye

Tim LaHaye, a longtime evangelical spokesman and coauthor of the best-selling *Left Behind* series of Christian fiction, echoes the Fearmonger version of history and where it is leading. In his 1994 book *Faith of Our Founding Fathers*, LaHaye first fixes the blame for America's social problems:

> [Humanism's] antimoral philosophy has created such an emptiness in our children that sexual permissiveness, unwed pregnancy, and venereal disease are rampant among junior and senior high schoolers, and suicide is the second highest cause of death among our nation's youth.
>
> Whom do you blame? Don't blame the church; we still warn young people about the consequences of such activities. Don't blame parents! They don't want their children living like humanistic animals who have evolved from lower life forms. I blame the secular humanists, who have expelled traditional American moral values that were an integral part of our school curriculum for the first 150 years of our nation's history. Since the humanists gained virtual control of education in this country (about fifty years ago), not only have academic levels declined but moral levels have radically deteriorated as well. Doing away with moral absolutes, they introduced "situation ethics" and "moral relativism," helping to create a wave of permissiveness that has given them the excuse to further attack our nation's youth by teaching a radical and explicit form of sex education in mixed classes without benefit of moral values. The ensuing moral holocaust could well destroy America if a cure is not found.[52]

The familiar dualism of the Fearmongers and their version of American history are clearly evident in LaHaye's cultural analysis:

> The most burning issue in America today is whether this is "One nation under God," based on the Bible and Judeo-Christian principles, or a secular nation

> without fixed moral absolutes that functions independent of any god other than human reason. . . .
>
> If we as a nation do not soon return our official public policy to the Christian consensus of our Founding Fathers and the Biblical principles of law that have provided the freedoms we've enjoyed for over two hundred years, it is just a matter of time before we lose those freedoms. . . .
>
> The future of America is up for grabs and will be determined before the twenty-first century. It could go either way—to the left and let an elitist minority of secularists continue to lead this nation into impotence, stagnation, and slavery—or to the right and return it to the control of those who continue the spirit of our Founding Fathers . . . .[53]

Although this picture may seem bleak, at least LaHaye gives us the comfort of knowing that the future of America has by now, in the twenty-first century, been conclusively "determined." All that remains is for LaHaye to inform us what the determination is.

David Barton

David Barton, founder and president of the deceptively-titled WallBuilders organization,[54] is the authority perhaps most often quoted by the Fearmongers to prove their version of American history. Barton has most recently served as a consultant to the Republicans, advising them on how to court evangelicals in preparation for the 2004 elections.[55] He has written many tracts and several books published by WallBuilder Press, all dealing with the subjects of the pious founding era, current American depravity, and the imperative for Christians to become politically active—particularly in light of the benighted secular humanism controlling the decisions of the U.S. Supreme Court:

> According to the [U.S. Supreme Court], to obey the Ten Commandments—things like "do not steal" and "do not kill"—would be to obey religious teachings at school, and surely the Founding Fathers would never have wanted students to be exposed to such teachings at school! . . .
>
> . . . [Our] Founding Fathers had forewarned of the societal consequences of excluding religious influences from the public arena. . . . It is now evident that they were right and that, statistically speaking, we have lost our national morality.
>
> [When] the public teaching of the Bible is restricted, crime and violent behavior escalate. Since 1963 (the year that the Court—for the first time in American history—ordered the Bible from the public school classroom), violent crime has increased 794 percent faster than population growth; metal detectors and uniformed police officers are now common sights in schools . . . . Nevertheless, despite such alarming trends, we still can't let students see things like

"don't steal" and "don't kill" since they might obey these "religious" commands![56]

And all this is just the tip of the iceberg. Space does not permit consideration of the views of other prominent evangelical Fearmongers, such as Don Wildmon of the American Family Association, D. James Kennedy, Senior Pastor at Coral Ridge Presbyterian Church, Beverly LaHaye of Concerned Women for America, and others. Suffice it to say that Fearmongering is alive and well among prominent evangelicals, particularly those on the political Right. There are other evangelical voices gaining an audience; time will tell if they can topple the Fearmongers from their place of ascendancy in evangelical discourse.[57] For now, however, it seems foolish to doubt that Fearmongering is exerting a powerful effect on many American evangelicals: 58 percent of self-identified American evangelicals claim affiliation with the Republican party;[58] 92 percent of them claim "we are seeing a serious breakdown of American society";[59] 87 percent of them agree that "the U.S. was founded as a Christian nation";[60] and 55 percent of them agree that "Christian morality should be the law of the land even though not all Americans are Christians."[61]

Of course we should be careful not to extrapolate this current of feeling to all evangelicals, or to assume that the political preferences of all evangelicals have been influenced by the Fearmongers. As Christian Smith counsels, "evangelical leaders do not simply give voice to the thoughts and feelings of millions of ordinary evangelicals. . . . To talk about a single view [even] among evangelical leaders is simply nonsensical."[62]

But at the same time, it would be foolish to ignore the common themes articulated by so many evangelicals in books, pamphlets, websites, and pulpits all over the country. Nor can there be any doubt that evangelicals are organizing at the grassroots level and influencing electoral outcomes in politically conservative directions. The 2004 elections dramatically demonstrate the power of organized groups of evangelicals acting on their religious beliefs in the political arena. At the national level, members of Congress, and perhaps the president and vice president of the United States, won elections in 2004 due to evangelical support; at the state level, eleven states, with strong influence from evangelical groups, ratified state constitutional amendments designed to ban gay marriage.[63] There is something important going on in evangelical rhetoric, among the leadership and at the grassroots level, and it is sometimes resulting in political action as well as other forms of witness to a sinful culture. Significant numbers of evangelicals apparently see themselves locked in a conflict with the dominant American culture of moral relativism and secularism, a culture that necessarily includes many self-identified Christians who are not moral absolutists. And many of the evangelicals are waging this war at the ballot box. The cultural and political pronouncements of the Fearmongers surely lie behind much of this political action.

AN AGENDA FOR POLITICAL CHANGE

One is particularly struck by the Fearmongers' exaggerations (intentional hyperbole, one hopes) and the uses they make of history. Their diatribes contain an important element of truth, perhaps, but they vastly overstate the case. It is true that America is today experiencing a variety of social problems that were not present in our country on a large scale before the middle of the twentieth century. It is also true, sadly, that these problems often cause harm to those directly involved and to others as well. Further, many of these problems might be diminished, or even eliminated, if our culture widely shared certain assumptions about morality, moral teachings which happen to be contained in the Bible (and sometimes in other religious texts and traditions too). Majorities of Christians and Non-Christians alike can probably agree with all of this. Most Christians might go even further: if everyone in our culture followed the precepts of Jesus, most of our social problems would vanish. The fearmongering Christians say these things, but they do not stop there. Unfortunately they feel compelled to launch out from these broadly supported views to make sweeping generalizations, to make exaggerated cultural and historical comparisons that mythologize the American founding, to expose those individuals or groups responsible for this mess and demonize them. The fearmongering has the appearance of oversimplified cultural analysis, which it is. But its potential mischief may be greater, for the flawed cultural analysis is often used to support some plea for political action on God's behalf.

Quite often the Fearmongers' calls to political action are more impassioned than specific. The following exhortation to evangelical pastors from Vision America is typical in this regard:

> [Pastors should] speak to the crucial moral issues of the day and communicate why Christians must be active citizens, influencing public policy on matters with Biblical perspective. . . . Congregations must be informed of their American religious heritage, understand the original intent of the U.S. Constitution, and know how to become involved in the citizenship process.[64]

This sort of plea is deeply felt, surely, but is rather lean on specific policy proposals or litmus tests. Instead, Vision America here calls Christians to "understand the original intent of the U.S. Constitution" and to vote "with Biblical perspective," leaving it to the audience to determine what intent the Founding Fathers had in framing the U.S. Constitution, why that matters, and which particular laws or resolutions the Bible calls true Christians to support.

On the other hand, the call to arms is sometimes disturbingly specific. In 1980, Tim LaHaye set forth a "Moral Minimums Test" which listed the beliefs that Christians should require of an elected official before supporting him. According to this test, any prospective government official should have to go on record as believing (among other things) that "this country was founded on a belief in God and the moral principles of the Bible"; that "abortion-on-demand" should be allowed only when the mother's life is endangered by the pregnancy; that the Equal Rights Amendment should be opposed; that there should be "stricter laws relating to the sale of pornography"; that marijuana should be outlawed; that "known homosexuals" should not be permitted to "teach school"; that parents have the "right" to send their children to private schools; that capital punishment should be a viable penal option for capital crimes; that schoolchildren should not be bused out of their neighborhoods to achieve racial integration; that government spending should never exceed government revenues unless there is a war or some other "dire emergency"; and that taxes should be reduced.[65]

In LaHaye's view, Jesus seemingly has specific desires even on issues as mundane and esoteric as the regulations governing certain business licenses. On the subject of the Christian view as to the proper scope for FCC regulation, LaHaye writes:

> Traditional family values should be recognized as official public policy by this government for education and entertainment in a secular society. These should include honesty, loyalty, patriotism, . . . respect for both adults and children, and sexual expression reserved for adulthood and confined to marriage. Promiscuity of all kinds should be discouraged for the sake of health, emotional and mental well-being, and the protection of our society. [The] Federal Communications Commission should be instructed to renew the radio, television, and cable license of only those stations that conform all programming to the above policy.[66]

Specific legislative proposals like these are rare among today's Fearmongers. Of course, the more specific the legislative proposals, the more narrow the Fearmongers' appeal, among evangelicals or anyone else. Rather than conjuring up for America an explicitly "evangelical heritage" or a "Protestant heritage," our American heritage is usually described as "Christian," or even more often nowadays, "Judeo-Christian." (As noted earlier, a "Judeo-Christian" heritage may be used to support government endorsements of "God," but not "Jesus" or "Christianity.") Similarly, the Fearmongers' proposals for specific civil and criminal laws are mostly left unstated, with the possible exceptions of laws disallowing homosexual marriage (which have broad majoritarian support and are already in place almost everywhere) or abortion (laws of a sort that cannot be passed until *Roe v. Wade* is overturned—which is why so many evangelicals are eager to direct their attention instead to influencing the confirmation of an abortion rights opponent to the U.S. Supreme Court).

Rather than getting into the dirty details of policy preferences on issues like balanced budgets, censorship, and women's rights, as LaHaye did in 1980, many Fearmongers today are content to rail against the moral relativism which is infecting not only our hearts and our culture, but our government. All moral absolutists are called to "stand up for God" in the voting booth. It is assumed that a true Christian will know what to do when he or she gets there. Without including many specific instructions on how to vote, the message is nonetheless clear: Stop sitting on the sidelines and get involved. In the words of Rick Scarborough of Vision America, it is time for Christians in America to decide "enough is enough."[67] When evangelicals act on such pleas, even in the absence of more specific policy guidance, the results often turn out to be one-sided: in the 2004 presidential election, for example, evangelicals cast almost four times as many votes for President Bush as they did for all other candidates combined.[68]

So it is that the Fearmongers have described their differences with the surrounding culture as a struggle between absolute truth and moral relativism, between moral absolutists on the one hand and moral tolerationists on the other. It is important to see the implication here. This sort of rhetoric makes it appear that evangelicals must side with the Fearmongers and their legislative agenda or else renounce moral absolutes, and by logical extension, evangelicalism itself. Referring to the federal court's decision in Roy Moore's case, Pat Robertson writes:

> Why are [the judges who decided against Roy Moore, and their sympathizers,] offended by the Ten Commandments? The answer is painfully obvious: They perceive any system of moral absolutes that defines or restrains their choices as antiquated and oppressive, dangerously limiting their rights. Simply put, the Ten Commandments represent absolute truth, and that cramps their style.[69]

The implication? If you support moral absolutes, you ought to support governmental display of the Ten Commandments; if you oppose such a display, it must be because you deny absolute truth, opposing any system of moral absolutes because it "cramps your style."

Complicating this picture is the fact that some who desire legal toleration are in fact libertines who want to live impure lives themselves. Some pointed arguments from the tolerationist camp against temperance, sexual purity, and the like have turned the situation into a sort of public debate on moral absolutes, if not an all-out culture war. But one does not have to listen long to the "moral absolutist versus tolerationist" debate in order to realize that the sides are mostly incomprehensible to each other. They speak different languages and cite different sources of authority for their knowledge. As communication between the two sides breaks down, the war of words sometimes becomes a political battle. To wage this battle the tolerationists, who (according to stereotype) are tolerant of everything except intolerance, have sometimes attempted to impose their own brand of intolerant legislative agenda—supporting, for example, various new sorts of anti-discrimination laws (which, after all, are essentially "morals laws" forbidding private actors from refusing to associate with someone on grounds morally unacceptable to the drafters of the laws).

Since World War II, many evangelicals (and other moral absolutists) have begun (again) to turn to politics. Perhaps this is because they are bewildered and frightened by the culture around them, a culture that not only rejects particular truths dear to evangelicals but also rejects the very possibility of "truth" as evangelicals have understood that term. They feel like outsiders, strangers in their own country—a country which, they are sure, was founded on evangelical footing. They are not even certain they understand the language any more. In the words of James Dobson and Gary Bauer:

> The span between 1990 [and 1994] is a mere four years. . . . For Americans who hold traditional values, however, these years have marked a watershed in our history. In 1990, the government was still officially on our side. [But] today, it is as if an alien force has taken control of the government, a force determined to press a broad attack on the family on all fronts.[70]

Bewildered and shocked by a culture that doesn't even understand their criticisms, a culture slipping away from them, a culture which in the words of one of their favorite social commentators is "slouching towards Gomorrah,"[71] significant numbers of evangelicals, swayed to some extent by the Fearmongers, are falling back on politics in a last ditch effort to stop the slide and restore sanity and moral consensus to the culture. They are, in short, trying to reclaim America.

ALMOST PERSUADED?

As I have already suggested, there is some question as to whether evangelicals in the main have been persuaded by the Fearmongers to believe the myth about America's pious founding, or to take specific political action aimed at prohibiting sin or propping up Christianity. In a book published in 2000, Christian Smith reports the findings of the 1996 Religious Identity and Influence Survey, a national level telephone survey funded by the Pew Charitable

Trusts. When asked whether they agreed that the U.S. was founded as a Christian nation, 87 percent of self-identified evangelicals agreed. But so did two-thirds of all other respondents. If the myth has been successfully purveyed to evangelicals, it has not fallen on entirely deaf ears elsewhere either.[72] But when asked whether they agreed that Christian morality should be the law of the land even though not all Americans are Christians, only 55 percent of evangelicals agreed (still a majority, it must be noted). When the question was watered down to ask whether they agreed that the federal government should "promote traditional values" in our society, a full 68 percent of evangelicals agreed.[73]

In other words, as we have suggested, the support for the Fearmongers' legislative agenda declines as that agenda becomes more specific. At the "promote traditional values" level of generality, over two-thirds of evangelicals will support the cause, even if the action is to be taken at the federal government level. Make the appeal more specific, though—as in "legislate Christian morality on even the unbelievers"—and 13 percent of evangelicals (about one-fifth of the original supporters) disappear. Make the appeal even more specific—as in "outlaw fornication" or "substantially redistribute wealth"—and the evangelical numbers might just drop through the basement, at least on many issues.

It is at least true that some vocal evangelicals, even those on the political Right, have explicitly repudiated the Fearmongers and their tactics. Cal Thomas, a popular evangelical radio personality and author, used to be a leader of Moral Majority and a close associate of Jerry Falwell. He has since coauthored the book *Blinded By Might: Can the Religious Right Save America?*, in which he argues that Christians would do well to spend less time on political activism and more time on personal evangelism and other forms of individual outreach to the world. In an interview after the book was published, Thomas reports that in earlier days:

> I was a regular Bible reader, but . . . I was letting charismatic people who were very persuasive and could have sold me a vacuum cleaner, even if I didn't need one, interpret and "spin," in the words of modern politics, the Bible to say things that it didn't mean. But when I got into the Bible for myself and really sought what God expected of believers, I found something completely different from what I have been told.[74]

Interestingly, Thomas points to fundraising pressures as the cause of many of the seeming inconsistencies in the Fearmongers' legislative agenda:

> Preachers who argue against homosexual marriage—which I am against—and legitimizing the gay lifestyle—which I oppose—don't speak a lot and don't

> preach a lot about the consequences of divorce, abandoned children and women who are making less money after they divorce. I find these to be a greater threat to the family. However, you can't raise money on those issues, and that's the whole point.[75]

So Thomas, his coauthor Ed Dobson, and some other evangelicals are encouraging the evangelical community at large to think critically about the claims and agenda of the Fearmongers.

On the other hand, the Roy Moore controversy in Alabama and the victories won in the 2004 elections seem to have sparked renewed interest among evangelicals in using politics and government to endorse the Christian faith and even to punish more sins. At an August 2003 rally in support of Moore, Rev. Rick Scarborough of Vision America described Moore's fight as a battle to reverse forty years of moral decline in America, and pledged, "This is not the end of this. This is the beginning of the movement."[76] Several thousand people came from all over the country to attend the rally.[77] Time will tell whether this "movement" will attract the greater part of evangelicals to its mythology or its specific plan for political action. But there can be little doubt that these are the aims. Certainly evangelical successes in the 2004 elections, regarding homosexual marriage amendments and races for key House and Senate seats as well as the presidency, have encouraged evangelical political momentum on the political Right. Focus on the Family, for example, plans to promote ballot initiatives outlawing same-sex marriage in up to 15 more states over the next two years.[78] And Jim Wallis's new bestselling book *God's Politics*, while perhaps encouraging critical evaluation of the evangelical Right's political agenda, will certainly encourage the evangelical Left for future political action on behalf of what might be termed a different sort of legal intolerance, the kind that forces unwilling citizens, in Jesus' name, to divert their resources to the benefit of the poor, the working class, and the environment.

So while some evangelical leaders may be rethinking their commitments to the legislation of morality, others—on the Left and the Right—have apparently recommitted themselves and their ministries to influencing Christians to flex their political muscles in the name of laws that explicitly endorse God, punish sinners, or coerce charity. Tom Minnery, the Vice President for Public Policy at Focus on the Family, has recently published a book arguing that Christians who wish to be "salt and light" as Jesus commanded (and is there any other kind of Christian?) will join with other believers to influence public policy and organize boycotts of immoral private businesses and groups. (Let us set aside the question of why an evangelical ministry to families needs a Vice President for Public Policy.) Minnery is apparently upset that Cal Thomas and his ilk have been saying Christians should stop trying to use politics so often to change the sinful culture. He views such thinking as cowardice.

Jim Wallis, the author of *God's Politics* and editor of *Sojourners* magazine, has taken much the same position regarding religious activism, albeit in favor of a different set of coercive laws:

> Never has there been a clearer role for the churches and religious community. . . . The truth is that there are more churches committed to justice and peace than belong to the religious Right. It's time the voice of those congregations be heard and their activism be mobilized to become the conscience of American politics in a time of crisis.[79]

But Wallis sees a great difference between his message and that of the Fearmongers. He writes:

> Al Qaeda, the Taliban, and American fundamentalists like my old debate partners Jerry Falwell and Pat Robertson are, indeed, all theocrats who desire their religious agenda to be enforced through the power of the state. And that is, primarily, a religious mistake.[80]

There is much to praise in Wallis's book, and he cannot fairly be called a "Fearmonger" as I have been using that term. But here, Wallis has it wrong in two different ways. First, Jerry Falwell and Pat Robertson are not "theocrats," desiring a complete merger of church and state. In particular, any "theocracy" worthy of the name (including the former Taliban regime) forbids even rudimentary freedom of worship for dissenting religious minorities, a freedom Falwell and Robertson broadly support (including freedom for Muslims, Hindus, Buddhists, and so on). But second, and more to the point here, Wallis has failed to appreciate the way in which his own legislative agenda is just as intolerant and coercive as theirs. Yes, Falwell and Robertson desire parts of their religious agenda to be enforced on unbelievers through the power of the state; but so does Jim Wallis. Laws taxing the rich to feed the poor are just as coercive as laws forbidding sodomy. One need not endorse sodomy to oppose sodomy laws; and one need not endorse greed or become callous toward poverty in order to oppose poverty laws.

Both sides, Left and Right, are calling for Christian activism of a sort that remakes culture by coercing those who do not share Christian values. If a Christian disagrees with the immoral culture but remains silent and does nothing, argues Minnery, he is being hypocritical and abandoning his Master's business. So far so good, and almost any Christian who is serious about the faith could agree. But then comes the implication. Minnery and Wallis (and many other evangelicals) argue that the way we are required to confront the culture is (at least in part) by using coercive laws to shape the culture in more Christlike ways.

Minnery says Christians must involve themselves politically so as to impose God's will upon unbelievers, especially (in Minnery's view) those who try to have an abortion:

> Admittedly, we can't force anyone to acknowledge God or willingly obey Him. But like it or not, they either have to accept God's ideas about what's right and wrong or pay the consequences. We've just said that biblical morality—no lying, cheating, stealing, murdering, etc.—is good for society, and we should be pleased that our forefathers had enough sense to translate these godly principles into laws. Those principles work well for everybody, because they reflect what is true about human nature.
>
> Today, the side that doesn't want God's standards to prevail has the upper hand on some issues and has begun passing laws and angling for court decisions that reflect immoral standards. . . . This is where we are on the issue of abortion.[81]

Again, one notes the familiar dualism of the Fearmongers, the "Us vs. Them" mentality that oversimplifies Christian disagreements and demonizes all opposition.

But this sort of call is not limited to the evangelical Right, or the Fearmongers. On the Left, Wallis utilizes a similarly dualistic argument, coupled with dire predictions for the future:

> [It's] not hyperbole to say that our political system is for sale to the highest bidder. Events like [the Enron scandal] show how the very nature of democracy in America is under threat. We now have a system of big corporations, big accounting firms, big law firms, and big politicians scratching each other's backs while millions of Americans struggle just to get by.[82]
>
> In America, people who work should not be poor, but today many are. We must ensure that all people who are able to work have jobs where they do not labor in vain, but have access to quality health care, decent housing, and a living income to support their families. . . . We must also ensure that those who are unable to work are cared for by our society. . . . [We] will pray together and work together for policies that can achieve these goals.[83]

In Wallis's view, the enemy is private concentrations of power and wealth, and God's special concern has always rested with the poor and powerless in society. Therefore, enacting taxation and spending laws that forcibly redistribute resources, eroding concentrations of wealth in favor of the poor and the working class, must be a step in the "righteous" direction. Essentially, greed and the hoarding of wealth must be outlawed. Mercy and charity must be legally required, in God's name.

This theological view of the uses of law is nowhere more common than among the Fearmongers. Focus on the Family trumpets a different list of cultural vices than Wallis, but the call to coercive legislation is much the same. Minnery writes in a Focus on the Family newsletter:

> The sort of political involvement that ends slavery—or abortion, or pornography—reflects the life of the Christian who has completely surrendered his or her life to Christ.[84]

Slavery, abortion, pornography—it's all the same to God, implies Minnery. It's all sin, and the legislative response ought to be the same: outlaw it all. So who is it that votes to censor *Playboy* magazine? The Christian who has completely surrendered to Christ. And who is it that thinks that any just and righteous government should allow both the Focus on the Family empire and the *Playboy* empire to sell periodicals and photographs as they choose? Well, that would be those who have *not* surrendered their lives to Christ.

It is clear from his book that Minnery believes there are many more issues besides abortion and pornography that also cry for attention from Christian legislators, issues upon which the "side that doesn't want God's standards to prevail" has induced the government to "reflect immoral standards." Yet characteristically, it is difficult to know, from reading his book, just what changes Christians should support. While he names a number of specific sins rampant in our culture, one is left to wonder what specific laws Minnery thinks are so desperately needed, beyond abortion laws (of a sort that would currently be doomed to fail in the courts) and widely approved laws already in place, such as those against "lying, stealing, cheating, and murdering." And even here one is in foggy territory, for the fact is, our laws do not forbid "lying," if we mean all the lying God hates. In truth, our laws prohibit only a very small percentage of all the lying that goes on in our culture. Is Minnery satisfied with these laws, or not? Is he saying we should outlaw all the lying God hates, or only some of it? What about outlawing other behaviors God hates, such as divorce, idol worship, and gluttony? Minnery, like the other Fearmongers, bypasses these difficult questions, assuming, perhaps, that true Christians will know the answers. In any event, the idea seems to be that Christians should stop thinking so much and get involved.

The Fearmonger diatribes are not representative of all recent Christian social commentary, certainly, but they *are* representative of a much larger body of popular work in the same vein. In fact, statements like these are so ubiquitous that they may fail to surprise us any more. And they have arguably become what most Americans think of first when someone mentions "the evangelical position" in politics. Whether or not most evangelicals would agree with the Fearmongers—and as we have noted, there is some reason to think that many evangelicals would not agree with any strong and intolerant legislative agenda—the Fearmongers seem to have won the shouting contest among evangelicals, at least for now. Moreover, it seems indisputable that their efforts are having an effect on electoral outcomes all over the country.

So where does this leave evangelicals? Some evangelicals are, in fact, persuaded to be disciples of the Fearmongers. Armed with faulty history and a persecution complex, they have set out to proselytize others—if not through reasoned persuasion, then via the ballot box. Another unwelcome result, though, is a possible backlash against virtue-talk. There is a recognizable distinction between calling individuals (or even "our culture") to repentance for homosexual activity, on the one hand, and calling for laws against all sexual contact between consenting adults of the same sex, on the other. But such distinctions have been ignored by the diatribes of the Fearmongers. Likewise, it seems plausible that from a biblical point of view there is no distinction between the immorality of heterosexual adultery and the immorality of homosexual marriage. Yet the Fearmongers have created a distinction, talking about the latter almost incessantly, and the former not at all, when they talk about what our laws should say.

As a result, it may be that there are significant numbers of religious and non-religious people in our culture who might otherwise be more vocal proponents of virtue, but who have been silent on values issues (or have even renounced the "cultural virtue" agenda altogether) because they have been so soured on the subject by the inaccuracies, incivility, and intolerant legislative agenda of the Fearmongers. If there is only moral relativism on the one hand, or the Fearmongers and their laws on the other, many may understandably feel there is no truly Christlike position one can take.

RECLAIMING AMERICA

What should thoughtful Christians, indeed thoughtful evangelicals, make of all this? How are Christians living in a democracy supposed to minister to a surrounding culture that may well be steeped in moral relativism and secularism? The rest of this book is an attempt to provide at least a partial answer to that question. However, an initial response might be useful here.

All of us—evangelicals and others—need to realize that a commitment to evangelicalism does not require one to subscribe to the tenets or tactics of the Fearmongers. While the Fearmongers may be the dominant evangelical voice on social issues in America today, there are other evangelicals who have remained truly evangelical, and even socially engaged, without partaking of the Fearmongers' excesses. Jim Wallis, Tony Campolo, and others illustrate the possibility of evangelical political involvement without a mythological view of American history, a warmongering ethos, or a sweeping set of laws regulating private sex choices. But it is also possible to conceive of an evangelical who remains engaged in an active ministry to culture without endorsing morals legislation of any kind. Such a position is one intellectually respectable alternative to the current evangelical political orthodoxy, as I will attempt to show in this book. For thoughtful evangelicals, this is liberating news, for it may signal an end to the understood political orthodoxy within evangelicalism. And this may in turn counsel non-evangelicals to stop stereotyping evangelicals, to recognize the potential for political diversity within evangelicalism. While evangelical tenets probably demand the adoption of some form of moral absolutism and an acceptance of the primacy of the Bible, they do *not* in any way require one to embrace legal moralism, or to believe that law can transform culture by coercing people in godly directions. Evangelicals must minister to a broken culture, but they need not share John Calvin's faith that human governments are ordained by God to overtly praise him and extend his reign on earth.

A word now to evangelicals specifically. Many of the dominant evangelical voices today—Fearmongers and others also—are encouraging Christians to engage in a self-consciously political ministry to their culture. Many are encouraging other forms of ministry, too, but much attention is given to political and legal ministry strategies. These strategies are doubtless well-intentioned in most cases, but we should examine them critically before accepting any of them as our own. To the extent a ministry is political and legal in its focus, it is necessarily coercive, threatening as it does the exercise of physical, temporal power. Evangelicals who advocate this kind of ministry may be compared to Peter in John 18:8–11. The passage recounts the arrest of Jesus in the garden of Gethsemane.[85] John tells us that Judas led certain Jewish religious leaders with an armed detachment of soldiers into the garden to arrest Jesus. Upon their approach, Jesus identified himself and placed himself in their custody. Bewildered by this sudden turn of events and zealous to defend his Lord, Peter drew his sword and swung at Malchus, a servant of the high priest, cutting off his ear.

Like Peter, many evangelicals today are bewildered by the "sudden turn of events" they believe they are witnessing all around them. Zealous to defend their Lord from the advancing assault, they are resorting to the use of physical, temporal power, drawing their swords and striking off ears, so to speak, through their political activism. No one may fairly doubt their zeal for Christ. Neither did Christ doubt Peter's zeal. But hear Jesus' response to Peter: "Put your sword back into its place; for all who take the sword will perish by the sword" (Matt. 26:52).

Rather than acting upon our first impulse, trusting our experiences and common sense intuition to know the appropriate response to the circumstances surrounding us, we evangelicals would do well to heed Jesus' instruction to Peter and look before we leap. Evangelicals have long been known for pious *action*—mission efforts, benevolence work, and a host of other laudable projects. But to be honest, we have not often been known for deep reflection or considered judgment. Evangelical Christians possess the zeal of Peter in spades; but we too often partake of his thickheaded impulsiveness and arrogance as well. Jesus counsels Peter, and us, to examine matters more carefully. If we are convinced that our culture has problems of spiritual deficiency, we must take the time to contemplate how best to approach our culture, how to fix what is broken. Legislation may be one possible way; but it is not the only way, and it may not always be the best way. Subsequent chapters will illustrate the many ways in which legislation fails to minister to a broken culture. In the worst case, our legislative strategies may even backfire, creating the precedent for a stifling legal regime in which the law ultimately comes to forbid our own faith practices. Sure enough, it turns out that those who take the sword often perish by the sword. Or our coercive morals legislation may actually interfere with a spiritual revival afoot within certain elements of our culture.

But short of these fearful results, the law may be simply ineffective in producing what we hope to achieve in ministry. For most evangelical Christians, changing the laws cannot be a spiritual end in itself. A legal change is only desirable to the extent that it successfully advances real spiritual ends, like personal conversion or spiritual growth. But we must recognize that the proposals for legal change which currently dominate evangelical discourse may in fact be completely powerless to advance real spiritual ends like these.[86] Surely, if all we have to offer the surrounding culture is new laws and lawmakers, the spiritual void around us will go unfilled. Or to say it another way, school violence will not end just because we pass a law requiring daily prayer in public schools. And ending poverty (even if laws could accomplish this) will not end greed, materialism, and abuses of power. The problems go deeper than this, and therefore our challenge in reclaiming American culture for Christ is greater. It is to spark a renewal of hearts and minds—or more precisely, to pave the way for God to do this.

In the Bible, Christians ministered to their culture by living godly, quiet lives and by telling others about Jesus.[87] These Christians were not "do-nothings," practitioners of a socially unaware and impotent faith. Quite the opposite—theirs was apparently an active and powerful cultural ministry. And their simple counter-cultural strategy ultimately revolutionized the world around them. We must consider the possibility that these methods are still the ones that work, and the only ones to which God has called us. Perhaps government, in the end, is poorly suited to the task of evangelism.

NOTES

1. Jerry Adler, "In Search of the Spiritual," *Newsweek*, 5 Sep. 2005, 48; "Faith-Based Funding Backed, But Church-State Doubts Abound," Pew Forum Survey of American Views on Religion, Politics and Public Policy, April 2001, by the Pew Forum on Religion and Public Life and the Pew Research Center for the People and the Press, <http://people-press.org/reports/display.php3?ReportID=15> (28 Oct. 2005) (hereinafter "Pew Forum Survey, April 2001").

2. Pew Forum Survey, April 2001; see also Adler, "Spiritual," 48 (reporting that 33 percent of Americans self-identified as "Evangelical Protestant"). Other surveys, using a classification scheme related to denominational affiliation rather than belief system or self-identification, have yielded similar results. See John Green, James Guth, Lyman Kellstedt, and Corwin Smidt, "Akron Survey of Religion and Politics in America" (1992), cited in Mark Noll, *The Scandal of the Evangelical Mind* (Grand Rapids, Mich.: William B. Eerdmans Publishing Co., 1994, paperback ed. 1995), 9 (finding that over 30 percent of American adults could be classified as evangelicals).

3. See Pew Forum Survey, April 2001. See also Barry A. Kosmin and Seymour P. Lachman, *One Nation Under God* (New York: Harmony Books, 1993), 295.

4. David Bebbington, *Evangelicalism in Modern Britain: A History from the 1730s to the 1980s* (London: Unwin Hyman, 1989), 2–19, cited in Noll, *Scandal*, 8. Professor Noll recognizes that this definition is incomplete for some purposes, but it captures the ideological distinctiveness of evangelicals, and it is that distinctiveness which concerns us here.

5. From this definition it is obvious that the term "moral absolutist" is not synonymous with "evangelical." Some evangelicals are *not* moral absolutists, and many non-evangelicals are. In particular, conservative Catholics (among the non-evangelical Christians) and orthodox Jews (among the Non-Christians) are important non-evangelical religious groups having a majority of members who might fit into the moral absolutist category. Some non-religious people might conceivably be classified moral absolutists as well, since religion is not the only possible source one could embrace for moral authority. In other words, one does not have to be "religious" in order to, for example, morally condemn the Nazis for the Holocaust.

6. Interestingly, a nationwide poll conducted in August of 2005 revealed that 68 percent of self-identified evangelicals believe that "more than one faith can be a path to salvation." Adler, "Spiritual," 52. While such findings do not show that most evangelicals have no belief in "absolute truth," they at least suggest that many people who currently call themselves "evangelicals" might not fully subscribe to the traditional tenets of evangelicalism, including the centrality of Jesus' death and resurrection, and individual belief in these, as the keys to human well-being.

7. Christian Smith, *Christian America? What Evangelicals Really Want* (Berkeley: University of California Press, 2000), 200.

8. Adler, "Spiritual," 54.

9. Adler, "Spiritual," 54.

10. The social critiques published by Jerry Falwell, Tim and Beverly LaHaye, Pat Robertson, James Dobson, and other prominent evangelicals are full of lists of sins (along with scripture references to support these) and calls for cultural recognition and repentance. See also James Davison Hunter, *Culture Wars: The Struggle to Define America* (New York: Basic Books, 1991), 107–58, for documentation of the public arguments in America regarding the possibility of absolute moral truth.

11. In the Pew Forum Survey, April 2001, fully 55 percent of *all respondents* (both religious and non-religious) said they thought religion as a whole was losing its influence on American life, and although no breakdown by religious affiliation was initially reported for answers to this question, it is reasonable to assume that this percentage would be somewhat higher among evangelicals. Additionally, 53 percent of white evangelicals, and 51 percent of black Protestants, reported a belief that the news media unfairly portray people of their religious faith. In the category of "highly committed" evangelicals (based on reported levels of church attendance, frequency of prayer, and importance of religion in one's life), 62 percent reported feeling this way. When asked whether Hollywood and the entertainment industry portray them unfairly, 68 percent of white evangelicals, and 58 percent of black Protestants, said yes. 65 percent of "highly committed" religious respondents agreed. Roughly one-fourth of each of these three groups (white evangelicals, black Protestants, and "highly committed" religious respondents) say they think of themselves as members of a "minority group" because of their religious beliefs. One-third of white evangelicals expressed concern over a growing number of non-religious people in America. One-third of "highly committed" religious respondents expressed the same concern. These data lend some support for extending the results of a survey of Moral Majority activists in Indiana, reported in Clyde Wilcox, *Onward Christian Soldiers?: The Religious Right in American Politics*, 2d ed. (Boulder, Colo.: Westview Press, 2000), 102–103. In the Indiana survey, 40 percent of the activists admitted to feeling "alienated" or "on the fringe of society."

12. Robert Wuthnow, *The Struggle for America's Soul* (Grand Rapids, Mich.: William B. Eerdmans Publishing Co., 1989), 49 (citing *Emerging Trends* (April 1987): 5; *Emerging Trends* is a monthly publication of the Princeton Religion Research Center, an affiliate of the Gallup Organization in Princeton, New Jersey).

13. Wuthnow, *Struggle*, 49 n. 19 (citing *Emerging Trends* (March 1987): 1, and ibid. (April 1987): 5).

14. Smith, *Christian America*, 200.

15. Smith, *Christian America*, 202.

16. "Survey: America's Evangelicals," Religion and Ethics NewsWeekly, March 2004, <http://www.pbs.org/wnet/religionandethics/week733/results.pdf> (4 Nov. 2005), 12.

17. For arguments that some form of culture war is currently being waged in America, see Hunter, *Culture Wars*; Gertrude Himmelfarb, *One Nation, Two Cultures: A Searching Examination of American Society in the Aftermath of Our Cultural Revolution* (New York: Vintage Books, 2001); Wuthnow, *Struggle*. For critiques of this

view, see Alan Wolfe, *One Nation, After All: What Americans Really Think About God, Country, Family, Racism, Welfare, Immigration, Homosexuality, Work, The Right, The Left and Each Other* (New York: Penguin Press, 1999); John A. Hall and Charles Lindholm, *Is America Breaking Apart?* (Princeton, N.J.: Princeton University Press, 1999). Note that if a culture war is indeed occurring it seems unclear in any event which side might be winning.

18. Several times in Acts, Paul asserted his legal rights. See Acts 16:35–40; Acts 22:23–29; Acts 25:6–12. Occasionally, he seems even to have voiced criticism of pagan culture, to an audience of pagans. See, for example, Acts 17:29–31.

19. Some of the best examples of this scholarship include Richard John Neuhaus, *The Naked Public Square*, 2d ed. (Grand Rapids, Mich.: William B. Eerdmans Publishing Co., 1984); Stephen Carter, *The Culture of Disbelief* (New York: Basic Books, 1993).

20. For one collection of evidence about such problems, see William J. Bennett, *The Index of Leading Cultural Indicators: Facts and Figures on the State of American Society* (New York: Simon & Schuster, 1994).

21. For example, Plato, *Republic*, bk. 4; Aristotle, *Politics*, bk. 5, ch. 9; ibid., bk. 7, ch. 1; Niccolo Machiavelli, *Discourses on the First Ten Books of Titus Livius*, bk. 1, ch. 11–12; Edmund Burke, "Letter to a Member of the National Assembly, dated January 19, 1791," in *The Works of Edmund Burke*, vol. 2 (Bohn's British Classics Series, London: Bell & Daldy, 1871), 555 ("Men are qualified for civil liberty in exact proportion to their disposition to put moral chains upon their own appetites . . . . It is ordained in the eternal constitution of things, that men of intemperate minds cannot be free. Their passions forge their fetters.").

22. See, for example, Lev. 26; Deut. 28, 30; Ps. 37; Hos. 10:9–15.

23. See, for example, Alexis de Tocqueville, *Democracy in America*, trans. Henry Reeve, vol. 2 (The World's Great Classics Series, rev. ed., New York: The Colonial Press, 1899), sec. 2, ch. 8; Edward Gibbon, *The Decline and Fall of the Roman Empire*, vol. 1 (New York: John B. Alden, 1885), ch. 20.

24. Biographical information about Moore and his awards is available online at <http://www.morallaw.org/roymoore.htm> (21 Oct. 2005). See also Roy S. Moore and John Perry, *So Help Me God: The Ten Commandments, Judicial Tyranny, and the Battle for Religious Freedom* (Nashville, Tenn.: Broadman & Holman, 2005), inside back cover flap.

25. Chris Cillizza, "Republicans Page Dr. Cheney," *Washington Post*, 4 October 2005, sec. A, p. 3.

26. Roy Moore, interview by Pamela Pearson Wong, as reported in " 'Moore' Justice: An Interview with Alabama Chief Justice Roy Moore," *Family Voice* (May/June 2002): 17.

27. Moore, as reported in Wong, " 'Moore' Justice," 17.

28. Moore and Perry, *So Help Me God*, 108–9.

29. Moore and Perry, *So Help Me God*, 87.

30. Moore and Perry, *So Help Me God*, 92.

31. Moore and Perry, *So Help Me God*, 254, 259.

32. As reported in John F. Harris, "God Gave U.S. 'What We Deserve,' Falwell Says," *Washington Post*, 14 September 2001, sec. C, p. 3. Robertson's response is quoted in context in a press release issued on September 13, 2001, by People for the American Way, available online at <http://www.pfaw.org/pfaw/general/default.aspx?oid=1817> (21 Oct. 2005); see also Barbara Mikkelson and David P. Mikkelson, "Falwell and Above," *Urban Legends Reference Pages*, <http://www.snopes.com/rumors/falwell.htm> (21 Oct. 2005). It should be noted that, in the wake of immediate criticism of these remarks, Robertson claimed to have not understood Falwell's remarks or why he would make them, while Falwell himself told CNN, "I would never blame any human being except the terrorists, and if I left that impression with [anyone], I apologize." Quoted in "Falwell Apologizes to Gays, Feminists, Lesbians," CNN.com, 14 Sept. 2001, <http://archives.cnn.com/2001/US/09/14/Falwell.apology/index.html> (21 Oct. 2005).

33. Jerry Falwell, Foreword, in Gene Wolfenbarger, *When Hollywood Says Yes, How Can America Say No?* (Green Forest, Ark.: New Leaf Press, 1998), 8–9.

34. Wolfenbarger, *Hollywood*, 187–188, 191–192, 194–195. Most of the quote comes from a longer passage entitled "I Saw America the Other Day," which Wolfenbarger approvingly quotes in full and attributes to a 1997 unpublished manuscript written by Elizabeth Collins.

35. Dan Gilgoff, "The Dobson Way: An Evangelical Leader Steps Squarely Into the Political Ring," *U.S. News & World Report*, 17 January 2005, 64.

36. Gilgoff, "The Dobson Way," 62.

37. Gilgoff, "The Dobson Way," 64, 66. Dobson's worldwide audience seems to have grown dramatically, even since 1999. See Greg Barrett, "Why James Dobson's $120 Million Ministry is a Household Name," *The Detroit News*, 3 May 1999, A12, cited in Wilcox, *Christian Soldiers*, 64.

38. James C. Dobson, as quoted in Isaac Kramnick and R. Laurence Moore, *The Godless Constitution* (1996; reprint, New York: W.W. Norton & Co., 1997), 23.

39. James C. Dobson, as quoted in Kramnick and Moore, *The Godless Constitution*, 23.

40. James C. Dobson, "The Second Great Civil War," in James C. Dobson and Gary L. Bauer, *Children at Risk: The Battle for the Hearts and Minds of Our Kids*, 2d ed. (Dallas: Word Publishing, 1990), 22–24, 39.

41. See Karen Breslau, "A Rising Tide, Rocking Boats," *Newsweek*, 17 May 2004, 43. The results of the election are reported at "2004 Primary Election Results," *Statesman Journal (Salem, OR)*, 20 May 2004, sec. A, p. 2.

42. James C. Dobson, Speech Before the Council for National Policy, 7 February 1998, <http://www.wildershow.com/dobson.htm> (21 Oct. 2005).

43. James C. Dobson, as quoted in Sam Kastensmidt, "Nation Rallies for Moore," *The Inside Track*, 18 August 2003, <http://www.reclaimamerica.org/PAGES/NEWS/newspage.asp?story=1329> (21 Oct. 2005). *The Inside Track* is a publication of D. James Kennedy's Center for Reclaiming America, an evangelical political organization. Dobson did personally attend a similar rally for Moore in downtown Montgomery on August 28. Moore and Perry, *So Help Me God*, 230.

44. The particular texts selected for inclusion on Moore's monument can be found online at <http://www.morallaw.org/monument.htm> (21 Oct. 2005).

45. See Pat Robertson, *The Ten Offenses* (Nashville, Tenn.: Integrity Publishers, 2004).

46. For the story surrounding the Miers nomination, including Dobson's involvement and Bush's statements about her religion, see Peter Baker and Charles Babington, "Role of Religion Emerges as Issue," *Washington Post*, 13 October 2005, sec. A, p. 8; Howard Fineman and Richard Wolffe, "Harriet's Hail Mary," *Newsweek*, 24 October 2005, 37–38.

47. Pat Robertson, *The New Millennium* (Dallas: Word Publishing, 1990), 187–188.

48. Robertson, *Offenses*, ix–xii.

49. Robertson, *Millennium*, 166–167, 298 (emphasis in original).

50. Robertson, *Offenses*, xii–xiii.

51. Adler, "Spiritual," 48; Pew Forum Survey, April 2001.

52. Tim LaHaye, *Faith of Our Founding Fathers* (Colorado Springs: Master Books, 1994), 4.

53. LaHaye, *Founding Fathers*, 190, 196, 200.

54. The "Wallbuilders" name is intended as a reference to Nehemiah, who rebuilt the wall of Jerusalem. The Wallbuilders organization is "dedicated to the restoration and rebuilding of the values on which America was built and which, in recent years, have been seriously attacked and undermined." (The quote is from the biographical sketch of David Barton featured on the back cover of David Barton, *America's Godly Heritage*, 2d ed. (Aledo, Tex.: Wallbuilder Press, 1993)). The name "Wallbuilders" is somewhat misleading in that most people who associate the term "wall" with this debate probably have in mind the "wall of separation between Church and State" popularized by Thomas Jefferson's 1802 letter to the Danbury Baptist Association. Barton and his "Wallbuilders" propose anything but a building or strengthening of that wall of separation.

55. Gilgoff, "The Dobson Way," 63.

56. David Barton, *The Foundations of American Government*, 2d ed. (Aledo, Tex.: WallBuilder Press, 2000), 11–12 (endnotes omitted).

57. One thinks especially of Jim Wallis of Sojourners magazine and his new best-seller, *God's Politics: Why the Right Gets It Wrong and the Left Doesn't Get It* (New York: HarperCollins, 2005).

58. Adler, "Spiritual," 54.

59. Smith, *Christian America*, 200.

60. Smith, *Christian America*, 200.

61. Smith, *Christian America*, 200.

62. Smith, *Christian America*, 7.

63. See James Dao, "The 2004 Elections: The Electorate—Gay Marriage; Same-Sex Marriage Issue Key to Some G.O.P. Races," *New York Times*, 4 November 2004, sec. P, p. 4, col. 5; James Dao, "Flush With Victory, Grass-Roots Crusader Against Same-Sex Marriage Thinks Big," *New York Times*, 26 November 2004, sec. A, p. 28, col. 1. See also Gilgoff, "The Dobson Way," 62–71.

64. Vision America, *The AMERICA Plan*, available online at <http://www.visionamerica.us/site/PageServer?pagename=AmericaPlanLanding> (21 Oct. 2005).

65. Tim LaHaye, *The Battle for the Mind* (Old Tappan, N.J.: Fleming H. Revell Co., 1980), 239–240.

66. LaHaye, *Founding Fathers*, 198.

67. Rick Scarborough, *Enough is Enough: A Call to Christian Involvement* (New Kinsington, Pa.: Whitaker House, 1996).

68. Gilgoff, "The Dobson Way," 62.

69. Robertson, *Offenses*, xiii.

70. Dobson and Bauer, *Children*, viii. Many perhaps will note that during the time period Dobson and Bauer are describing, when they felt "as if an alien force has taken control of the government," Bill Clinton began his first presidential term, replacing the Republican George H.W. Bush.

71. From Robert Bork, *Slouching Towards Gomorrah* (New York: ReganBooks, 1996).

72. Smith, *Christian America*, 200. Much of the explanation for these figures may lie in the ambiguity of the phrase "founded as a Christian nation." For those who have been persuaded by the Fearmongers' version of history, however, the phrase is much more than a claim that most Americans called themselves Christians in 1789.

73. Smith, *Christian America*, 200.

74. Cal Thomas, as quoted in John W. Whitehead, "Turning Back to the Things of God," *Oldspeak* (an online journal of the Rutherford Institute), 21 October 2002, <http://www.rutherford.org/oldspeak/articles/religion/oldspeak-calthomas2.asp> (21 Oct. 2005).

75. Thomas, as quoted in Whitehead, "Turning Back."

76. Rick Scarborough, as quoted in Dana Beyerle, "Thousands Rally to Back Moore," *Tuscaloosa News*, 17 August 2003, <http://search.tuscaloosanews.com/apps/pbcs.dll/article?AID=/20030817/NEWS/308170383/1007/ARCHIVES01> (21 Oct. 2005).

77. According to unnamed "observers" at the rally, between 3,500 and 10,000 people attended the August 16 rally. Beyerle, "Thousands Rally." Many similar rallies, attended by thousands of people, were held in Montgomery in the days between August 15 and September 3, 2003. Moore and Perry, *So Help Me God*, 225–31.

78. Gilgoff, "The Dobson Way," 64.

79. Wallis, *God's Politics*, 77.

80. Wallis, *God's Politics*, 67–68.

81. Tom Minnery, *Why You Can't Stay Silent: A Biblical Mandate to Shape Our Culture* (Wheaton, Ill.: Tyndale House, 2001), 68–69.

82. Wallis, *God's Politics*, 261, 266.

83. Wallis, *God's Politics*, 240 (quoting Call to Renewal's *Unity Statement on Overcoming Poverty*, May 2004).

84. Tom Minnery and John Eldredge, "Christian Activism," *Focus on the Family Citizen*, <http://www.communityimpactspokane.org/activism.htm> (21 Oct. 2005).

85. John and Luke refer to the place of arrest as an unnamed "olive grove" across the Kidron Valley from Jerusalem (John 18:1), and as an unnamed location on the

Mount of Olives (Luke 22:39), respectively. Matthew and Mark tell us the place was called "Gethsemane." Matt. 26:36; Mark 14:32.

86. This, in fact, is the informed conclusion of former Moral Majority leaders Cal Thomas and Ed Dobson. They report that the political agenda of the Christian Right successfully claimed national attention but then failed to accomplish its spiritual goal of reforming society. Both men now seriously question the wisdom of Christian political activism. See Cal Thomas and Ed Dobson, *Blinded By Might: Can the Religious Right Save America?* (Grand Rapids: Zondervan, 1999).

87. 1 Pet. 2:11–17; 1 Tim. 2:1–4; 1 Pet. 3:15–17.

Chapter Two

A Selection of Significant Christian Thought About Government

Christians want to know God's will for them in the political realm. We ought to be cautious, searching with humble hearts and open minds, but we must seek God's will in this area of life as in any other. We want to know whether God desires Christians living in a democracy to become politically engaged, and if so, in what way. For evangelicals, the primary evidence to consider must be the text of the Bible, for evangelicals believe the Bible is the ultimate authority regarding the will of God. Yet other sources might also contribute to our understanding of God's will. It turns out that many other sources are available to us, for we are not the first Christians to have considered these questions.

LEARNING FROM OTHERS

In the past some evangelicals have proceeded as if they could learn nothing from outsiders, or even each other, about the meaning of the text. We have sometimes been so keen to prioritize the Scripture above the words of men that we have seemingly gloried in our ignorance of Christian thinkers and their ideas. Determined to know nothing *except* the Bible in all its pristine purity, we have short-changed ourselves of the wisdom of some of the wisest Christians of the ages, and condemned ourselves to ignorance of our own historical roots in the process.

It is important to prioritize the Scriptures, but we go too far when we mistake the *inferiority* of other sources for an *irrelevance*. God speaks to us through the Bible, but also through people. The Bible is inerrant, while people err frequently; and yet, people sometimes rise above error to "speak as the oracles of God" (1 Pet. 4:11, King James Version), and surely the conveyed wisdom and experiences of others can contribute significantly to our understanding of the Bible. The spiritual blessings we have received from the words of others in home Bible studies, Sunday schools, and sermons are eloquent testimony to this truth. And if the insights of living people can help us, so can the written reflections of those who have fallen asleep. Without canonizing these other sources at all, we ought to stop hiding our eyes from them. We ought to seek them out. Respecting them for what they are—fallible human beings' opinions regarding authoritative Scripture—we should affirm their value in enhancing our understanding of the biblical text.

Many prominent Christians through the centuries have thought and written about the purposes of government. This chapter summarizes just the tip of this iceberg. What follows is a brief description of the political theology of five influential Christians from history. A treatment like this is admittedly quite shallow and cannot do justice to the variety of Christian thought on this subject, either as a thematic or historical study. I have not attempted to present a fully representative sample of theological positions, or of time periods in the development of Christian thinking; rather, I have included a few authors of historical significance whose theologies illustrate some major divisions within Christian thought. Perhaps this brief exploration will provide a context for further reflection and study, and especially for wrestling with the Scriptures to be confronted in subsequent chapters.

AUGUSTINE OF HIPPO

Augustine of Hippo, better known as Saint Augustine, is generally regarded as the most gifted and influential Christian thinker of the entire first millennium after Christ.[1] He lived seventy-six years, from A.D. 354 to 430. Born and reared in North Africa during the waning years of the Western Roman Empire, he was a pagan who led a licentious life until, at about the age of 33, he became an orthodox Christian. Eight years later he was elected bishop of Hippo, a coastal city just west of Carthage in what is today Algeria, and from that time he began his tireless lifelong ministry of preaching and writing. He had showed early intellectual promise and therefore had received a thorough classical education despite his provincial upbringing, developing an expertise in logic and rhetoric. As a Christian convert he brought this expertise to bear in the name of Christ. Apparently he also possessed a charismatic and forceful personality that naturally drew a great number of followers. His theology was to greatly influence the church, from his own day until ours.

Augustine is perhaps best known today for his attempts to harmonize Christianity and Platonic philosophy. He was a devoted student of Plato as well as Christ, and although it is clear whom he regarded as having the prior claim on his allegiance, his understanding of Christianity was undoubtedly influenced by his prior intellectual commitments to Platonism. In his two major works, *Confessions* and *The City of God*, as well as many lesser known writings, he presents the ancient Greek understandings of truth as a kind of foreshadowing of Jesus, the One Truth (or Logos) which permeates and sustains all things.

Augustine holds that the material universe exists as a series of imperfect emanations from the central perfect unity, the Transcendent One. To Augustine, this is Jesus, the "Logos" of the first chapter of John. The material world, then, is a corrupted copy of a perfect heavenly model—just as Plato said. Each material thing in the world is an imperfect copy of a perfect heavenly form or ideal of that thing. Hence, Augustine tends to find some value even in the corrupted things of this world, since they are imitations of perfection. At the same time, he is not prone to view the world through rose colored glasses; he does not ascribe perfection to anything on earth or in actual human experience, since perfection is only attainable in heaven.

In his most political work, *City of God*, Augustine explains that the "city of God" or "heavenly city" is his allegorical reference to the worldwide community of human beings who live according to God's will (albeit imperfectly) and are destined for salvation in the hereafter. This he contrasts with the "earthly city," composed of all the individuals who live according to human standards and are destined for eternal punishment. Although in the Middle Ages Augustine's "city of God" was widely interpreted to be the institutionalized Church, Augustine is clear that many who wear the name "Christian" will not be saved and thus are not a part of what he is describing as the city of God. Additionally, the city of God is not a prescription, but a description, and perhaps an idealized description at that; Augustine never believed the city of God, as an operational community, could be realized on earth, and his purpose is not to set forth a political program. The "city" metaphor has perhaps caused some confusion in this regard, since cities are often thought to be governments; but Augustine is using "city" to refer to a group of people united only in the sense of being part of God's true family, people who may not act in concert or even know each other and who are not all under the control of a single human government or social institution.

Augustine's view of earthly governments was informed by his beliefs about not only the nature of God, but also the nature of man. He held that human beings are corrupt and sinful by nature because of man's fall from grace in the Garden of Eden. Sin entered the world through Adam and Eve, and all humanity became corrupted thereafter. For Augustine, then, human governments are a necessary, limited response to the sinful and depraved human condition, but they are incapable of providing a perfect solution for the world's imperfection. They treat the symptoms of the human disease—the wrongs that humans do to one another—but not the cause. Even in this limited goal, governments sometimes fail, because they are dependent on fallen human beings. But civil government is part of God's plan. God in fact ordains governments comprised of human beings, and these governments are both the result of sin and a means of assuaging its effects. Without sin, no government would be necessary; but in a sinful world, government has a purpose: to punish evildoers. Not all evil, however, will be punished. Quite contrary to the classical Greek understanding, human governments cannot aim at anything as high-minded as making men good or virtuous; it is quite enough if the government punishes outward acts of violence and theft against others. It is even too much to expect a human government to be just, since true justice can only be realized in heaven, where justice is not a corrupted copy of true justice but the real thing. The end of the state is not true justice, but a limited peace and order—at best an imperfect copy of justice.

Thus far Augustine's thought squared well with the writings of the Church fathers who had preceded him. Influential Christian thinkers like Origen and Tertullian had reinforced the early church's view that earthly kingdoms have little to do with the kingdom of God and are to be obeyed but otherwise mostly ignored by Christians.[2] Human governments were thought to be ordained by God as an imperfect but necessary response to man's sinful nature. For the Ante-Nicene fathers, who saw no wide opportunities in their days for Christian influence over government policy, the primary civic duty of Christians was to obey the state, by paying taxes and so on. And yet, living as they did in the midst of waxing and waning persecutions at the hands of the Roman state, they recognized that governments are sometimes corrupt, unfair, and ungodly. For this reason they instructed Christians to look to God, not governments, for true justice and happiness. Christians were instructed to obey the state, but only insofar as the state did not require them to violate their prior loyalty to God. If such were required, Christians were instructed to peacefully disobey the state rather than rebel, and to suffer martyrdom if necessary rather than transgress God's will. This they apparently did in sobering numbers.

But when the state began to encourage or even prescribe Christianity, Christians were faced with new questions about civic duty. An opportunity arose for rethinking the part of the early doctrines that advocated passivity or indifference toward government. Augustine did much of this work, for he stood at the historic boundary between the era of Christian persecutions and the era of the Christian state, an entity destined to dominate European politics for the next one thousand years. Only four years before Augustine's conversion to orthodox Christianity, the emperor Theodosius the Great had proclaimed Christianity the official religion of the Roman Empire; thus it is not surprising that Augustine, unlike the New Testament authors and the earlier Church fathers, discusses at some length the duties of Christians who have political power.

According to Augustine, "those who, by a talent for business, are fitted for government, must for the public benefit consent to bear the burden and suffer the hardships of public life. . . ."[3] A monarchical form of government is assumed, and Augustine argues that God desires Christians who are suited to the task to actually seek to be appointed to political office. Christian rulers are to acquire this power in order to praise God "by using it for the greatest possible extension of His worship."[4]

What did Augustine mean when he instructed Christian rulers to use their political power to extend men's worship of God to the greatest possible extent? How did he square this view with his assertion that governments are not intended to make men virtuous or to change hearts, but only to maintain peace and order? On this subject Augustine's writings appear contradictory. In his earlier writings, from about 391–398, he decries any attempt to use state force to compel the Donatists (a heretical group) to conform to orthodox Christianity. He insists on freedom of conscience on the ground that government is unsuited to the task of changing men's hearts.[5] But beginning in about 399 or 400, he begins to approve the use of state coercion to punish the Donatists. At first he only recommends limited punishments such as moderate fines, but by about 409 he advocates any punishment short of death, including exile and forfeiture of property.[6]

How did Augustine justify his later attitude toward state coercion in light of the Scriptures? First, he refers to the example of Christ when Christ "persecuted even with bodily chastisement those whom He drove with scourges from the temple. . . ."[7] Second, he relies on Jesus' parable of the great banquet, as recorded in Luke 14:16–24, in which a wealthy man invited many guests to a great feast but each of them made excuses and did not appear. The householder grew angry at this and ordered his servant to instead invite whatever poor and disabled people he found in the streets of the city. When the servant had obeyed, he reported to the master that there was still room, and the master responded, "Go out into the highways and along the hedges, and compel them to come in, so that my house may be filled" (Luke 14:23) (New American Standard Bible). Augustine interpreted this command figuratively to refer to God's will toward heretics who had once embraced the true faith but had later left it for the "highways and hedges" of false doctrine; they might wish, says Augustine, to be left alone to enter orthodoxy again (if at all) of their own free will, but the Lord's command to the church is to "compel them to come in."[8] This is why Christians may use the machinery of the state to punish heresy. Augustine further asserts that the reason there is no example in the New Testament of Christians asking the state for aid against heretics is that the New Testament was written during the age of the apostles and martyrs, whereas the present age is the age of godly kings, prefigured in the story of King Nebuchadnezzar's edict prohibiting slander against the God of Shadrach, Meshach, and Abednego (Daniel 3:28-29).[9] Despite these biblical references, however, Augustine ultimately admitted that it was not the Scriptures which changed his mind regarding the state's treatment of heretics; rather, it was the practical consideration of the number of instances in which Donatists who had been subjected to state punishment for their heresy had eventually claimed to repent and embrace orthodox Christianity.[10]

Thus, by the end of his life Augustine concluded that the state is ordained by God not only to maintain peace and order, but also to encourage Christian orthodoxy. Although Augustine never assumed the state could change people's hearts or make them virtuous, and he continued to maintain that the state was the result of evil and had limited purposes in a fallen world, he did later in his life assume that state coercion had a role to play somehow in bringing heretics back to the fold. Augustine's interpretation of the parable of the great banquet would be cited a number of times by the medieval Church in an attempt to justify various religious persecutions.

THOMAS AQUINAS

If Augustine was the primary intellectual influence on the Church during the first millennium, the thought of Saint Thomas Aquinas dominated the Middle Ages.[11] Born around 1225 near Naples, he was schooled in a Benedictine monastery between the ages of five and thirteen, at which time he entered the newly emerging university at Naples. There he was exposed to the teaching of a new monastic order called the Dominicans. The Dominicans were studying the works of Aristotle, most of which had just become available in the West. After seven years of study with the Dominicans in Naples, he went to Paris and joined their order, studying theology and Aristotelian philosophy under Dominican masters. By 1256 he was granted a license to teach by the Chancellor of the University of Paris and joined the theology faculty there. He became a devotee of Aristotle. Around 1272 he completed his most important work, the work that became the standard text for theology instruction in Catholic universities all over Europe: the *Summa Theologiae*. He died two years later, at about the age of fifty, having composed over one hundred works besides the *Summa*.

While Augustine is remembered for attempting to harmonize Christianity and Platonism, Aquinas is known for his attempts, particularly in the *Summa*, to harmonize Christianity with Aristotelian philosophy. His additional challenge was to reconcile his theology with that of the widely revered Augustine, who by Aquinas's day had been quoted for more than eight hundred years as a singularly important authority on Christian doctrine. Aquinas did not always succeed at this attempted synthesis, perhaps, but what resulted was a more rational and inductive approach to discovering God's will. For Aquinas, God was rational and had created the world according to certain rational rules. Aquinas therefore emphasized the rationality and goodness of the natural world, rather than its imperfection. Men can understand the rational rules of nature because God created men to be rational. The set of rules, or natural law, exists independently of man's law but is discoverable by men inductively, as they gather evidence from the world around them. Natural law encompasses every field of study, including theology and ethics; thus Aquinas's basic epistemological approach is the same whether one is pondering the composition of rain, the purpose of government, or the morality of contraception.

Aquinas, unlike Augustine, views government as a positive good more than a necessary evil. For Aquinas (and Aristotle), governments are not the unfortunate result of evil in the world, as Augustine would have it; instead, they are the natural consequence of man's social nature. "Man is by nature a political and social animal,"[12] says Aquinas in a paraphrase of Aristotle, and so "it is natural for man to live in association with his fellows."[13] And thus there must be government, for "in every group, there must be something that rules."[14] The natural order is created by God to be good, and governments are part of that divinely ordained order.

Yet government's sphere of authority is still distinct from that of the church; the church reigns supreme even over the state regarding "those things pertaining to the salvation of souls," while the state and not the church ought to command the Christian's highest allegiance in "those things which pertain to civic welfare."[15] As support for this claim, Aquinas quotes Jesus' admonition to "render to Caesar the things that are Caesar's, and to God the things that are God's" (Luke 20:25) (New American Standard Bible).

However, Aquinas's vision of church-state separation is not as neat and tidy as it at first appears. While he believes that government is not capable of directing men to eternal life, he still claims that it has some role to play in furtherance of that end. For Aquinas, government, like every other part of the divine order, is intended by God to further a particular rational end, and the rational end to which human society is directed is "the virtuous life."[16] But Aquinas distinguishes between "ends" and "final ends." "The final end of organized society [is] not [merely] to live the life of virtue but through a life of virtue to attain the enjoyment of God,"[17] he writes. "Divine, not human rule, will lead to that end."[18] Thus Aquinas believes that human government is powerless to bring about the final, highest end of organized society, the enjoyment of God; the most human government can do is to bring about an *intermediate* end—the virtuous life—in pursuit of that highest goal. In this context, Aquinas writes, "Those who are responsible for intermediate ends"—that is, the secular state—"should be subject to the one who is responsible for the ultimate end"—that is, the Pope—"and be directed by his command."[19] Just as the pilot of a ship directs the shipbuilder how to build a ship best suited to a certain task, and the soldier directs the blacksmith how to craft a suitable weapon, so priests ought to direct kings how to guide citizens in virtue so that the society may reach its highest end, the enjoyment of God.[20] Perhaps, then, Aquinas believes the church does have some authority over the state, even in "those things which pertain to civic welfare."

Despite his allusions to church-state separation, Aquinas clearly envisions an important role for human governments (perhaps under some degree of church control) in discouraging vice and encouraging godliness. "It is the duty of the king to promote the good life of the community so that it leads to happiness in heaven—so that he should command the things that lead to heavenly bliss and as far as possible forbid their opposite."[21] In the *Summa Theologiae*, Aquinas clarifies the process by which governments can encourage virtue:

> Man has a natural aptitude for virtue, but the perfection of virtue must be acquired by man by means of some kind of training. . . . Now, it is difficult to see how man could suffice for himself in the matter of this training . . . . [As] to those young people who are inclined to acts of virtue by their good natural disposition or by custom, or rather by the gift of God, paternal training suffices, which is by admonitions. But since some are found to be depraved and prone to vice and not easily amenable to words, it was necessary for such to be restrained from evil by force and fear in order that they might at least desist from evil-doing and leave others in peace, and that they themselves, by being habituated in this way, might be brought to do willingly what hitherto they did from fear and thus become virtuous. Now this kind of training which compels through fear of punishment is the discipline of laws. Therefore, in order that man might have peace and virtue, it was necessary for laws to be framed . . . .[22]

Hence Aquinas seems to be advocating something close to a theocracy—in fact, a kind of theocracy that outlaws sinful acts and encourages righteous acts—controlled by either the Pope or Christian kings who follow the recommendations of priests. But a series of caveats further complicate Aquinas's theocratic prescription. For example, Aquinas opposes laws against sin, even when the sin is easily detected, if the sin is not serious or if the majority of citizens are incapable of restraining themselves from it:

> Now, human law is framed for a number of human beings, the majority of whom are not perfect in virtue. Wherefore, human laws do not forbid all vices from which the virtuous abstain but only the more grievous vices from which it is possible for the majority to abstain and chiefly those that are to the hurt of others, without the prohibition of which human society could not be maintained; thus human law prohibits murder, theft, and suchlike.[23]

There is also a caveat for situations in which outlawing the vice would cause a greater evil of some kind:

> God, who is omnipotent and supremely good, permits some evils which he could prevent to exist in the universe, because if he did so a greater good might be taken away or worse evils follow. So also in human government it is right for those who are in authority to tolerate some evils so as not to prevent other goods or to avoid some worse evil from occurring. As Augustine says, "Suppress prostitution and the world will be torn apart by lust."[24]

Augustine's choice of prostitution as an example is particularly interesting and clarifies both his position and that of Aquinas, who quotes Augustine approvingly here. Both men are clear that prostitution is sinful. Yet apparently it is the sort of vice they both believe should *not* be outlawed. Outlawing it would only serve to tear society apart through the increased prevalence of the sin of lust, which Aquinas evidently regards as a "worse evil" than prostitution.

Another caveat allows religious freedom to non-Christians, but despite the caveat, religious freedom would be denied to former Christians and current Christian dissenters:

> There are some unbelievers such as the Gentiles [referring to non-Christian, non-Jewish citizens] and the [non-Christian] Hebrews who have never accepted the Christian faith. These should in no way be forced to believe, for faith is a matter of the will. Appropriate force may be used by the faithful to prevent them from interfering with the faith through blasphemy, or evil inducements, or open persecution. [However] there are other unbelievers such as heretics and all apostates who once accepted and professed the faith. These are to be compelled, even by physical force, to carry out what they promised and to hold what they once accepted.[25]

Aquinas, following Augustine's later writings, seems to think the state has an especially important role to play in suppressing heresies:

> [Heretics] have committed a sin that deserves not only excommunication by the church but their removal from the world by death. . . .

> The church, however, is merciful and desires the conversion of those who are in error. Therefore she does not condemn them immediately "but after a first and second admonition," as the Apostle [Paul] teaches [at Titus 3:10]. However if the heretic still remains pertinacious the church, despairing of his conversion, provides for the salvation of others by separating him from the church by the sentence of excommunication and then leaves him to the secular judge to be exterminated from the world by death.[26]

Thus Aquinas argues that human governments and laws are tools to be used actively by the church for promoting the virtuous life in society and ultimately leading the society to a fuller knowledge of God. Whether Aquinas's ideal state could properly be called a "theocracy" is open to some doubt, but at least he is clear that the state's objects are openly religious ones. Perhaps the state cannot lead citizens directly to God, but under the counsel of the church, the state is to train its citizens in virtue (and away from vice) so that the *church* can more easily lead them to God. Additionally, the church may draw on the coercion of the state to prevent and punish unorthodox Christian doctrines and practices among the population.

All in all, Aquinas departed significantly from Augustine's negative view of the state. While Augustine, like Aquinas, would have the state punish heretics, he strictly limited the state's role in fostering virtue and continued to stress the fallibility and limits of the state. Aquinas, on the other hand, adopted wholesale the Aristotelian view that the state is a positive good capable (by design) of engineering virtue into the citizenry. In doing so, he perhaps unknowingly presented a theology that would be used to justify many wars and persecutions carried on during the following centuries in the name of Christ.

MARTIN LUTHER

Martin Luther,[27] who lived from 1483-1546, is widely regarded as the most influential of the leaders of the Protestant Reformation.[28] Many would even credit him with beginning that religious movement, which had profound implications for the political, economic, and social orders as well as the religious one. Lutherans now bear his name, but all Protestants are to some extent influenced by his thought and actions.

Luther was educated as a monk in the Augustinian order, but for most of his career, he was a professor and chair of biblical theology at Wittenberg University, in what is today northern Germany. As he began teaching, he led a movement to shift his university's curriculum back toward the doctrines of the early Church fathers—especially Augustine—and away from the Aristotelianism of Aquinas. Success in this endeavor encouraged him to make known other misgivings he had about Catholic creeds and practices. In 1517, just five years into his teaching career, he composed and distributed a list of "Ninety-five Theses" of protest against the Pope and the Catholic Church (reportedly nailing these to the door of the Wittenberg Castle Church). This watershed event, more than any other, is traditionally regarded as the beginning of the Reformation. The newly invented movable type printing press was used to produce many copies of the Theses, which were circulated all over Germany and beyond. The Theses, and various reactions to them, propelled Luther to the spotlight and ultimately forced him into a protracted struggle against the Pope, a struggle that continued until he died. For the remainder of his life, he pressed the attack on what he saw as corruption within Catholicism, writing a number of tracts and preaching a reformed theology.

Luther's view of the state was of course influenced greatly by Augustine's writings.[29] Like Augustine, Luther held that the state was ordained by God in response to a need called forth by man's sinful nature. The purpose of the state is to prevent and punish certain types of sin, in order to compel the wicked to be orderly. True Christians, who are already presumably living virtuous and orderly lives, need no earthly law; the law is for all the *other* people, who are undoubtedly much more numerous. The state cannot make men virtuous, since virtue is a matter of the soul, and so the state, in contrast to the church, does not aim to create virtuous citizens. Thus Luther departs from Aquinas's Aristotelian view of the purposes of the state. He attempts to draw a sharper distinction between the kingdom of God and that of men. But even though the true Christian does not need secular law, it still demands his respect because it is ordained by God. The Christian's duty to the secular state is complete obedience insofar as the state does not require a violation of God's will. Christians are to pay taxes, honor government officials, and even serve in military and government offices when called upon, as a ministry to one's fellow men. The state is not perfect, but it is quite preferable to anarchy in a fallen world and must be respected. Luther's idea is that the state is both the result of sin and its partial remedy, and in this too he represents a shift away from Aquinas and a return to Augustine.

Like Augustine, however, Luther seems to have had conflicting thoughts regarding the proper treatment of heretics and other teachers of false doctrine. On the one hand, in most of his writings on the subject, including his important tracts "On Temporal Authority" (1523) and "To the Christian Nobility of the German Nation" (1520),[30] Luther states a view in concert with that represented above: man's conscience cannot be coerced. "Heresy can never be restrained by force," he writes in a famous and characteristic passage. "One will have to tackle the problem in some other way, for heresy must be opposed and dealt with otherwise than with the sword. Here God's word must do the fighting. If it does not succeed, certainly the temporal power will not succeed either, even if it were to drench the world with blood."[31] Yet on the other hand, in various letters he allows or even requests temporal punishments for false teachers. In one letter he writes: "I cannot advise or permit that false teachers be put to death. It is sufficient to banish them."[32] In another letter, he asserts that if unbelievers have been instructed in the truth and yet persist in their erroneous views, they should be forcibly prohibited from proclaiming those views and also compelled by the state to attend sermons on political and household affairs.[33] He writes in 1525 that "princes should prohibit public crimes such as perjury, manifest blasphemy of the name of God, and the like, without considering whether the culprits believe or not or whether they curse God in private."[34] In March of 1530, he even authorized the death penalty for Anabaptists.[35]

Luther also recommends outlawing certain sins that neither Augustine nor Aquinas would probably have prohibited through the secular law. For example, in his "To the Christian Nobility of the German Nation," Luther recommends laws against prostitution, extravagant clothing, overuse of spices, and excessive eating and drinking.[36]

Thus Luther's vision of the state remains somewhat unclear. While he wants to maintain a clear distinction between the affairs of the soul and the affairs of state, in the end he is not willing to completely forbid a role for the state in soul matters. He would use the machinery of state to punish heretics and compel men's consciences as well as to censor their false religious doctrines. As we have seen, his mentor Augustine partook of the same intellectual conflict. But in some ways Luther's state exceeds Augustine's in attempting to promote virtue and punish vice. Augustine specifically disclaimed any desire to outlaw prostitution and similar vices, and it is difficult to imagine him supporting sumptuary laws. Moreover, he never, as far as we know, approved the penalty of death for heretics, as Luther did for the Anabaptists.

JOHN CALVIN

John Calvin was a French contemporary of Martin Luther and was, like Luther, a widely influential leader of the Protestant Reformation.[37] Born in 1509, he was educated in religion and law at several leading French universities. His major work, *Institutes of the Christian Religion*, completed in 1535, was to become history's most influential systematic statement of Protestant theology. For most of his public life he preached and helped govern the city of Geneva, Switzerland, ultimately establishing there a system of government modeled on his understanding of God's will for the secular state. He died in 1564.

While Calvin and Luther were both reformers, they were far from agreeing on all theological matters. The realm of political theology was no exception. "While Martin Luther emphasized more the negative role of the state as a curb on evil and its care for the bodily welfare of its subjects, Calvin, on the contrary, considers the state in terms of a *Kulturstaat*, that is, a civilizing agency, whose duty it is, under God, to assure the harmonious life of individuals and society."[38] In this view Calvin represents the thinking of Aquinas more than he does Augustine or Luther. One can almost hear Aquinas himself in the words of Calvin:

> As man is naturally a creature inclined to society, he has also by nature an instinctive propensity to cherish and preserve that society; and therefore we perceive in the minds of all men general impressions of civil probity and order. Hence it is that not a person can be found who does not understand, that all associations of men ought to be governed by laws, or who does not conceive in his mind the principles of those laws.[39]

For Calvin, as for most Christian thinkers through the centuries, the primary civic duty of a Christian citizen is to obey the laws of the land completely insofar as they do not require the Christian to violate God's law. Calvin would require this type of obedience even to magistrates who are infidels or tyrants, because in obeying the ruler the Christian is obeying God.[40] But he earnestly desires that the government leaders be Christians, as is only fitting in all institutions of God.

Luther and Calvin agree that God is the source of temporal government. But while Luther remains generally pessimistic about the prospects for godly government or for changing men's hearts through the law, Calvin sees the divine origin of government as a cause for optimism on these fronts. Calvin refuses to "consider the whole system of civil government as a polluted thing, which has nothing to do with Christian men."[41] Although God's kingdom is "spiritual and internal,"[42] so that the kingdom of God and civil government "are things very different and remote from each other," Calvin stresses that "they are in no respect at variance with each other."[43] In fact, Calvin believes that they should vigorously support one another. He holds that the civil government has a very active role to play in promoting God's purposes in the lives of believers and unbelievers alike:

> Civil government is designed, as long as we live in this world, to cherish and support the external worship of God, to preserve the pure doctrine of religion,

> to defend the constitution of the Church, to regulate our lives in a manner requisite for the society of men, to form our manners to civil justice, to promote our concord with each other, and to establish general peace and tranquility.[44]

Earthly kingdoms, though excluded from direct lordship over the heart, are nevertheless entrusted with promoting an environment conducive to Christian faith and orthodoxy. According to Calvin, civil governments must make laws providing for "the due maintenance of religion." Calvin distinguishes such laws from "laws respecting religion and the worship of God," which he says are beyond the purview of the temporal authorities.[45] One way to interpret the government's duty of "due maintenance of religion" might be to say that the government must protect the church as it would protect any other member of society, perhaps even funding the church on top of that. But Calvin clearly rejects this interpretation as too weak; his idea of "maintenance of religion" encompasses much more than funding and protection from abuse. The duty to maintain religion means the duty to regulate society so that "idolatry, sacrileges against the name of God, blasphemies against his truth, and other offenses against religion, may not openly appear and be disseminated among the people."[46] The "maintenance" Calvin envisions, then, is a maintenance of outward doctrinal orthodoxy and religious homogeneity in the society. Nevertheless, he (somewhat confusingly) holds that governments doing this are still short of making "laws respecting religion and the worship of God," which would be impermissible for them.

Calvin's understanding of the purposes and duties of secular government is stated against the backdrop of the "two tables" dispute. The name refers to the two tables of stone upon which the Ten Commandments were written.[47] According to tradition, the first five commandments were written on the first table, and the second five commandments were written on the second table. By Calvin's day, the "first table commandments" were interpreted by many Church leaders to be "religious duties" or "duties to God,"[48] while the "second table commandments" were thought to involve "civil duties" or "duties to others."[49] Virtually all Christians agreed that civil government should enforce the second table, but some disputed whether it should enforce the first table, particularly upon unbelievers and infidels. Calvin believed, as Luther reputedly did not, that civil government should widely enforce some commands from the first table as well as the second.[50] The first table command "You shall not make for yourself an idol," for example, was vigorously enforced by civil magistrates in Geneva and other Calvinist communities.

All in all, Calvin's ideal state looks very much like something most Americans today would call a theocracy, despite his protests to the contrary. He claims that the spheres of civil government and the kingdom of God are completely separate; but the only apparent limitation on state intrusion into the religious sphere is that the state may not make laws "respecting religion and the worship of God." Given the scope of his recommendations for outlawing heresy, blasphemy, idolatry, and the like, it is very difficult to see what laws would be out of bounds under this standard. Indeed, in the name of protecting the church, Calvin supported government edicts of banishment, forfeiture of property, public whippings, and even the death penalty (most memorably in the case of the heretic Servetus, who was prosecuted by Calvin personally and then burned at the stake). One commentator has summarized Calvin's political attitudes as follows:

> It was Calvin's mission to assert that a State has no right to the name of Christian unless it consistently and constantly aims at procuring the moralization of the society and community under its control in accordance with the ethical code revealed in Scripture. . . . Calvin's conception of the State was simply that of the organ through which God ruled the nations for the advancement of His kingdom of righteousness.[51]

So it is that Calvin's thought represents the more militant spirit of the Reformation, the branch of the movement that affirms and extends the political theology of Aquinas.

ROGER WILLIAMS

The ideal for human government that Roger Williams embraced has undoubtedly obtained wide influence around the world today, and particularly in American political culture. It is unclear how much of this influence we can attribute to Williams himself. But whether or not he personally influenced history to the extent of the other authors we have thus far examined, he deserves study as one of the earliest exponents of a highly influential ideal never truly advocated or practiced by the others: the thorough separation of church and state. And he demanded a religiously neutral state not despite, but because of, his extreme zeal for the Christian faith.

Williams was born in London in the early seventeenth century to middle class parents.[52] He was educated at Cambridge through the patronage of Sir Edward Coke, the great English jurist and author of the English Bill of Rights of 1628, who believed Williams showed great intellectual promise. During his studies at Cambridge Williams was influenced by a sect of Calvinism called the Puritans, who got their name by demanding the continued purification of the Anglican Church (itself a Reformation-era breakaway from the Catholic Church). Upon completion of graduate training at Cambridge, Williams became a Puritan minister and chaplain to Sir William Masham, through whom he became acquainted with Oliver Cromwell, John Winthrop (later governor of Massachusetts Bay Colony), and other leading Puritans of his day. Within two years, he had built a great reputation (as a gifted minister or a religious extremist, depending on who was describing him) and had attracted the attention of William Laud, the Anglican Bishop of London and Chancellor of Oxford, soon to become Archbishop of Canterbury, who had begun ordering the torture and imprisonment of leaders of various Christian sects that expressed disagreement with Anglican doctrines. As a particularly zealous Puritan, Williams partook of a heritage critical of the Anglican and Catholic Churches and was also known to associate with Anabaptists and Mennonites. Threatened with imminent persecution, in 1630 he and his wife sailed from Bristol for New England, arriving in Boston Harbor early in 1631. He arrived to find the religious dissidents of New England already divided amongst themselves on religious questions. Massachusetts Bay Colony, centered in Boston and Salem, was a community of Puritan nonseparatists, meaning those Puritans who were unwilling to break fellowship with the Anglican Church despite their criticisms of it; meanwhile Plymouth Colony, on the shores of Cape Cod, was a group of Separatist Puritans (today often called "Pilgrims") who believed the Anglican Church was so corrupt that it could not be considered the true church, and therefore true Christians should not have fellowship with it.

At the time of his arrival in Boston, Williams was only in his late twenties; but already he had built such a reputation in the Puritan community of England that William Bradford (governor of the Pilgrims' colony of Plymouth) described the new arrival as a "godly and zealous" young minister. And John Winthrop, now governor of the Puritan colony of Massachusetts Bay and probably the most powerful American colonist of the seventeenth century, described Williams in his diary as a "godly minister" newly arrived from England.

Williams was immediately invited to be the teacher of the church in Boston, which was the most influential and prestigious position for a clergyman in all of the English-speaking New World. He refused, however, because the Boston Puritans were nonseparatists. Williams was adamant that true Christians should not choose to fellowship Anglicans. The Puritans of Boston, as in most of Massachusetts Bay Colony, were in fellowship with the Anglican Church; but the Separatists of Plymouth Colony were not. He therefore accepted a pastorship with the church in Plymouth instead. But after about two years there, he was dismissed by that congregation for teaching that the colony did not have a moral right to the land they possessed, despite whatever charter the king may have granted, because they had not purchased the land from the Indians in a free exchange.

Upon his dismissal from Plymouth the church of Salem immediately hired him as an assistant teacher, and a number of Plymouth settlers followed him there. In Salem he continued his claims that refusing to pay the Indians for New England land amounted to theft; he also began preaching the novel (and none-too-Calvinistic) doctrine that civil power should not be used to enforce religious opinions. Within one year the General Court of Massachusetts Bay Colony, headed by Winthrop, informed the church at Salem that Williams was subverting the colonial government and that the Court intended to take away some of the land currently allotted to Salem if it did not break with Williams. After appealing unsuccessfully to other Puritan churches for aid against the Court, the church of Salem ultimately capitulated and dismissed him. To avoid arrest by the civil authorities, he fled in the dead of winter to the southern wilderness and the protection of certain Indians with whom he had developed a friendship during his various evangelistic excursions. In 1636 he founded Providence Plantation in Narragansett Bay to the south. This was the beginning of what became the colony of Rhode Island, which at its inception was the only colony to grant complete legal toleration of religious belief. He soon began publishing a series of written responses to those who had written against him, including John Cotton, the influential teacher of the church of Boston. For the rest of his life he made Providence his permanent residence, working as a minister and government official, teaching and writing religious tracts and attempting to evangelize the Indians. His most important written work is considered to be a tract entitled *The Bloudy Tenent, of Persecution, for Cause of Conscience, discussed, in A Conference between Truth and Peace* (1644), which was an appeal, grounded in biblical texts, for the separation of church and state. He died in 1682 or 1683, at about the age of eighty, critical to the end of what he regarded as a Puritan theocracy in Massachusetts.

Turning to his views on government, the first thing to understand about Williams is that he was a theologian first and a political theorist second. In that respect, he followed in the footsteps of Augustine, Aquinas, Luther, and Calvin—not Aristotle, Machiavelli, Hobbes, or Jefferson, some of whom indeed added theological arguments to other evidence in support of their political analysis. Williams's understanding of the Scriptures seems to have absolutely dictated his political views, rather than serving as mere supplemental evidence for them. In fact, he was by education and experience a Puritan Calvinist minister, and as divergent as his political conclusions are from those of Calvin, he apparently was no less sincere an exponent of his Christian faith.

Williams saw government as divinely ordained but created by the assent of men and completely secular in its intended function. In Williams's view, Rom. 13:1–7 stipulates that God ordained civil government, but no more so than any other element of his creation. From this passage and 1 Pet. 2:13–17, Williams deduced (in agreement with the other writers we have seen) that out of respect for God, Christians are to obey civil government authorities insofar as their laws do not require violation of God's commands. But unlike the others (except possibly for Luther), Williams taught that the divine ordination of the state gave it no warrant to enforce an orthodoxy of religious practice. Thus for Williams, "religious and political life were both under the direct supervision of the divine power. But Christ and his disciples taught that the church and state are two distinct authorities, each requiring and deserving obedience within its particular sphere of influence."[53] As further support, Williams cites Christ's injunction to "render to Caesar the things that are Caesar's, and to God the things that are God's" (Luke 20:25) (New American Standard Bible). If Jesus himself taught separation of the two kingdoms, Williams reasoned, it would ill befit the state to attempt some sort of limited cooperative merger in which the state executed or enforced God's law.

In fact, Williams would have the separation so complete as to totally eliminate state funding of religion. In *The Bloudy Tenent*, he writes:

> *Truth.* If any man professing to be a Minister of Christ Jesus, shall bring men before the Magistrate . . . for not paying him his wages or his due: I ask (if the voluntary consent of the party hath not obliged him) how can either the officers of the Parish, Church, or of the Civil State compel this or that man to pay so much (more or less) to maintain such a Worship or Ministry? . . .
>
> *Peace.* Yea but (say they) is not the Labourer worthy of his hire?
>
> *Truth.* Yes, from them that hire him, from the Church, to whom he laboureth or ministereth, not from the Civil State: no more than the Minister of the Civil State is worthy of his hire from the Church . . . . We find two ways of maintenance for the Ministry of the Gospel, proposed for our direction in the New Testament. First, the free and willing contribution of the Saints . . . . Secondly, the diligent work and labor of their own hands . . . .[54]

For Williams, state compulsion in religious matters is completely forbidden, whether it takes the form of criminal penalties for false doctrines or the forcible taxation of citizens to support a church or doctrine with which they disagree.

Williams challenged his readers: "I desire Mr. Cotton and every soul to whom these lines may come seriously to consider, in this controversy, if the Lord Jesus were Himself in person in old or New England, what church, what ministry, what government He would set up, and what persecution He would practice toward them that would not receive Him?"[55] For Williams, the key question for Christians was not, "What did the Church fathers say?" or "What is most natural or expedient?" but always, "What would Jesus do?" And the answer, as he derived it from Scripture alone, was not persecution, but persuasion. "If thou huntest any for cause of conscience, how canst thou say thou followest the Lamb of God who so abhorred that practice?"[56] In this theological objection to punishing heresy through government force, he was arguing against not only John Cotton of Boston, but also John Calvin, Thomas Aquinas, and even Augustine, not to mention many centuries of church tradition.

Importantly, Williams did not derive his theology from some kind of infatuation with the liberal idea of "toleration." Certainly he did not ground any appeals for legal toleration on moral relativism or indeterminacy; in fact, he grounded his pleas on the presumption of unalterable, knowable moral truth. And he did not appeal for every kind of toleration imaginable. Theologically he was anything but tolerant. With respect to the divinely stipulated truth, there could be no compromise, no moral relativism, no agreement to simply disagree and drop the matter. For Williams, the moral requirements of God and Scripture were clear. True Christians should not have fellowship with Anglicans, or indeed with anyone who *did* fellowship Anglicans. True Christians must be born again, regenerated by Christ and his Spirit. True Christians must accept the Bible as the inerrant word of God. True Christians should not practice infant baptism. True Christians are not respecters of persons or races. True Christians should not countenance evil deeds, but expose them. On these and many other doctrinal issues Williams would not compromise. In his view, those who called themselves Christians were already compromising too much, and most of them would no doubt be condemned to eternal damnation. His inflexibility on religious matters bound him to endless debates, social ostracism, tireless and unpopular advocacy on behalf of the Indian tribes, loss of income and employment, and banishment. Yet as intolerant as his separatist theology was (and it was much stricter and less inclusive than the nonseparatist John Cotton's), he was not willing to use the coercive machinery of the state to enforce his theological views. Quakers, for example, thrived in Rhode Island unmolested by the law, although Williams himself passed up no opportunity to publicly refute their heresy, believing they were damned to hell and that their dangerous theology might drag others along with them. Theologically he was an uncompromising moral absolutist; but *his* understanding of moral absolutes committed him, among other things, to *legal toleration*. And this is where Williams differed not only from John Cotton, but from virtually every other Christian on earth in the seventeenth century.

Williams perceived a great danger from allowing civil magistrates to enforce religious rules. And the danger was primarily a religious one. "The church of the Christians under the New Testament [was created] separate from the world; and . . . when they have opened a gap in the hedge or wall of separation between the garden of the church and the wilderness of the world, God hath ever broke down the wall itself, removed the candlestick, and made His garden a wilderness, as at this day."[57] Thus, the "wall of separation," according to Williams, is divinely ordained. (Roger Williams used this metaphor over 150 years before Thomas Jefferson so famously incorporated it in his letter to the Danbury Baptists.) And when Christians breach the wall, granting civil authorities the power to enforce even a few religious rules, true religion is the loser. As Williams puts it, God breaks down the *remainder* of the wall of separation between church and state and gives the church what it is asking: a full-blown theocracy. But theocracies corrupt the faith. When church and state merge, God does not make the wilderness a garden; he makes the garden a wilderness. The church, formerly God's garden, becomes as worldly, debased, and corrupt as the state. For the protection of the church and the faith, civil government must be kept out of religious affairs, as God planned.

Yet Williams was no anarchist. The government restricted from religious legislation would still have plenty to do. The chief object of a state is the "commonweal or safety of [the] people in their bodies and goods."[58] Laws toward these objects are permissible. Thus Williams could write that if one considers the commonwealth as a ship at sea, with a diversity of religions represented among the sailors and passengers, there is nevertheless by necessity and divine will a captain, who is entrusted with commanding the ship so as to reach its (secular) destination safely. The captain ought not compel the sailors or passengers to worship or believe a certain way, but he may nonetheless impose rules designed to bring the ship safely to port—and this notwithstanding any incidental burden on their religious beliefs. In a famous passage, Williams writes:

> If any of the seamen refuse to perform their services, or passengers to pay their freight; if any refuse to help, in person or purse, towards the common charges or defense; if any refuse to obey the common laws and orders of the ship, concerning their common peace or preservation; if any shall mutiny and rise up against their commanders and officers; if any should preach or write that there ought to be no commanders and officers, because all are equal in Christ, therefore no masters nor officers, no laws nor orders, nor corrections nor punishments;—I say, I never denied, but in such cases, whatever is pretended, the commander or commanders may judge, resist, compel and punish such transgressors, according to their deserts and merits.[59]

Williams believes the civil government has an important job to do. Notice that he would go so far as to allow government censorship of anarchist or seditious speech, even when the speaker is motivated by religious belief. But he also holds that the government's job of promoting "safety" must be viewed in secular, not religious, terms. Its task is to protect people's "bodies and goods," not their souls or minds.

CONCLUSIONS

Without thoroughly evaluating the relative merits of each view we have examined, it may be worthwhile here to summarize and to draw a few tentative conclusions.

The mainstream view of the early church, represented by the writings of Ante-Nicene Fathers like Tertullian and Origen, stressed the differences between the kingdom of God and the worldly kingdoms. Their writings emphasize the duty to obey secular law as long as it does not require violation of God's will, in which case peaceful disobedience, not rebellion, is advised. The Fathers are clearly deferential to secular authority, praying for rulers and wishing them well on all occasions. The early Church seems to have had little interest in speculating about God's will for government. All this is perfectly understandable, since Christians at that time had no political power and were at pains to demonstrate to their pagan persecutors that they were obedient citizens who posed no danger to the state. This noninvolvement pressed to the final degree, however, results in a doctrine of apathy about the political realm that Augustine only slightly modified.

Historically and theologically, Augustine bridges the gap between the eras of "Christianity the persecuted sect" and "Christianity the state religion." He mostly maintains the attitudes of the earlier Church fathers toward the state, holding that it is worldly and corrupt and quite distinct from the kingdom of God. For Augustine, like the earlier Church fathers, Christian civic duty consists mainly of obedience to the state, insofar as possible consistent with God's will—although Augustine would also add that Christians with business and leadership skills should seek political office. His furthest departure from earlier Church tradition, however, is found in his zeal for destroying damaging heresies, a zeal that seems to have increased with age. As Herbert Deane has noted, "[Augustine's] defense of the principle of using state coercion against heresy . . . constitutes [his] most important break with the outlook and beliefs of the early Church."[60] No doubt Augustine saw his view not as an illogical or unfaithful shift of any sort, but rather as a rational reaction to the improved political status of Christianity. Nevertheless, he set a long-standing precedent for the use of civil government force in the discouragement and punishment of unorthodox religious doctrine, and many have noted that his willingness to use the state this way seems in tension with his views of the nature and purpose of government.

Aquinas was not a student of Augustine or Plato, but of Aristotle. He sought and assumed a divine rationality and order in the natural world, including human institutions like government, that would have befuddled Augustine. Further, Aquinas wrote at a time and place when Christianity was the *only* socially acceptable and widely professed religion, when the Church was already a civil power unto itself that also held sway over many other powerful worldly kingdoms and baronies. While giving lip service to the idea that church and state are separate kingdoms with separate goals, it is fair to say that both his precept and practice reflected a substantial integration of the two. Aquinas would allow the church to use the state to define religious orthodoxy and punish doctrinal variations, to encourage virtue as defined by the church, to punish vice as defined by the church, to censor ideas deemed by the church to be dangerous, and generally to enforce the rule of God on earth, subject to certain caveats that were to be defined on a case by case basis by the church. He even gave easy approval to the death penalty for unwavering heretics, something Augustine could never bring himself to advocate. Separation of the kingdoms, for Aquinas, just meant that the church shouldn't try to tell the state how to punish theft, and the state shouldn't try to define religious orthodoxy for the church. There was a hierarchy of authority between the two kingdoms that changed from situation to situation, dependent on whether the subject under regulation was "religious" or "secular"; but there was no question that the kingdoms would be working together to achieve whatever purpose the higher of the two authorities commanded.

If Augustine and Aquinas represent two broad and somewhat contradictory strains of political theology within traditional Catholicism, John Calvin and Martin Luther represent, in many ways, the Reformation's divided response to that contradiction. Perhaps it is natural that Luther, subjected to more persecution in his lifetime than Calvin, would be the Reformation's exponent for a return to a more Augustinian attitude toward government. Luther, trained as an Augustinian monk, viewed civil government as a corrupt part of a corrupt world, and his writings are full of doubts about its efficacy as a religious tool. Over and over again he advises secular authorities to tolerate religious diversity—although it seems his actual practice did not always match his ideals. Calvin, on the other hand, had no qualms about using the civil government as a tool to advance the aims of the church and the Christian faith. In the style of Aquinas, he pays lip service to the differences between the nature of earthly kingdoms and the kingdom of God, but then constructs a polity in which the state is the tool of the church to protect pure religious doctrine, support the external worship of God, punish blasphemy and idolatry, and the like. Most of the Calvinists who migrated to Massachusetts Bay Colony and Plymouth Colony apparently took Calvin's vision to heart, as evidenced by a string of notorious religious persecutions, including the Salem Witch Trials, the banishment of Anne Hutchinson, and the public execution of four Quakers in Boston Common.

It is well documented in the pages of history that those who cry loudest for official toleration are the powerless—those who are currently being persecuted or those for whom the threat of persecution is as real and immediate as their local magistrate. On the subject of religious toleration by Christians, almost all toleration literature has been authored by members of minority groups, or at any rate those who are powerless to persecute. Sometimes it has happened in the course of time that those who were formerly powerless gain power over their erstwhile oppressors, and their newfound authority becomes a test of the depth of their devotion to the principle of toleration. History indicates that most fail the test; the persecuted who obtain power usually become persecutors themselves. The Catholic Church of the fourth and fifth centuries, the Lutherans in northern Germany, the Puritan experience in New England, and many other historical examples confirm this truth. However, if there were nothing else to commend Roger Williams to us, he would be worth studying as a sort of historical counterexample to this general truth. In his day all the state churches of Europe, except those in Holland and Turkey, actively persecuted dissenters.[61] After being persecuted for his faith and driven out of England and two colonies, he at last gained temporal power over a colony of his own—but he did not use this power to persecute those with whom he disagreed. Instead, he used his influence to protect religious minorities, who flocked to Rhode Island in droves. Standing halfway between John Calvin and the American Revolution, Williams was a strict moral absolutist who bucked the conventional wisdom of his day and helped to usher in the wave of religious toleration that became so fashionable in the New World one hundred years later, in the American Founding era. His support of religious toleration was not contingent upon his own ongoing victimization. Nor was it due to any religious apathy on his part, as one might plausibly claim with regard to a Thomas Jefferson; on the contrary, he was as devoted to Christ and to uncompromising biblical truth as any of his contemporaries. In fact, he believed it was this absolute biblical truth that dictated a civil government neutral toward religion.

One thing we learn from a study of these thinkers is how easily we may be deluded into internally inconsistent and even hypocritical views about government. Each of the five thinkers we have studied would claim that government and religion are quite separate kingdoms which operate in completely different spheres of authority. None of them claimed to be advocating a theocracy in the style of ancient Israel. And yet I suspect that from the perspective of most Christians today, state punishment of religious heretics, a policy supported from time to time by four of these five, is quite inconsistent with their stated desire to separate church and state. It is especially striking how different the specific policies of these thinkers turn out to be, given that they all claim to support "separation of church and state." The separationist position is used as a foundational assumption behind everything from the strict separationism of Roger Williams to what might be called the quasi-theocracy advocated by John Cotton and John Calvin. One might wonder that Calvin, Aquinas, and others never seemed to understand the inconsistencies inherent in their various claims about civil government. In light of history, we might be wise to reexamine our own political theology, to see just how consistent our own claims are.

It is true that most Christians today probably oppose the idea that the government should discover and punish heresy. American Christians are likely, in fact, to view such an idea as positively un-American as well as unchristian. Of the five influential theologians we have studied, only Roger Williams agrees completely. That, of course, does not make Roger Williams right. But it may not be out of place at this point to suggest that Williams's doctrine presents a unique and appealing prospect, one that the other theologies do not.

Notice that "separation of church and state" means something very particular for Williams, something that we will miss if we do not attend his argument carefully. To keep secular government's laws "secular," separated from religion and the church, is not necessarily to create a "naked public square" of some sort, a public policy debate closed to religious considerations. Williams represents the idea that religious opinions about politics should be not only legally tolerated, but respected. For Williams, separation of church and state does not imply that religion has nothing to say about law, or that political leaders should be religiously unaffiliated, or even that they should keep their religious views to themselves. In fact, if Williams the political leader had been prohibited from introducing *religion* into political discussions, he would have had nothing whatever to say about politics. To him, religion was not just one relevant consideration for government; it was in a key sense the *only* relevant consideration for government. And yet he advocated as strict a separation of church and state as the world had ever known. His theology suggests the interesting possibility of a *religiously informed* separation of church and state: a separation that recognizes the primacy of the kingdom of God over all things and therefore recognizes that God might have something to say about how Caesar is to rule *within his secular jurisdiction*, while still forbidding Caesar to function (or be used) as the executive branch of the kingdom of God. Separation need not entail the naked public square, or a church forbidden to speak about politics, or the ecumenical acceptance of all religious views as equally valid. It *can* mean any or all of these things, of course; but it *need* not. It simply requires that government do nothing that cannot be fairly justified *outside* the faith, on some secular ground. It means a serious, honest commitment to limiting Caesar's power to his own jurisdiction.

This chapter has included just a tiny sampling of some salient Christian political theologies from history. If this brief analysis accomplishes nothing else, hopefully it prepares us in at least two ways to investigate God's will for politics. First, our historical analysis might suggest some ways of understanding God's will that we have not considered seriously before. Second, it might help us place ourselves and our views in historical context by showing us some of our theological ancestry. Preparation of this sort is surely worthwhile for anyone who will be interpreting the biblical text. In the next chapter we will begin doing just that.

NOTES

1. For the discussion of Augustine, I have drawn from Herbert A. Deane, *The Political and Social Ideas of St. Augustine* (1963; 2d printing, New York: Columbia University Press, 1966).

2. Regarding the attitudes of the early church and the Ante-Nicene Fathers to the Roman state, see, for example, T.M. Parker, *Christianity & the State in the Light of History* (London: Adam and Charles Black, 1955), 35–40; J. Philip Wogaman, *Christian Perspectives on Politics*, rev. ed. (Louisville, Kentucky: Westminster John Knox Press, 2000), 35–38.

3. Augustine, *Contra Faustum Manichaeum* 22.58, translated in Philip Schaff, ed., *A Select Library of the Nicene and Post-Nicene Fathers*, 1st series, vol. 4 (1886–1890; reprint ed., Grand Rapids, Mich.: Eerdmans Publishing Co., 1978–1979), 294.

4. Augustine, *City of God* 5.24, Marcus Dods, trans., vol. 1 (New York: Hafner Publishing, 1948), 223.

5. See Augustine, *Epistula* 23.7, translated in Schaff, ed., *A Select Library*, vol. 1, 244; Augustine, *Epistula* 34.1, translated in Schaff, ed., *A Select Library*, vol. 1, 262; Augustine, *Epistula* 44.5.10–11, translated in Schaff, ed., *A Select Library*, vol. 1, 288–89.

6. See Augustine, *Retractationum* 2.5; Augustine, *Epistula* 93.5.17, translated in Schaff, ed., *A Select Library*, vol. 1, 388; Augustine, *Epistula* 93.3.10, translated in Schaff, ed., *A Select Library*, vol. 1, 385; Augustine, *Epistula* 7.25–26, translated in Schaff, ed., *A Select Library*, vol. 4, 642–43; Augustine, *Epistula* 89.6–7, translated in Schaff, ed., *A Select Library*, vol. 1, 375–76.

7. Augustine, *Contra Litteras Petiliani* 2.178, translated in Schaff, ed., *A Select Library*, vol. 4, 571.

8. Augustine, *Sermo* 112.8, translated in Schaff, ed., *A Select Library*, vol. 6, 449.

9. Augustine, *Epistula* 93.3.9, translated in Schaff, ed., *A Select Library*, vol. 1, 385.

10. Augustine, *Epistula* 93.5.16–17, translated in Schaff, ed., *A Select Library*, vol. 1, 388. There is significant evidence that Augustine exaggerated the effectiveness of the punishments in bringing about Donatist conversions. Even if not, however, it would be in no way surprising if a number of people who were being persecuted for their sincere religious beliefs suddenly disclaimed those beliefs. Whether they truly changed their minds is, of course, another question.

11. For the material on Thomas Aquinas, I have relied on Paul E. Sigmund, trans. and ed., *St. Thomas Aquinas on Politics and Ethics* (New York: W.W. Norton & Co., 1988); George H. Sabine, *A History of Political Theory*, 3d ed. (New York: Holt, Rinehart and Winston, 1961), 247–57; Donald G. Tannenbaum and David Schultz, *Inventors of Ideas: An Introduction to Western Philosophy* (New York: St. Martin's Press, 1998), 90–96.

12. Thomas Aquinas, *On Kingship*, ch. 1, in Sigmund, *St. Thomas Aquinas*, 14.

13. Aquinas, *On Kingship*, ch. 1, in Sigmund, *St. Thomas Aquinas*, 14.

14. Aquinas, *On Kingship*, ch. 1, in Sigmund, *St. Thomas Aquinas*, 15.

15. Thomas Aquinas, *Commentary on the Sentences* 2.44.4, in *On Law, Morality, and Politics*, ed. W.P. Baumgarth and R.J. Regan (Indianapolis: Hackett Publishing Co., 1988), 259–60.

16. Aquinas, *On Kingship*, ch. 14, in Sigmund, *St. Thomas Aquinas*, 27.

17. Aquinas, *On Kingship*, ch. 14, in Sigmund, *St. Thomas Aquinas*, 27.

18. Aquinas, *On Kingship*, ch. 14, in Sigmund, *St. Thomas Aquinas*, 27.

19. Aquinas, *On Kingship*, ch. 14, in Sigmund, *St. Thomas Aquinas*, 28.

20. Aquinas, *On Kingship*, ch. 14, in Sigmund, *St. Thomas Aquinas*, 27.

21. Aquinas, *On Kingship*, ch. 15, in Sigmund, *St. Thomas Aquinas*, 28.

22. Thomas Aquinas, *Summa Theologiae*, I-II, q. 95, a. 1, in *St. Thomas Aquinas on Law, Morality, and Politics*, William P. Baumgarth and Richard J. Regan eds. (Indianapolis: Hackett Publishing Co., 1988), 57.

23. Aquinas, *Summa*, I-II, q. 96, a. 2, in Baumgarth and Regan, *St. Thomas Aquinas*, 67.

24. Aquinas, *Summa*, II-II, q. 10, a. 11, in Sigmund, *St. Thomas Aquinas*, 62 (quoting Augustine, *On Ordination* 2.4).

25. Aquinas, *Summa*, II-II, q. 10, a. 8, in Sigmund, *St. Thomas Aquinas*, 61.

26. Aquinas, *Summa*, II-II, q. 11, a. 3, in Sigmund, *St. Thomas Aquinas*, 63–64.

27. The material on Martin Luther is drawn from Mark U. Edwards, *Luther and the False Brethren* (Stanford: Stanford University Press, 1975); Luther Hess Waring, *The Political Theories of Martin Luther* (1910; reiss. Port Washington, N.Y.: Kennikat Press, 1968); Sabine, *Political Theory*, 358–62.

28. See, for example, Michael H. Hart, *The 100: A Ranking of the Most Influential Persons in History*, rev. ed. (Secaucus, N.J.: Carol Publishing Group, 1992).

29. For Luther's view of the nature of the state and the necessity of maintaining the distinction between religious and temporal power, see Martin Luther, "Temporal Authority: To What Extent It Should Be Obeyed" (1523), in Walther I. Brandt, ed., J.J. Schindel, trans., *Luther's Works*, vol. 45 (Philadelphia: Fortress Press, 1962), 81–129.

30. Luther, "Temporal Authority"; Martin Luther, "To the Christian Nobility of the German Nation, Concerning the Reform of the Christian Estate" (1520), in James Atkinson, ed., Charles M. Jacobs, trans., *Luther's Works*, vol. 44 (Philadelphia: Fortress Press, 1966), 123–217.

31. Luther, "Temporal Authority," Part 2, in Brandt, ed., *Luther's Works*, vol. 45, 114.

32. Martin Luther, "Letter to Wenceslas Link, Dated July 14, 1528," in the Weimar edition of Luther's collected letters, *Briefe*, vol. 4, 498 f, cited in Ewald M. Plass, ed., *What Luther Says*, vol. 2 (St. Louis: Concordia Publishing, 1959), 648.

33. Martin Luther, "Letter to Thomas Löscher, Dated August 26, 1529," in Gottfried G. Krodel, ed. and trans., *Luther's Works*, vol. 49 (Philadelphia: Fortress Press, 1972), 233–34.

34. Martin Luther, "Letter to George Spalatin, Dated November 11, 1525," in the Erlangen edition of Luther's collected letters, vol. 5, 271, quoted in William A. Mueller, *Church and State in Luther and Calvin: A Comparative Study* (Nashville, Tennessee: Broadman Press, 1954), 62.

35. John T. Noonan, Jr., and Edward McGlynn Gaffney, Jr., *Religious Freedom: History, Cases, and Other Materials on the Interaction of Religion and Government*, 2d ed. (New York: Foundation Press, 2001), 117, citing Joseph Lecler, *Toleration and the Reformation*, trans. T.L. Weslow (New York: Association Press, 1960), vol. 1, 162; Mueller, *Church and State*, 62.

36. Luther, "To the Christian Nobility of the German Nation," 27, in Atkinson, ed., *Luther's Works*, vol. 44, 212–15. Regarding prostitution, Augustine had specifically disclaimed any willingness to outlaw the practice, and Aquinas quoted him favorably on this principle, as noted earlier in this chapter. See Aquinas, *Summa*, II-II, q. 10, a. 11, in Sigmund, *St. Thomas Aquinas*, 62 (quoting Augustine, *On Ordination* 2.4).

37. For the material on John Calvin, I have relied on A. Mitchell Hunter, *The Teaching of Calvin: A Modern Interpretation*, 2d ed. (Westwood, N.J.: Fleming H. Revell Co., 1950); Mueller, *Church and State*, 73–163; John C. Bennett, *Christians and the State* (New York: Charles Scribner's Sons, 1958), 40–43; Tannenbaum and Schultz, *Inventors*, 132–34.

38. Mueller, *Church and State*, 142.

39. John Calvin, *Institutes of the Christian Religion*, bk. 2, chap. 2, par. 13, in John Allen, trans., *Institutes of the Christian Religion, by John Calvin*, 6th American ed., vol. 1 (Philadelphia: Presbyterian Board of Publication and Sabbath-School Work, 1921), 245.

40. See Calvin, *Institutes*, bk. 4, chap. 20, par. 23–32, in Allen translation, vol. 2, 655–63.

41. Calvin, *Institutes*, bk. 4, chap. 20, par. 2, in Allen translation, vol. 2, 634.

42. Calvin, *Institutes*, bk. 4, chap. 20, par. 2, in Allen translation, vol. 2, 634.

43. Calvin, *Institutes*, bk. 4, chap. 20, par. 1, in Allen translation, vol. 2, 633.

44. Calvin, *Institutes*, bk. 4, chap. 20, par. 2, in Allen translation, vol. 2, 634.

45. Calvin, *Institutes*, bk. 4, chap. 20, par. 3, in Allen translation, vol. 2, 635.

46. Calvin, *Institutes*, bk. 4, chap. 20, par. 3, in Allen translation, vol. 2, 635.

47. The Ten Commandments are found at Exod. 20:1-17. According to Deut. 4:13, they were originally written by God on two stone tablets.

48. The first five commandments are: (1) You shall have no other gods before me; (2) You shall not make for yourself an idol; (3) You shall not make wrongful use of the name of the Lord your God; (4) Remember the sabbath day, and keep it holy; and (5) Honor your father and your mother. (Exod. 20:3–12)

49. The second five commandments are: (6) You shall not murder; (7) You shall not commit adultery; (8) You shall not steal; (9) You shall not bear false witness against your neighbor; and (10) You shall not covet you neighbor's wife, or anything that belongs to your neighbor. (Exod. 20:13–17)

50. Mueller, *Church and State*, 128; but see Calvin, *Institutes*, bk. 4, chap. 20, par. 14–16, in Allen translation, vol. 2, 648–50, where Calvin disclaims at length any attempt to impose the law of Moses *in its entirety* through the civil state.

51. Hunter, *Calvin*, 264.

52. The material on Roger Williams comes from Noonan and Gaffney, *Religious Freedom*, 124–31; Isaac Kramnick and R. Laurence Moore, *The Godless Constitution: The Case Against Religious Correctness* (New York: W.W. Norton and Co., 1997), 46–66; James E. Ernst, *The Political Thought of Roger Williams* (Seattle, Wash.: University of Washington Press, 1929).

53. Ernst, *Political Thought*, 32.

54. Roger Williams, *The Bloudy Tenent, of Persecution, for cause of Conscience, discussed, in A Conference between Truth and Peace* (1644), in Samuel L. Caldwell, ed., *The Complete Writings of Roger Williams*, vol. 3 (New York: Russell & Russell, 1963), 304–5 (italics deleted and spelling revised to conform to modern English).

55. Roger Williams, *Mr. Cotton's Letter Lately Printed, Examined and Answered* (1644), in Perry Miller, *Roger Williams: His Contribution to the American Tradition* (Indianapolis: Bobbs-Merrill, 1953), 100.

56. Roger Williams, *Bloudy Tenent*, in Miller, *Roger Williams*, 109.

57. Roger Williams, *Mr. Cotton's Letter*, in Miller, *Roger Williams*, 98.

58. Roger Williams, *Bloudy Tenent*, in Caldwell, ed., *Complete Writings*, vol. 3, 354 (italics deleted and spelling revised to conform to modern English).

59. Roger Williams, "Letter to the Town of Providence, Dated January, 1654–1655," in Noonan and Gaffney, *Religious Freedom*, 130–31.

60. Deane, *Ideas of St. Augustine*, 228.

61. James Ernst, *Roger Williams: New England Firebrand* (New York: The Macmillan Co., 1932), 433.

Part II

POLITICS: DIVINE DUTY OR DIABOLICAL DISTRACTION?

Chapter Three

Examining the Case for Political Noninvolvement

So how is a Christian to decide what to do on election day? Presumably, the same way a Christian ought to decide what to do on any other day. That is, by (1) discovering God's will on the matter, if possible, and (2) obeying God. This sounds simple, perhaps, but of course it is much harder than it sounds. One problem may be our inability to determine God's will. But often the more nagging difficulty, if we are honest with ourselves, is our apathy toward God's will. For we human beings are notoriously, stubbornly insistent on doing things our own way.

The question of the moment comes down to this: Have we reached our political conclusions because of our understanding of God's will, or have we molded our understanding of God's will to fit our preexisting political preferences? It is essential, before we begin the search for God's will about politics, to clean the slate, if possible, of any political creeds we may already hold. We must remind ourselves why we are looking for God's will, and we must recommit ourselves to following his will even before we know specifically what it is.

"MERE" CHRISTIANITY

Christianity, on New Testament terms, is a demanding religion. The New Testament teaches that it is impossible to be a casual Christian. Jesus himself said, "Whoever loves father or mother more than me is not worthy of me; and whoever loves son or daughter more than me is not worthy of me; and whoever does not take up the cross and follow me is not worthy of me" (Matt. 10:37–38). In another place Jesus says, "Any of you who does not give up everything he has cannot be my disciple" (Luke 14:33) (New International Version). This is strong language, for a strong religion. Perhaps one can take a casual interest in learning and subscribing to the philosophy of Immanuel Kant or Plato. But "casual Christianity" is, according to the New Testament, an oxymoron, an inherent contradiction. Being a follower of Jesus means giving oneself fully to him, sacrificing one's own will fully to his in every aspect of life.[1] Christianity is not for the dabbler.

Christianity requires deep commitment. And committed Christianity means the renewing of one's mind. It means basing one's ideas and actions on God's will, not choosing an understanding of God's will that fits one's preconceived ideology. True mind renewal, in fact, might entail not only an abandonment of sinful habits, but a revision of many of our old assumptions and intellectual commitments as well. It will definitely require us to jettison whatever old prejudices we might have. It means living and thinking *differently* than we otherwise would because of a relationship with Jesus and a knowledge of truth. In short, Christianity ought to cause a difference in who we are. We ought to be different people as Christians than we would be if we were not followers of Christ.

What does this tell us about committed Christianity and politics? Simply this: Committed Christians submit their will to God's will in *politics*, just as in every other aspect of life. God must be God. This means our political activities and preferences, as surely as our other activities and preferences, must bow to God's will.

This principle may not sound controversial, but it is a vitally important one. Before we even seek God's will in the realm of politics, we must make the commitment to live with what we find. For our findings may surprise us.

Committed Christians seek God's will, not a flawed understanding of God's will tainted by their own predispositions. The danger is clear: if we think we already know God, we may assume we already know his will in the political realm. If we cannot step outside what we think we know and let God speak to us afresh, we need not search for God's will at all, for it will do us no good. A search for truth under those conditions turns into a search for proof texts to support one's predetermined pet theory. Committed Christians cannot condone this approach. It is putting words in God's mouth. It is the height of arrogance.

So the committed Christian will commit herself to determining God's will in the most objective way possible, and then obeying God's will, whatever it is. Are we prepared to do this in the political realm? Are we prepared to search objectively for God's will and then to obey it regardless of what our political preferences *used* to be? Knowing Jesus—knowing the truth—sometimes demands radical change. When the Pharisees in Jesus' day were confronted with the truth, they wouldn't believe it, because it was so different from their traditions and preconceived notions about God. By now, we ought to know better.

We must begin our search open to the possibility that God wants us to radically change the ways we think and act politically. For instance, God may desire that we change our political party affiliation. Or that we vote only for candidates who espouse a certain religious doctrine. Are we willing to obey him under those circumstances? Or he may want us to become pacifists. Or to spend our afternoons picketing abortion clinics. Or to oppose capital punishment. Or to abolish the First Amendment. Or to lobby for increased funding for welfare programs. Or he might want us to stop voting altogether. Are we prepared to obey God, no matter what? Committed Christianity demands no less.

PASSAGES DIRECTLY ADDRESSING THE CHRISTIAN'S RELATIONSHIP TO CIVIL GOVERNMENT

Having made the commitment to search for God's will and to live with the results, the next step for evangelicals must be an honest analysis of the Bible. And for those who believe the Bible is the most authoritative statement of God's will for Christians, the most straightforward way to begin any inquiry into God's will would surely be to examine those biblical passages that directly address the subject at hand. While we must guard against simple "proof-texting" or reading passages without taking account of their larger context, it is nonsensical to ignore or discount clearer textual instructions in favor of passages containing analogies, allegories, or some other general truth supposedly relevant to the subject under investigation. Whatever has been said directly to the issue ought to be considered first, and every other arguably relevant text evaluated in light of the more direct statement. So our search of Scripture must begin with Scriptures that speak explicitly about human government.

A word now about the Old Testament. Many Old Testament passages speak explicitly about government, but for Christians the New Testament, especially where it provides instruction or approved examples for a Christian audience, ought to be regarded as better evidence of God's will for modern governments than any Old Testament passages. One reason is that commands and examples written for a Christian audience are more directly the subject of our inquiry and will not be found in the Old Testament. Another reason is that (as most Christians agree) it is now possible to be pleasing to God by accepting Jesus under the New Covenant, without adhering to all the strictures that bound the Jews under the Old Covenant.[2] In particular, most Christians believe the New Testament writings clearly teach that the New Covenant supersedes the governmental and legal forms commanded for the Jews under the Old Covenant. When pressed, evangelicals in particular are not likely to warm to the notion of incorporating all of the Torah's prohibitions or governing institutions into American law. In fact, most evangelicals are probably uncomfortable with any general suggestion that the Old Testament should be a source of authority for Christian behavior, much less a model for law or government; we tend rather to emphasize, with the author of Hebrews, that the Old Testament is obsolete (Heb. 8:13). Most Christians in America do not feel obligated to keep a Saturday sabbath or offer animal sacrifices, nor do they embrace socio-political institutions like the monarchy and the inherited priesthood. Since few evangelicals embrace the entire Old Testament as a pattern for social or political institutions today, those who wish to copy its provisions only selectively must justify each of their particular selections, in light of some authority outside the Old Testament itself.

Thus, when we read an Old Testament command or example pertaining to ancient Israel's government—such as the command to impose capital punishment for blasphemy[3]—we cannot assume it reflects God's desire for human laws enacted by Christians today. In fact, if we truly live under a New Covenant, one might argue that the assumption ought to run in exactly the opposite direction, that no command or example from the Old Testament is binding on Christians unless confirmed somehow by the New Testament.[4] This is not to say that the Old Testament should be ignored, or that the God of the Old Testament is a different God. The Old Testament may indeed tell us something important about God's nature, but it may not be the best source for determining God's will for our social institutions (including laws and government), since it is precisely the social institutions of the Old Covenant, and their function in bringing man into relationship with God, that the New Covenant was designed to obviate.

So let us begin our textual analysis by posing the following question: Which passages from the New Testament, written for a Christian audience, speak most directly to the question of the Christian's relationship to civil government? Four passages seem uniquely to fit into this category, judging not only by their content but also by the number of times they were cited by the early Fathers when those men wrote about civil government. The passages are Rom. 13:1–7, 1 Pet. 2:11–17, 1 Tim. 2:1–4, and Luke 20:19–26 (with its parallels in the other gospels).[5]

Of these four passages, the most extended treatment of the subject of civil government is found in Paul's letter to the Romans:

> Let every person be subject to the governing authorities; for there is no authority except from God, and those authorities that exist have been instituted by

> God. Therefore whoever resists authority resists what God has appointed, and those who resist will incur judgment. For rulers are not a terror to good conduct, but to bad. Do you wish to have no fear of the authority? Then do what is good, and you will receive its approval; for it is God's servant for your good. But if you do what is wrong, you should be afraid, for the authority does not bear the sword in vain! It is the servant of God to execute wrath on the wrongdoer. Therefore one must be subject, not only because of wrath but also because of conscience. For the same reason you also pay taxes, for the authorities are God's servants, busy with this very thing. Pay to all what is due them—taxes to whom taxes are due, revenue to whom revenue is due, respect to whom respect is due, honor to whom honor is due. (Rom. 13:1–7)

The second of the passages is very much along the same lines. It comes from the first letter of Peter:

> Beloved, I urge you as aliens and exiles to abstain from the desires of the flesh that wage war against the soul. Conduct yourselves honorably among the Gentiles, so that, though they malign you as evildoers, they may see your honorable deeds and glorify God when he comes to judge.
>
> For the Lord's sake accept the authority of every human institution, whether of the emperor as supreme, or of governors, as sent by him to punish those who do wrong and to praise those who do right. For it is God's will that by doing right you should silence the ignorance of the foolish. As servants of God, live as free people, yet do not use your freedom as a pretext for evil. Honor everyone. Love the family of believers. Fear God. Honor the emperor. (1 Pet. 2:11–17)

The short passage from Paul's first letter to Timothy adds the instruction to pray for government leaders:

> First of all, then, I urge that supplications, prayers, intercessions, and thanksgivings be made for everyone, for kings and all who are in high positions, so that we may lead a quiet and peaceable life in all godliness and dignity. This is right and is acceptable in the sight of God our Savior, who desires everyone to be saved and to come to the knowledge of the truth. (1 Tim. 2:1–4)

The fourth passage is a bit different. It takes the form of a narrative, not an instructional letter. It recounts a saying of Jesus himself when he was asked to give a religious opinion about a political controversy:

> The scribes and the chief priests tried to lay hands on [Jesus], and they feared the people; for they understood that He spoke [a certain populist] parable against them. So they watched Him, and sent spies who pretended to be righteous, in order that they might catch Him in some statement, so that they could deliver Him to the rule and the authority of the governor. They questioned Him, saying, "Teacher, we know that You speak and teach correctly, and You are not partial

> to any, but teach the way of God in truth. Is it lawful [according to God's law] for us to pay taxes to Caesar, or not?" But He detected their trickery and said to them, "Show me a denarius. Whose likeness and inscription does it have?" They said, "Caesar's." And He said to them, "Then render to Caesar the things that are Caesar's, and to God the things that are God's." And they were unable to catch Him in a saying in the presence of the people; and being amazed at His answer, they became silent. (Luke 20:19–26) (New American Standard Bible)

Perhaps we should begin our analysis of these passages by suggesting some of their more obvious, less controversial meanings.[6] First among these is that God wants Christians to be generally obedient to civil government and its laws. Obedience to the secular state is in fact a central message in the passages from Romans, 1 Peter, and Luke. How far a Christian should take that obedience is another question, a question that may not be addressed in these passages. Surely not *all* the state's laws must be obeyed—otherwise, early Christians would have been obliged to obey laws requiring emperor worship and the like—but these passages *at least* lay down a general principle that obedience to the law is important to God, that Christians should obey secular law if obedience does not require violation of God's will in some other respect.

This may in fact suggest that Christians are not free to disobey a law just because it is unwise or because it fails adequately to promote virtue, truth, justice, liberty, equality, or godliness. Note that Paul probably wrote his instructions to the Romans during the reign of the Roman emperor Nero, who would not yet have begun to persecute Christians but was already far from a paradigm of virtue or Christian values.[7] Many Roman laws, made by Nero or those like him, had nothing to do with virtue or godliness but apparently were nevertheless to be obeyed by Christians. For example, in the passage from Romans, Paul (as Jesus had done in the Luke passage) directly instructs Christians to pay taxes to Rome—taxes that would be used to finance Nero's vain pleasure palaces and entertainment venues, his armies making war on other nations for no other cause than greed and glory, his civil government administration which routinely erected and staffed pagan temples as part of a large and powerful civic religion.[8]

Considerations like these caused many Jews, particularly those of the Pharisee sect, to oppose the payment of Roman taxes altogether on religious grounds.[9] But not Jesus, and not Paul. They taught Christians to pay taxes to a government that would undoubtedly use some of the money to promote sins like pagan idolatry and the greedy slaughter of innocents on the imperial frontier. In a larger sense, Jesus and Paul taught obedience to laws that (we assume) they would not have imposed themselves. Perhaps neither Jesus nor Paul meant to suggest that literally every Roman law must be obeyed. But both Paul and Jesus tell Christians to pay taxes that would be put to some sinful uses. It seems clear from the passages above that those Christians wishing to justify disobedience to particular secular laws, including tax laws, must prove something more than the fact that the law somehow promotes evil or fails to promote righteousness.

Already we may be on some uncomfortable ground. If the foregoing interpretation is correct, the New Testament is making a fairly strong statement about God's will with regard to civil disobedience and rebellion, a statement which for Christians may call into question the moral justification of some widely applauded events of American political and social history. For example, what was the American Revolution except a disobedient rebellion against clearly established governmental authority, upon the stated justification that the British laws were not promoting justice, liberty, and equality?[10] Consider the fiery Declaration of Independence: "Whenever any Form of Government becomes destructive of these Ends [for which men institute governments], it is the Right of the People to alter or to abolish it" (paragraph 2). Compare this to the deferential language of Rom. 13:1–2: "Let every person be subject to the governing authorities. . . . [W]hoever resists authority resists what God has appointed."

Or consider the "civil disobedience" of Henry David Thoreau or Martin Luther King, Jr. Although these men did not advocate violent rebellion, as did the Founding Fathers, they nevertheless preached and practiced intentional disobedience of laws they considered unfair or ungodly, even when those laws did not require them to actively participate in sinful acts (like emperor worship). Thoreau, for example, opposed the payment of taxes to support a government he viewed as corrupt and a war he viewed as unjust and contrary to the teachings of Christ.[11] King advocated disobedience of laws requiring racial segregation, a policy he viewed as hateful and unchristian.[12] As unconscionable as these laws might have been (and there can be no doubt that the racism giving rise to our segregation laws, for example, was completely antithetical to the mind of Christ), it was probably not a sin for someone to do the acts the laws required (say, paying taxes, or avoiding a particular public place designated for members of another race). So from a Christian perspective, were Thoreau or King morally justified in purposefully disobeying the laws? These and other principled stands against government may be open to some moral doubt if we interpret Romans 13 and the other passages to mean that God wants Christians to obey laws that do not require the Christian to sin.

But however we view conscientious civil disobedience, it seems clear that part of every Christian's civic duty is some level of obedience to the laws of the land, just because they are the laws of the land. Paul and Peter are perhaps not trying to specify the proper reaction to every conceivable law, no matter how evil or unjust. But surely they are at least announcing a general *presumption* that Christians are to obey the laws, even laws we find distasteful, out of respect for God.

Beyond the instructions to obey the government generally and to pay taxes, the passage from Romans (and the 1 Peter passage to some extent) suggests something about the origin and authority of government. For one thing, Paul indicates a connection between God and government at some level. *In some sense*, it must be true that God "instituted" all the governments that exist and that "there is no [government] authority except from God" (Rom. 13:1). A Christian, then, cannot view civil government as something *entirely* human, an institution in which God has had and can have no involvement. God had a hand in establishing all governments, and for this reason, Paul says, the person who opposes any government's authority is, generally speaking, opposing God himself. And in the letter to Timothy, Paul implies that God may even intervene somehow in government affairs if this is requested through prayer. So in some sense God had past involvement in establishing governments, and in some sense he may continue to be involved with them if Christians pray for this.

The *implications* of God's involvement in the establishment of governments are less clear. Perhaps one's view depends upon what one interprets the nature and extent of that involvement to be. For example, we have noted that some Christian theologians have interpreted Romans 13 to mean that government, as a divinely ordained institution, should promote doctrinal purity and outlaw religious heresies. Others have contended that God "established" or "ordained" civil government only in the same sense in which he "ordains" and "establishes" other human organizations and institutions, and thus that such divine "establishment" can tell us nothing about how Christians should vote or what government should do. There are, of course, other points of view as well. This debate about government origins is crucial. It has important implications for how we view the purposes and proper sphere of government, and thus for what laws and public policies Christians should favor. We will return to this discussion in more detail later; for now we are simply considering whether Christians are to form or express political opinions at all.

God's involvement in government origins may suggest that politics is not a forbidden zone for Christians. But there are other possible interpretations. Many Christians over the years have argued that Christians should not participate in civil government in any way other than the ways specifically commanded in the New Testament ("honoring" and praying for leaders, paying taxes, and obeying laws that do not command sin). This was essentially the position of the Anabaptists during the Reformation. In this the Anabaptists and their theological descendants follow the teachings of many of the Ante-Nicene Fathers, teachings that we have already noted. This understanding would prohibit Christians from (among other things) running for political office, joining or contributing to a political party, or even voting. The primary arguments for noninvolvement are discussed in the remainder of this chapter.

However, as will become clear, I believe a plausible case can be made from the biblical text, not only that Christian political involvement is permissible, but that it is a positive duty of Christian stewardship in a democracy. I believe this position is not refuted by the Scriptures or by the arguments for noninvolvement. The remainder of this chapter examines the arguments opposing Christian involvement in politics and government, concluding that each of these arguments is ultimately unpersuasive. The next chapter sets forth the positive textual case for Christian political involvement, by presenting the Scriptural basis for political stewardship.

GOVERNMENT AS AN "OTHER"

Some Christians reason that Christian political involvement is impermissible because Christians are commanded to be in subjection to government, and one cannot be in subjection to oneself. Commandments to be in subjection to something or someone necessarily exclude exercising power over that other person or thing. More broadly, the New Testament as a whole seems to regard civil government as an "other," distinguished from Christians, who are supposed to be subject to it. Christians are described as "aliens and exiles" (1 Pet. 2:11) who are citizens of a heavenly kingdom, not an earthly one (Phil. 3:18–21; Heb. 12:25–29). Christians are told to set their minds on heavenly things, not earthly things (Matt. 6:19–33; Col. 3:1–4). The civil government, by contrast, is portrayed in the New Testament as an "earthly thing," a regime of this world that is destined to pass away. The few times civil government is even mentioned in New Testament writings, it is described as something completely outside the circle of the saved, exercising temporary power over them but not known or influenced by them.

It is true that the New Testament writers present the civil government this way; but it is hard to know whether that means anything. Perhaps they could not very well do otherwise, considering their immediate audience and culture. As far as we know, Christians living in the first century simply had no opportunity to participate in government. Living as we do, in the midst of an unparalleled expansion of democracy around the globe, it is sometimes difficult to remember or appreciate that self-government is, historically, a great oddity. Systems guaranteeing real voting rights do not occupy much of the historical landscape. Instead, the norm of history has been an iron-fisted reign of the very few over the very many. The Roman Empire which held sway over Christians in the first century had little in common with the earlier Roman Republic so lauded by Cicero, and much less in common with systems of widespread suffrage like the one obtaining in the United States today. And Christians during the first century were most often viewed by their surrounding culture as a fringe mystery cult, not even part of "mainstream society"—a designation which would have meant little enough power over imperial government in any event. So how else would first century Christian authors describe civil government, this aloof, powerful, and (to them) uncontrollable force that kept the peace, collected taxes, and occasionally turned the lives of God's people upside down?

Christians clearly had little to do with setting public policy or running governments in the first century. This fact explains why the New Testament writers would not have said much about how Christians are to participate in government, but it hardly proves that God frowns on Christian political involvement. Christians today have been blessed with *many* opportunities—not just self-government—that our first century brothers and sisters could barely have imagined, and the New Testament does not speak of these other opportunities either. For example, the New Testament does not (directly) tell Christians how to manage a business. In fact, the New Testament does not even suggest that owning a business with paid employees is permissible in God's sight. Would it for that reason be sinful for a Christian to own a business? (Or to buy shares of stock and become a partial owner of a business?) And how should one operate the business? If the labor market becomes saturated with available workers during a recession and wages go down all over the country, what is a fair wage to pay one's employees—the depressed market wage, or the wage required for the employees to care for their families, or the minimum wage set by the government, or what? What is a fair price for the product one sells? The fact that the New Testament does not specify an appropriate wage (as a function of housing expenses, etc.) or price is hardly a reason to think that God forbids the payment of wages—or that the Bible has nothing to say to us about how to set wages and prices.

But it is argued that the New Testament clearly teaches subjection to the government authorities (but not to businesses), and since one cannot be subject to oneself, Christians must be implicitly forbidden to participate in politics or government. The problem with this argument, it seems to me, is that one *can* in fact be subject to oneself in the sense implied here. It is perfectly ordinary, in fact predictable, for someone occasionally to be bound, or feel herself bound, to follow rules that she herself has made. On a mundane level, people constantly set rules for themselves—in the nature of New Year's resolutions and the like—which they follow with conviction. Teachers make rules for the conduct of a class, publish these rules in a written syllabus, and feel bound by them for the rest of the semester. The members of a private club may vote on when to have their next meeting, and yet be submissive to the will of the club as a whole by meeting at whatever time the majority chooses. In the New Testament, slaves are commanded to be submissive to their masters (Col. 3:22–24; Eph. 6:5–8), and yet they are also encouraged to gain freedom from their masters if they can do so legally (1 Cor. 7:21–23); and even if they could not gain their freedom, surely many slaves were given positions of trust by their masters in which they were allowed to set rules governing an entire household, including themselves. Wives are commanded to be submissive to their husbands in everything (Eph. 5:22–24), and yet surely a Christian wife may have a voice in setting the goals, plans, and rules of her particular marriage and household. And at the government level, legislators routinely make laws that they themselves are required to obey. In fact, the concept of "the rule of law," so prized in the United States, is in essence a requirement that our rulers bind themselves along with everyone else when they make and enforce the laws. In short, one *can* submit to oneself in the sense of being submissive to rules that one had a share in creating. Thus, it is difficult to understand how the biblical command to submit to government authority can be construed as a command forbidding the one who submits to have any say in that authority or the rules it makes.

What would be helpful for Christians considering political involvement is a letter from Paul (or some similar authority) to Caesar, upon Caesar's conversion to Christ. If Caesar had been converted, we might surely expect him to ask all sorts of questions about how his new faith should affect his daily responsibilities as head of state. Christians who oppose political involvement on biblical grounds are asking us to believe that in such a situation, Paul would instruct Caesar to abdicate the throne and have nothing more to do with government. Even aside from the practical reality that this instruction would constitute a virtual death sentence for Caesar in the world of first century Roman politics, it is hard to believe that this would be Paul's attitude. In light of Rom. 13:1–7, 1 Cor. 7:17–24, and other passages to be discussed in the next chapter, I rather think Paul would advise Caesar on the proper way to exercise his supreme political power. Romans 13 says that rulers are in some sense God's agents. Where is the inconsistency between being an agent of God and being a Christian? 1 Cor. 7:17–24 makes the point that physical appearance and social relationships and positions are generally not to be changed just because of one's conversion to Christ—so the wife who becomes a Christian is to remain married to her unbelieving spouse, the uncircumcised are to remain uncircumcised, the slave is not to run away or feel inferior in Christ (but to gain his freedom if he can do so legally), the free man is to stay free, viewing himself as Christ's slave, and so on. "Let each of you remain in the condition in which you were called," Paul says (1 Cor. 7:20, repeated in 7:24). Thus it seems unlikely that Caesar would have been instructed that his new bond to Christ obligated him to relinquish all government power. And if the tenets of Christianity would not have required Caesar to stop being Caesar, then surely Christ's followers today are not obliged to relinquish the much lesser power of voting.

GOVERNMENT, VIOLENCE, AND VENGEANCE

Those opposing Christian political involvement have also raised the argument that civil governments exercise powers that Christians are expressly forbidden to exercise. More specifically, governments use violent force (or the threat of it) to enforce laws and to protect their citizens. To give one example, the government protects our collective security by using an army to violently repel foreign invasions. Is this sort of violence and killing permissible by the Christian individually? If not, why is it permissible for Christians to *vote* to wage wars or fund armies? Similarly, lawbreakers are imprisoned and sometimes wounded or even killed by the state (if not through capital punishment, then at least occasionally when perpetrators are fleeing, resisting arrest, or trying to escape custody). Would it be permissible for Christians to do these things on an individual basis—say, to imprison a man who stole my television? If not, what makes it all right for a Christian to order his government to do the same thing, by voting for a law to that effect? Paul says in Rom. 12:17–21:

> Do not repay anyone evil for evil, but take thought for what is noble in the sight of all. If it is possible, so far as it depends on you, live peaceably with all. Beloved, never avenge yourselves, but leave room for the wrath of God; for it is written, "Vengeance is mine, I will repay, says the Lord." No, "if your enemies are hungry, feed them; if they are thirsty, give them something to drink; for by doing this you will heap burning coals on their heads." Do not be overcome by evil, but overcome evil with good.

According to the immediately succeeding passage at Rom. 13:1–7, *government* is God's agent of wrath or vengeance on the wrongdoer; and (the argument goes) Christians are not to be part of that, leaving vengeance to God and his agents in the sinful government.[13]

It is important to note that this argument does not suggest that there should be no government; it recognizes, in fact, the necessity and divine approval of government but simply claims that Christians cannot be part of it. The essence of this argument is that all civil governments are, in God's eyes, somewhat like the ancient, sinful governments of Assyria and Chaldea, not *approved* by God but *ordained* by him for a particular purpose—that is, to punish wrongdoers (see, for example, Isa. 10:5–19; Hab. 1:5–15).

In considering this argument, imagine again that Caesar had been converted to Christ in Paul's day and that Paul had written the new convert a letter of instruction to answer his many questions. What would the letter say? Of course, we cannot know for sure, which is why some of these questions have been debated for so long. But perhaps we can rule out some possibilities. Those who believe political involvement is forbidden because of the inherent violence of government are asking us to believe that Paul would have told Caesar not just to resign the throne, but to free all the government's prisoners first. If this seems dubious, notice that if imprisonment of wrongdoers is wrong for *Christians*, it is wrong for *anyone*—in other words, the act is wrong without regard to the identity of the actor. Forceful imprisonment is so wrong, the argument goes, that Christians cannot even participate in a government that carries out such vengeance (although God has admittedly ordained government for just this purpose). The argument thus boils down to an assertion that while all criminal justice systems are sinful, it just so happens that God actually relies on this particular sin, systematically and routinely using it to his purposes, as he did the sins of the Assyrians and Chaldeans (or Pharaoh, or Judas, or a host of others). But that does not mean sin is permissible. It still isn't, which is the only reason anyone would claim that Christians cannot participate in the sinful activity of government. God used Judas's sin, too, but it was still sin. Likewise, the argument runs, when the jailer puts someone in jail pursuant to secular law, he is sinning, and God happens to be using that sin for his purpose of punishing the wrongdoer.

But if that is true, and Caesar now becomes a Christian, how can Caesar turn a blind eye to this sin he has been committing and encouraging? Caesar must free the prisoners. God may use sin all the time to accomplish his purposes, but that is no argument for committing or encouraging the sin. It seems the acme of irrational legalism to suggest that imprisonment is a sin but that the newly converted Caesar must renounce his political power *without* freeing the prisoners he had sinfully helped imprison. That would be to *participate* in the continuing sin of restraining those people in jail. Even Zaccheus, upon coming to faith in Jesus, not only renounced his old fraudulent ways but resolved to repay what he had stolen four times over (Luke 19:1–10). Could Caesar be expected to do any less, if in fact imprisonment of thieves is just as sinful as stealing itself? No—he must set all the thieves and murderers free if he has the power to do so. And if Romans 13 is any guide, that result certainly seems contrary to God's will.

If this prescription sounds too incredible to be followed, perhaps we should question its premise and reconsider whether imprisoning criminals is always a sin. What we must conclude here, I think, is that there might be a difference, to God, between Caesar's making a law requiring the imprisonment of thieves, and the private vengeance forbidden in Romans 12—that is, the scenario of a private citizen (or Caesar himself) who acts on his own initiative, outside the mantle of state authority, to personally grab a thief and lock her in his basement. Would it not be sinful, even for Caesar himself, to carry out vengeance in an individual capacity? Romans 12 certainly suggests that such behavior would be sinful, for this reason: Caesar would be *taking vengeance* without acting *as the state*, which appears to be the only human being or institution approved by God for punishing thieves. The facts that the thief is guilty and that Caesar exercises complete power over the state in his "day job" are irrelevant; Caesar's individual act in this example is still not the act of the state and does not carry its authority, so his imprisonment of the thief amounts to no more than a kidnaping. There would seem to be a big moral difference between this private type of imprisonment and the situation that occurs when a police officer (or Caesar) arrests a thief pursuant to law.

All this is not to argue that the state can do anything it wants, no matter how sinful those acts would be if done privately. Human governments cannot morally legitimize immorality. On the contrary, if an act would be a sin if done privately (say, the act of maliciously burning someone else's house down), that fact would seem to set up a rebuttable presumption that the act would also be sinful for the state, and would implicate in sin anyone who authorized the state to do it. (This is how we would have the moral ground for criticizing sinful government actions like the Holocaust or racial discrimination.) But when it comes to imprisoning a thief or some similar "wrongdoer" (Rom. 13:4), such punishments seem to be specifically approved by God when the state does them, and *not* when individual citizens do them. Rom. 13:4 says the state is "the servant of God to execute wrath on the wrongdoer" and that it "does not bear the sword in vain," strongly implying that God at least sometimes approves of the state's use of the sword. Thus Caesar could in good conscience enact laws against theft and provide punishments for thieves, even though he would *not* be justified in punishing thieves in his capacity as a private vigilante. This interpretation seems more plausible (and more palatable) than one that requires the newly converted Caesar to free all the state's imprisoned thieves.

But why would God view so many imprisonments by the state as permissible when he views private imprisonment as sinful? Why would he approve the state, and those controlling it, in the practice of things he would not want individuals to do? Perhaps the answer is found in the passage quoted above from Romans 12. Here Paul not only forbids Christians to take revenge, but he tells them why: "Do not repay anyone evil for evil, but take thought for what is noble in the sight of all" (Rom. 12:17). The "vengeance" that is forbidden to Christians is the kind that can fairly be called "evil," so that to avenge oneself is to repay "evil for evil." It is the kind of act that is not "noble in the sight of all." Locking someone up in my basement because they stole my television is that kind of act. It is the kind of response that announces, "I will get you back for what you did to me. I will make you sorry you ever messed with me." And if it is done by me and not the state, it is, in the eyes of most people, ignoble and improper. It is an evil and vindictive act. On the other hand, it is much more morally appropriate for me, in the words of Rom. 12:19, to "leave room for the wrath of God" and wait for the state, as a limited agent of God's justice, to capture and punish the thief. When the state captures and imprisons him, God approves, and I am morally blameless, even if I voted for the law that the thief violated—indeed, even if I am the arresting officer (assuming I enforce the law without partiality). This kind of imprisonment is "noble in the sight of all," at least in our society, and it is not repaying evil for evil. It is the fulfillment of a deterrent assurance made under law by an impersonal and powerful third party with no stake in this particular dispute—the assurance given by the state (and apparently approved by God) that theft will not go unpunished. And if state punishment of thieves is not sinful, Christians who participate in or authorize the state's function along these lines are merely helping the state perform its divinely authorized duty as God's minister to do people good.

In considering this a bit further, we may find that this is not an anomaly. In fact, the morality of an act of punishment *frequently* depends upon the legitimacy and authority under which it is imposed. For example, suppose the CEO of a corporation issues a new company policy via internal memorandum. He believes this policy, which requires a reduction of salary as a penalty for noncompliance, is necessary for the good of the organization. Upon discovering that an employee has fallen afoul of the new rule, he applies the penalty to the employee and docks the employee's pay. Assuming the new rule is not in itself immoral and the CEO is authorized under company policy and relevant law to take this action, has he taken "vengeance" on the employee within the meaning of Romans 12:19, in some sinful way? That seems doubtful. Clearly there are some *other* ways of accomplishing this result that *would* be wrong for the CEO—for example, to steal the money from the employee's desk—but this does not prove the CEO sins when he applies the duly enacted policy. Although in either instance he would accomplish the same result and would have acted for the same reasons, the fact that the CEO acted in his official, legal, corporately authorized capacity, rather than as a common thief, makes all the moral difference in the world. Similarly, when we evaluate whether Christians can participate in violent activities that punish wrongs against others, there seems to be a moral difference—a difference in God's sight, perhaps—between using violence by oneself and using (or voting for) violence used by the state, under its authority.

MORAL VALUES AND THE POLITICAL GAME

It is sometimes argued that Christians should not participate in politics because politics necessarily requires dishonesty, deception, and compromise of values in order to get results. By the very nature of politics, the argument goes, it is impossible to accomplish anything without building consensus with unbelievers and worldly people. Consensus support must be developed from time to time among, for example, a constituency, a party, or an assembly of politicians, any or all of which may be inundated with pagans. But to build this consensus, one must compromise—one must give in to some of the demands of the worldly. Inevitably, a Christian will be forced to renounce some of his Christian values in order to be effective or possibly even to keep his job. This is the "politics is dirty" argument. Christians must keep themselves "unstained by the world" (James 1:27), and that means politics, by definition, is forbidden to the Christian.

It seems plausible that politics, at least holding political office effectively, requires compromise. Whether it inevitably requires dishonesty or the compromise of one's religious or moral beliefs is an empirical question without a self-evident answer. But whatever the answer is, it would seem unlikely that the answer would be different for politics than for a whole host of other activities a Christian could undertake. Holding a position as the CEO of a major corporation requires compromise and consensus-building, too. So does holding a position as the manager of a baseball team, or indeed as the manager of a fast food restaurant. In fact, one might make a similar claim about any position in which one's effectiveness and longevity in the position require consensus support among ungodly people. If politics is forbidden to Christians on that basis, so are many other positions in society. Perhaps even Cornelius the Roman centurion[14] could tell us a thing or two about the necessity for building consensus support by reaching compromises with the ungodly—in his case, Roman soldiers. Yet Cornelius became a Christian and, as far as we know, was never instructed to resign his position of leadership in the army.

In short, those who would argue for a no-exceptions rule that politics is always too dirty for Christians will have to explain why other occupations requiring compromise with the ungodly are *not* always too dirty for Christians. Until then, this argument remains a sober warning to those Christians who would join with others to achieve political goals—and particularly to those Christians who would hold political office—but not, I think, strong evidence that voting or holding political office are sinful activities *per se*.

SILENCE OF SCRIPTURE AS PROHIBITION

Finally, we should note the argument that Christians are forbidden from political involvement by the silence of the Scriptures. The idea here is that the Christian must have biblical authorization for everything he does, and since the biblical text does not clearly authorize political involvement, the Christian should not be politically involved.

The New Testament, at least, certainly does seem to be silent with respect to individual political involvement. We are not told how to vote, which political party to choose, what laws to support, or what qualifications to look for in candidates; indeed, we are not even told very clearly whether to be involved at all, which is why this debate has continued with such vitality for so many centuries. But even if we agree the Scriptures are mostly or entirely silent on these questions, it is unclear which way that cuts.

Particularly, it is troubling to set a hermeneutic precedent that says, "Any activity not explicitly endorsed in the Bible is forbidden to Christians." This means, among other things, Christians may not play hockey, be bank presidents, or run a homeless shelter. Most Christians would view these activities as *permissible* because they are not *forbidden* by Scripture. The New Testament is not a rule book in any event, and so we should not expect it to state with precision each forbidden act and each permitted act.

I have heard people modify the hermeneutic principle to state, "Any *important* activity not endorsed in the Bible, *implicitly or explicitly*, is forbidden to Christians." Then one might argue that hockey is relatively unimportant, while being bank president and the like are *implicitly* endorsed in the Bible, through the passages instructing Christians to work to earn a living and so on.[15] The problem with this approach, as becomes immediately apparent, is that now we cannot be sure what Scripture is silent about and what it speaks about. If being bank president is implicitly endorsed by the Bible, then perhaps a profitable government career is too. The New Testament seems to have as much to say about one line of work as the other, and the Old Testament in fact says far more about working in the government.

The silence of the Scriptures (if it is silence) might not be meaningless, but the meaning of silence is certainly open to differing interpretations. Did God think the whole issue unimportant, or did he intend for Christians to avoid politics altogether, or did he think the answer was too obvious to require explanation? Or did the New Testament writers themselves simply see no occasion to write instructions for the politically empowered Christian, because there was no such thing in the first century? None of these divergent interpretations of silence seems, on its face, outlandish. How then can we conclude that the silence of Scripture clearly forbids Christian political involvement?

The arguments for an absolute ban on political involvement thus seem flawed. But surely this is not because the Bible clearly commands involvement. The New Testament authors, at any rate, simply do not address the question directly. In the next chapter we will consider whether the New Testament may contain some *indirect* guidance on this issue.

NOTES

1. New Testament writers often referred to this sacrifice as a "death" of sorts, reinforcing the totality of the required commitment. For example, the apostle Paul wrote to the Galatian church, "I have been crucified with Christ; and it is no longer I who live, but it is Christ who lives in me" (Gal. 2:19–20). See also, for example, Rom. 6:6 ("our old self was crucified with him"); 1 Pet. 2:24 ("He himself bore our sins in his body on the cross, so that we might die to sin and live to righteousness") (New American Standard Bible); Col. 3:5, 9–10 ("Put to death, therefore, whatever in you is earthly . . . seeing that you have stripped off the old self with its practices and have clothed yourselves with the new self").

2. See, for example, Rom. 10 and 11; Heb. 8–10, especially 8:13; Col. 2:13–17; Gal. 2:15–16; Gal. 3:23–29.

3. Lev. 24:16.

4. But note that some Christians, within the movement usually termed "Theonomy" or "Christian Reconstruction," argue that the judicial laws and penalties specified for Israel in the Old Testament should in the main be enacted and enforced across the United States today. (Incidentally, some within this movement do indeed support capital punishment for blasphemy.) See, for example, Rousas J. Rushdoony, *Institutes of Biblical Law* (Nutley, N.J.: Craig Press, 1977); Greg L. Bahnsen, *Theonomy in Christian Ethics* (Nutley, N.J.: Craig Press, 1977); Gary North, *The Sinai Strategy: Economics and the Ten Commandments* (Tyler, Tex.: Institute for Christian Economics, 1986). For a critical view of the movement, see William S. Barker and W. Robert Godfrey, eds., *Theonomy: A Reformed Critique* (Grand Rapids, Mich.: Academie Books, 1990).

5. These parallel accounts are found at Matt. 22:15–22 and Mark 12:13–17. The church of the first century apparently regarded this story as one of the more important and memorable events in Jesus' life, judging by its appearance in three of the four gospels. The popularity of this story among early Christians makes sense in light of the numerous attempts by the early church leaders to convince the Roman government that Christianity posed no threat to its power. The saying of Jesus recorded here—"render to Caesar what is Caesar's, and to God what is God's"—would tend to dispel the notions that the "kingdom" proclaimed by Jesus of Nazareth was a secular civil authority in competition with Rome, or that Jesus had preached rebellion against Rome.

6. The discussion which follows, especially that part which relates to the more commonly accepted meanings of Rom. 13:1–7, is adapted from my article, "Govern-

ment as God's Agent: A Reconsideration of Romans 12 and 13," *Stone-Campbell Journal* 8, no. 2 (Oct. 2005): 181–97.

7. Regarding the date for the composition of Romans, see Richard J. Cassidy, *Paul in Chains* (New York: Crossroad Publishing Co., 2001), 26; F.F. Bruce, *The Epistle of Paul to the Romans: An Introduction and Commentary* (London: Tyndale Press, 1963; 3d reprinting, 1967), 11–18. There is great scholarly consensus that Paul wrote Romans during Nero's reign. One can make a credible argument that the other epistles under consideration, 1 Peter and 1 Timothy, were also written during the reign of Nero. According to early church tradition, Peter and Paul were both executed during Nero's reign, and Peter wrote 1 Peter late in his life, which would indicate that Peter's instructions in 1 Peter were written during the reign of Nero. But since a great many scholars argue that 1 Peter was written pseudonymously after Peter's death, the writing of 1 Peter, unlike Romans, cannot with confidence be fixed within Nero's reign. A similar division of opinion exists respecting the authorship and date of 1 Timothy.

For a discussion of Nero's lifestyle, values, and public policies during the early years of his reign, see Cassidy, *Chains*, 144–62; and see generally Michael Grant, *Nero: Emperor in Revolt* (New York: American Heritage Press, 1970), and especially pages 35–51.

8. Grant, *Nero*, 60–71, 106, 112–16, 129–30, 149, 164–85, 187–95.

9. William Barclay, *The Gospel of Matthew*, The Daily Study Bible series, vol. 2 (Philadelphia: Westminster Press, 1957; 2d ed., 1958), 300–302.

10. In considering Romans 13 and Luke 20, it is particularly interesting to note that much of the rebellious sentiment in the colonies that gave rise to the American Revolution was stirred up around the issue of taxation. The American rebels regarded as illegitimate any tax imposed by a governing assembly, like Parliament, that did not contain a fair proportion of the colonists' own delegates; they also argued that they could never expect to be "truly and properly" represented in Parliament. See, for example, Samuel Adams, "The Rights of the Colonists" (1772), in *American Political Thought*, ed. Kenneth M. Dolbeare and Michael S. Cummings, 5th ed. (Washington, D.C.: CQ Press, 2004), 38. One wonders how the American revolutionaries would have felt about the Roman taxes levied upon the Jews in the first century—taxes which the Jews clearly had no voice in creating. The argument that justifies the American Revolution would presumably also justify the first century Jews, not only in refusing to pay the Roman tax (contrary to the teaching of Jesus), but in actually staging an armed rebellion against the Roman authorities.

11. See Henry David Thoreau, "Civil Disobedience," in *The Works of Thoreau*, Cambridge edition, ed. Henry Seidel Canby (Cambridge, Mass.: Houghton Mifflin Co., 1937), 789–91, 795, 797–98, 801, 804.

12. See Martin Luther King, Jr., "Letter from Birmingham City Jail," in *A Testament of Hope: The Essential Writings and Speeches of Martin Luther King, Jr.*, ed. James M. Washington (New York: HarperCollins, 1986; paperback ed., 1991), 293–95.

13. This argument is considered in more detail in Chapter 5.

14. For Cornelius's story, see Acts 10:1–11:18.

15. See, for example, 1 Thess. 4:11

Chapter Four

The Textual Case for Political Involvement

To judge by the passages we have examined so far, the gist of the New Testament message about government is that all governments are somehow approved by God for the purpose of punishing wrongdoers, and the Christian is supposed to submit to his government by paying taxes, showing honor to it, and generally obeying it whenever possible.

But do New Testament authors say anything else about a Christian's civic duty? There are a few other passages that arguably make some mention of civic duty or reputation among unbelievers. They are all very much in the same vein as the passages already considered:

> Remind them to be subject to rulers and authorities, to be obedient, to be ready for every good work, to speak evil of no one, to avoid quarreling, to be gentle, and to show every courtesy to everyone. (Titus 3:1–2)
>
> [Aspire] to live quietly, to mind your own affairs, and to work with your hands, as we directed you, so that you may behave properly toward outsiders and be dependent on no one. (1 Thess. 4:11–12)
>
> Pursue peace with everyone, and the holiness without which no one will see the Lord. (Heb. 12:14)

These passages send the consistent message that Christians are to be submissive and peaceful. Followers of Jesus should be model citizens, the kind the state never has to worry about. Of course, leading obedient and peaceful lives was the epitome of good citizenship for subjects of the Roman Empire. But might good citizenship in a twenty-first century democracy require something additional?

It should be clear by now that the New Testament does not explicitly answer this question, because it does not directly address the subject of Christian political involvement in a democracy. But despite this silence, I believe the New Testament may indicate that such involvement is not only permissible, but required of Christians as they have opportunity. This chapter presents that argument.

SILENCE OF THE SCRIPTURES

We have earlier examined the four primary New Testament passages that give instruction about civil governments. Even in these explicit references, the Christian's duty is expressed in terms of honor and obedience, with "government" and "rulers" portrayed as decidedly "other." The passages do not tell Christians what to do if the powers cease to be "other"—that is, if the Christians acquire political power. We have seen that some Christians view this silence as implying a lack of divine authorization, as if the Bible were intended to answer all questions about political involvement that might ever arise in any culture or time in which believers read it. But any argument that these passages were intended to specify the sum of the permitted involvement with government, for all governments in all times and places, ignores the cultural context in which the passages were written and assumes that context had no effect whatsoever on the text, aside perhaps from dictating that the language used would be Greek.

The social structure of the Roman world during the first century was quite different from our own. As John Stambaugh and David Balch have noted:

> In terms of power, influence, money, and the perceptions of the time, we can divide the population of the Roman world into two main categories, those with influence and those without it, the "honorable" and the "humble," those who governed and those who were governed, those who had property and those who did not. The upper category was very small, the lower one very large.[1]

This was the reality of life in the Roman Empire of the first century. For most people, including almost all Christians at that time, there was simply no power over government, or indeed many other aspects of their social environment. Positions of power in government were not typically filled by election, but were appointed or inherited positions. Even when elections were held, only certain privileged Roman citizens in the city of Rome were allowed to vote—and their votes were often controlled in fact by wealthy or powerful patrons from the senatorial class. Laws were made in Rome by the emperor or possibly the Senate, sometimes acting through the formality of a citizen assembly in the city but doing this less commonly as the first century continued. It is less clear who had power to make other, local laws, and the rule may have varied from town to town; but even the local laws were not influenced by the mass of the governed, and the social structure all over the empire makes it clear that the "have-nots" of society could not expect to have the least amount of control over government or law.[2] With the exception of perhaps a handful of converts,[3] the early Christians were decidedly "have-nots."

In that cultural context, what can we reasonably expect? What can the New Testament authors be expected to say about self-government? True, the New Testament is silent on the subject; but in light of the cultural context, that silence implies precious little. The New Testament authors are assuming, with good reason, that their audience *cannot* become politically effective through involvement with the system. Law existed; it was what it was. It was pointless to discuss how to make it because *no Christians could make it.* It was pointless to discuss how it could be better because *no Christians could change it.* This is the political and cultural reality into which Christianity was born. The unsurprising result is that New Testament authors do not address how law should be made, but merely whether existing law should be obeyed.

This may suggest how we are to interpret the silence of the Scriptures regarding questions of political involvement. If the early Christians were never instructed to try to inform themselves about political events or to move for political change, perhaps that omission was not the result of a plan to communicate divine disapproval of Christian involvement with such matters. Perhaps, instead, the Scriptures are silent about how to govern for the same reason other correspondence between Roman subjects of the time is silent about how to govern: the subject was moot for the average person. Questions about the proper extent or methods of political involvement never came up. Since the early disciples never had opportunity to affect the laws, they were not told God's will for laws, or for Christian involvement in law making.

This understanding is supported by New Testament teachings about worry. These teachings may be summarized as: Don't worry about things you cannot change, and don't worry about temporary needs like food and clothing, but don't quit your job either—just seek first God's kingdom and righteousness, and these other needs will be met as God wills.[4] The idea may be applied to the context of political concerns. It seems quite natural, in light of the Christian teachings on worry, that the New Testament authors would not spend time discussing the moral or social value of institutions, like laws and governments, that Christians could not change. Christians should not worry about such things—but not because these things are *unimportant* (clothing and food are important, too, and "your heavenly Father knows that you need all these things"),[5] but rather because *you cannot change them* ("Can any of you by worrying add a single hour to your span of life?").[6] So even if Jesus had explicitly addressed the subject of the Roman legal code, he might well have instructed his audience to obey the laws without worrying about them. Indeed, this may have been his audience's principal understanding of his instruction to "render to Caesar what is Caesar's, and to God what is God's."

Of course, Jesus did not issue such instructions, but the silence of Scripture does not necessarily imply that politics is unimportant or a waste of time, any more than it implies that food and clothing are unimportant—particularly food or clothing we might provide to our neighbor. (It is hard to imagine Jesus instructing his listeners not to worry about what *their neighbor* would eat or what he would wear.)[7] Christians are told not to worry about things they cannot change, or about things that merely satisfy their own material needs. But law has always been important, not only because of its effects on our own narrow interests but also because of its power to help or harm others; and if law has now, with the passage of time, become a matter that Christians can change, the silence of Scripture does not imply that they shouldn't.

Are we thus left with no biblical instruction at all on the subject of Christian involvement in politics? In fact, I think there are some passages that suggest our duties in this area. But we must look not only to the passages directly discussing government. We must also look to other biblical passages that may more indirectly suggest God's attitude toward Christian political involvement.

STEWARDSHIP

Consider these words of Jesus:

> There was a rich man who had a manager, and charges were brought to him that this man was squandering his property. So he summoned him and said to him, "What is this that I hear about you? Give me an accounting of your management, because you cannot be my manager any longer." Then the manager said to himself, "What will I do, now that my master is taking the position away from me? I am not strong enough to dig, and I am ashamed to beg. I have decided what to do so that, when I am dismissed as manager, people may welcome me into their homes." So, summoning his master's debtors one by one, he asked the first, "How much do you owe my master?" He answered, "A hundred jugs of olive oil." He said to him, "Take your bill, sit down quickly, and make it fifty." Then he asked another, "And how much do you owe?" He replied, "A hundred containers of wheat." He said to him, "Take your bill and make it eighty." And his master commended the dishonest manager because he had acted shrewdly; for the children of this age are more shrewd in dealing with their own generation than are the children of light. And I tell you, make friends for yourselves by means of dishonest wealth so that when it is gone, they may welcome you into the eternal homes.

> Whoever is faithful in a very little is faithful also in much; and whoever is dishonest in a very little is dishonest also in much. If then you have not been faithful with the dishonest wealth, who will entrust to you the true riches? And if you have not been faithful with what belongs to another, who will give you what is your own? (Luke 16:1–12)

This wonderful parable shows us something important about the meaning of our lives here on earth. Our lives in this temporary land have meaning and purpose to the extent we exercise shrewd stewardship over what God has entrusted to us.

The manager in the story is praised because he used his opportunities shrewdly, and it is this quality that Jesus recommends to us. The manager was definitely dishonest (Luke 16:8) and had apparently squandered someone else's property to get himself into this mess in the first place. So he is not worthy of emulation in every respect. But he was savvy enough to know an opportunity when he saw it and to make good use of it in a forward-looking way. He had authority as agent of the master to rewrite the terms of his master's contracts. Dishonest? Yes—but clever. He used the short time he had left as manager to alter the contracts, without his master's knowledge or consent, in ways that shifted wealth from the master to the other contracting parties. It is not unlike a situation that sometimes occurs today, when a salesman knows he is about to be fired and so cleans out the office, stealing all the company's trade secrets and client contact information and taking it with him to his new employer, a competing company that finds him an extremely attractive hire because he possesses all this stolen information. This kind of behavior makes employees even more odious to their former employers—but then the old boss hated them anyway, so the employees had nothing to lose—and it ingratiates the employees to others who can do them good. Jesus tells us that even though this conduct is reprehensible, we can still find something in it to praise: say what you like about these employees, but they certainly know how to take advantage of an opportunity.

Children of light also, Jesus says, sometimes have opportunities here on this earth, opportunities which may include wealth and power. The wealth and power is not really theirs; they are stewards or trustees of these things, which ultimately belong to God. If they are shrewd, like the dishonest manager, they will realize that one day their stewardship will come to an end, and they will plan ahead for that day as they exercise their stewardship. One day the Christian's home on earth will be gone, and he will want to be welcomed into eternal homes. How can he manage his trust now in order to assure his dwelling hereafter? By shrewdly making use of every opportunity on earth for the glory of God.

GLORIFYING GOD SHREWDLY

How do we glorify God shrewdly? Jesus provides the answer in another extended discussion of stewardship:

> Then the kingdom of heaven will be like this. Ten bridesmaids took their lamps and went to meet the bridegroom. Five of them were foolish, and five were wise. When the foolish took their lamps, they took no oil with them; but the wise took flasks of oil with their lamps. As the bridegroom was delayed, all of them became drowsy and slept. But at midnight there was a shout, "Look! Here is the bridegroom! Come out to meet him." Then all those bridesmaids got up and trimmed their lamps. The foolish said to the wise, "Give us some of your oil, for our lamps are going out." But the wise replied, "No! there will not be enough for you and for us; you had better go to the dealers and buy some for yourselves." And while they went to buy it, the bridegroom came, and those who were ready went with him into the wedding banquet; and the door was shut. Later the other bridesmaids came also, saying, "Lord, lord, open to us." But he replied, "Truly I tell you, I do not know you." Keep awake therefore, for you know neither the day nor the hour.
>
> For it is as if a man, going on a journey, summoned his slaves and entrusted his property to them; to one he gave five talents, to another two, to another one, to each according to his ability. Then he went away. The one who had received the five talents went off at once and traded with them, and made five more talents. In the same way, the one who had the two talents made two more talents. But the one who had received the one talent went off and dug a hole in the ground and hid his master's money. After a long time the master of those slaves came and settled accounts with them. Then the one who had received the five talents came forward, bringing five more talents, saying, "Master, you handed over to me five talents; see, I have made five more talents." His master said to him, "Well done, good and trustworthy slave; you have been trustworthy in a few things, I will put you in charge of many things; enter into the joy of your master." And the one with the two talents also came forward, saying, "Master, you handed over to me two talents; see, I have made two more talents." His master said to him, "Well done, good and trustworthy slave; you have been trustworthy in a few things, I will put you in charge of many things; enter into the joy of your master." Then the one who had received the one talent also came forward, saying, "Master, I knew that you were a harsh man, reaping where you did not sow, and gathering where you did not scatter seed; so I was afraid, and I went and hid your talent in the ground. Here you have what is yours." But his master replied, "You wicked and lazy slave! You knew, did you, that I reap where I did not sow, and gather where I did not scatter? Then you ought to have invested my money with the bankers, and on my return I would have received what was my own with interest. . . ."

> When the Son of Man comes in his glory, and all the angels with him, then he will sit on the throne of his glory. All the nations will be gathered before him, and he will separate people from one another as a shepherd separates the sheep from the goats, and he will put the sheep at his right hand and the goats at the left. Then the king will say to those at his right hand, "Come, you that are blessed by my Father, inherit the kingdom prepared for you from the foundation of the world; for I was hungry and you gave me food, I was thirsty and you gave me something to drink, I was a stranger and you welcomed me, I was naked and you gave me clothing, I was sick and you took care of me, I was in prison and you visited me." Then the righteous will answer him, "Lord, when was it that we saw you hungry and gave you food, or thirsty and gave you something to drink? And when was it that we saw you a stranger and welcomed you, or naked and gave you clothing? And when was it that we saw you sick or in prison and visited you?" And the king will answer them, "Truly I tell you, just as you did it to one of the least of these who are members of my family, you did it to me." (Matt. 25:1–40)

There are three stories here: the story of the bridesmaids, the story of the talents, and the story of the last judgment. It is no accident that these three stories appear in the same discourse, one immediately after the other. They each demonstrate the same imperative: shrewd stewardship. Time on earth is short, says Jesus, and you have no idea when your stewardship here will end. Prepare now so that you will be received into the eternal dwellings. Take a lesson from the wise bridesmaids: plan ahead for that time. Take a lesson from the productive slaves: use every opportunity available to you during your short time on earth. Take a lesson from the righteous "sheep" at the last judgment: stewardship for God means helping other people in need. If you would serve Jesus and invest his wealth productively, get busy using your every opportunity to serve others, for the truth is that Jesus has not gone very far away. Jesus is the homeless man, the downtrodden day laborer, the single mother with a sick child, the orphan no one wants, the drifter with no friends in town, the broken prisoner forsaken by everyone who ever loved him. The basic idea is this: If you have an opportunity to affect people, use it, whatever it is, to glorify God and help others.

POLITICS AS THE POWER TO DO GOOD

In a democracy, ordinary citizens have the power and opportunity to control government, at least through informed voting. As Christians, we are to use every opportunity to help others. Putting these two ideas together, it seems initially plausible that for Christians living in a democracy, political involvement might be an opportunity we should use to help others. But our time is short. Can politics do any good? Does this world even matter? Perhaps, someone might argue, our limited time and resources would be better spent on evangelism or direct benevolence, rather than trying to affect a political system that will always be imperfect, a system that is necessarily focused on the temporary here and now and is destined to pass away.

This argument, however, proves too much. True, we should not abandon evangelism and benevolence altogether in our pursuit of political ends; and it is clearly dangerous to place too much faith in "politics" as the answer for all people's problems. But we can easily get carried away "streamlining" our efforts for Christ, as if we are performing some sort of "Christian stewardship triage." The cry rises that only the most important needs should qualify for our limited resources of time and money. But if it is true that evangelism and benevolence are more important than politics, then it is also true that evangelism is more important than benevolence, since evangelism ministers to the soul rather than the temporary physical body. Does that prove we should abandon benevolence and focus all our attention on evangelism? And are benevolence and evangelism so separable?

Jesus was constantly concerned with the quality of people's lives on earth, in the here and now. It is unnecessary to cite the number of instances in which he used his limited time to alleviate people's physical needs—needs he knew would recur. He himself said, "You always have the poor with you";[8] yet he spent a good deal of his own time on earth trying to alleviate the effects of poverty. He was a constant evangelist; yet his "benevolence ministry" hardly took a back seat to his preaching.

Perhaps he was so keen on helping people, even physically and temporarily, because he viewed what happens on earth as having eternal significance. Sometimes in our desire for heaven and some kind of eternal perspective, we miss this simple point. Over and over the New Testament teaches that earthly life, while short and temporary, is important. One's eternal destiny is dependent on the choice to accept Jesus—a choice one makes in this temporary life. Other choices in this life might in turn influence that choice. What circumstances in this life might affect those choices? Surely one's family is one factor, economic condition is another factor—and the political environment is another. Like it or not, the civil state affects people dramatically. Change it, and you change people's lives. The law affects the range of choices reasonably available to people; it affects their opportunities, resources, health, and life span. It affects how long they have to spend on earth, and what they are able to do while they are here. This is serious, eternal business, and Christians should take it seriously.

If political involvement is one opportunity to affect the lives of others dramatically, and it is available to Christians, Jesus' teaching about stewardship strongly suggests we should use that opportunity to fullest advantage, shrewdly and without delay. The opportunity to affect government policies and rulers is an important source of power over others, just as money is. In Luke 16:9, Jesus told the "children of light" to use *secular money* ("dishonest wealth") to fullest advantage in securing "eternal dwellings." Can we afford to do any less with *political power*?

In fact, although Christians seem to have had little power over government in the first century, some of them did have wealth, social standing, or other means of exercising power over the lives of others. It is interesting that in every case of such power, the New Testament instruction is not to relinquish the power, but to use it as a faithful steward would, to help others. Slave holders, for example, were instructed by Paul, not to give up their slaves, but to do good to their slaves and treat them fairly, knowing that they themselves are slaves of God.[9] And in the teaching of John the Baptist, we find specific instructions to the wealthy, the tax collector, and the soldier, all of which possessed some measure of temporal power over others:

> And the crowds asked him, "What then should we do?" In reply he said to them, "Whoever has two coats must share with anyone who has none; and whoever has food must do likewise." Even tax collectors came to be baptized, and they asked him, "Teacher, what should we do?" He said to them, "Collect no more than the amount prescribed for you." Soldiers also asked him, "And we, what should we do?" He said to them, "Do not extort money from anyone by threats or false accusation, and be satisfied with your wages." (Luke 3:10–14)

None of these groups of powerful people are told to relinquish power; instead, they are told how to use power over others to glorify God.

Temporal power is an opportunity for those who have been blessed with it. Power is, so to speak, an investment opportunity for Christian stewards. The shrewd steward realizes that his stewardship is rapidly coming to an end, and he invests his talents and uses his opportunities, whatever they are, so as to assure for himself an eternal home. Moreover, he knows that service to Christ is service to his fellow man. "Whoever has the world's goods, and sees his brother in need and closes his heart against him, how does the love of God abide in him? . . . [For] the one who does not love his brother whom he has seen, cannot love God whom he has not seen" (1 John 3:17; 4:20) (New American Standard Bible). In this way political involvement can be understood as not only permissible, but a duty of stewardship for those who have been blessed with this trust.

CONCLUSIONS

It seems that those who say the Christian should not be involved in politics, even through informed voting, bear a heavy burden of proof. There is certainly no command or example to this effect. The subject, by and large, is simply not addressed in the New Testament. When an occupation or pursuit is not forbidden by the biblical text, we generally assume it is (at least sometimes) permitted for Christians—as in playing a sport, owning a business, or leading a civic group. Thus, those who claim that Christians should not involve themselves in politics must reason by inference from passages that stress the priority of the spiritual over the temporal. Yet these passages do not have to carry that implication, and there is much evidence from other passages, not inconsistent with the priority of spiritual things, that temporal affairs do have lasting significance and are important to God.

The passages we have examined in this chapter imply that what occurs in this world does matter eternally; that Christians with positions of worldly power are not bound to surrender those positions but to use them for good, with each person remaining in the position they were in when they were called to Christ; that Christians should be good citizens, with all that good citizenship may imply consistent with their walk with God; and most importantly, that Christians should be shrewd stewards of every opportunity at their disposal to do good to others, because the time is short. A good argument can be made that Christians ought to view informed voting, and indeed civic and political participation generally, as a duty related to the opportunity with which they have been blessed in a democratic society—in short, that the opportunity for political participation is a trust from God. At the very least, I would contend that we ought to allow for differences of opinion on this issue according to conscience, rather than insisting that all true Christians remain uninvolved.

But if we assume that God wants Christians to be informed political participants, the next logical questions are whether he wants us to favor any particular policies or agenda; and if so, which one(s). Again, the passages directly addressing civil government do not speak to political involvement at all. If these passages do not tell us *whether* to vote, surely they do not tell us *how* to vote either. The New Testament authors were not directly answering the questions, "How shall I vote?" or "What law shall I make?" but rather, "Shall I obey preexisting law?"

But committed Christianity demands that we seek to know God's will for how we live our lives. If we are to participate in politics, this includes our political lives. In order to govern as we ought, Christians must know God's will. Evangelical Christians, at any rate, will search for God's will in the biblical text. Again, the committed Christian will not conform his faith to his politics, but instead will conform his political views, his votes, and every other aspect of his life to his faith. We are slaves of God.

Perhaps God has no preferences in the realm of public policy; but on the other hand, if God wants Christians to vote, it is not unreasonable to assume that he might have some preference about how they vote. The upcoming chapters of Part III are devoted to analyzing Scripture and other arguments to try to answer the question, "Does God have a preference about how Christians vote or what laws and policies we favor?"

I believe that he might. But it behooves us to tread cautiously here. Historically, all those who have claimed to govern on God's behalf have believed that he had a preference and that they knew for sure what it was. In God's name many of them conducted persecutions that most of us would roundly condemn today. In God's name rulers have executed infidels and heretics; cut out the tongues of false teachers; tortured scientists, linguists, and philosophers; and imprisoned the deformed and the mentally ill. More recently, legal persecutions by Christians have been more limited—although justified, if at all, on many of the very same grounds. But God's true desires for public policy—if we could know them—might surprise us. Ultimately, we may have to rethink what it means to be Christian governors.

NOTES

1. John E. Stambaugh and David L. Balch, *The New Testament in Its Social Environment* (Philadelphia: Westminster Press, 1986), 110.

2. See generally Stambaugh and Balch, *Social Environment*, 30–36, 110–13.

3. Some have speculated that the converts Dionysius of Athens (a member of the Areopagus who is mentioned in Acts 17:34) or Erastus of Corinth (mentioned in Rom. 16:23 as the treasurer for the city of Corinth) may have been members of local aristocratic families. Stambaugh and Balch, *Social Environment*, 112.

4. See Matt. 6:25–34; 2 Thess. 3:6–12.

5. Matt. 6:32.

6. Matt. 6:27.

7. See, for example, Matt. 25:31–46; James 2:14–17.

8. Matt. 26:11.

9. See Eph. 6:9; Col. 4:1. For reasons not discussed here, I do not believe these passages show that God approves of the legal institution of human slavery. However, they do make the point quite clearly that having power over others imposes stewardship obligations on the powerful.

Part III

God's Will for Governors

Chapter Five

God and Caesar: Keeping Law in its Place

Now that we have examined the arguments for and against Christian political involvement in itself, it is time to consider what permissible, responsible Christian political involvement might look like. Assuming God wants Christians to become politically involved—an assumption that seems to have biblical support in light of our study so far—what policies should they favor? What principles should govern the government? What laws does God desire? Or can we know?

This chapter argues that there is a place for law, but that law should be kept in its proper place. These are two separate claims, and we should begin with the first: the claim that there is a proper place for coercive human laws.

A PLACE FOR LAW

The claim that law has a proper place would probably be endorsed by the majority of Christians in America today. Most of us agree that Christians ought to support at least some laws that punish violators. In other words, despite the moral importance of mercy in the life of a Christian, and despite the biblical prohibitions on personal vengeance, most Christians agree that Christians are permitted (or even required) to support laws that punish individual acts of force and fraud that victimize others. But no principle's correctness can be assured solely by its popularity. Before forming our own opinions or supporting a particular type of law, we should examine the biblical text to try to determine God's will. Is there a proper place for law? To answer this question, we must revisit a distinction has already been discussed in Chapter 3: the distinction between forbidden vengeance and permissible punishment.

Vengeance, Forgiveness, and Government Punishment

There are several reasons to think that Christians can support at least some state punishments for criminals. For one thing, there is an important moral distinction between private vengeance or vigilante-style punishment, on the one hand, and state authorized punishment under law, on the other. The Bible at least strongly implies that God approves certain government punishments of wrongdoers when those punishments are carried out under authority of state law. Recall Paul's description of civil government: "[Government] is God's servant for your good. But if you do what is wrong, you should be afraid; for the authority does not bear the sword in vain! It is the servant of God to execute wrath on the wrongdoer" (Rom. 13:4). Again, it is unlikely, for the reasons discussed in Chapter 3, that the punishments to which Paul refers are sinful acts that God wants to use for his purposes. Instead, it seems much more likely that state punishment is a righteous act in God's sight, if for no other reason than the fact that it is conducted under authority of the institution he ordained for exactly this purpose. Of course, this does not mean that *every* punishment done under state authority is morally permissible; it just means that surely *some* are.

If God approves of government punishments through law, one might wonder whether God is giving tacit approval to "vengeance" carried out by those who govern.[1] Is this the government's role as a "servant of God to execute wrath" (Rom. 13:4)? Recall that Paul forbids Christians from taking revenge on those who wrong them (Rom 12:17–21). Presumably, this is because revenge is sinful, whether the action is taken by a Christian or a Non-Christian. On the other hand, Paul states that governments are "servant[s] of God to execute wrath on the wrongdoer" (Rom 13:4). Is criminal law then a system of organized sinful vengeance at God's behest? Why is the sinful act of "vengeance" permissible for the government but not for individuals?

This is a slight rewording of an argument we examined in Chapter 3, where it was presented as a reason for Christians to avoid political involvement of any kind. As we have seen, the response to this argument is that what is forbidden in Romans 12 is *individualized* vengeance. The first verses of Romans 13 strongly imply that *collective* vengeance through the civil government is not only permissible, but is part of God's plan. This is not because Non-Christians happen to be in charge of the government. If punishing others is sinful, it is sinful for everyone. Rather, some governmental punishments are permissible because punishments done under state authority sometimes carry God's authority as well.

As we have already suggested, alternative interpretations are implausible. If we interpret Paul to mean that governments cannot legitimately punish, then they cannot effectively exist in any manner that satisfies God, even if

Christians control them. Yet Paul says God wants governments to punish. Paul says they are ordained by God in order to act on behalf of wronged individuals as God's agents of justice and punishment. If those very punishments are illegitimate, then Paul is describing a God who is using sin, not for a one-time rectification of wrong, but for a permanent dispensation of his justice. This sort of God is actually dependent on sin throughout the foreseeable future; he is counting on it. Could we really say of this God that he desires more people to come to know him? This sort of God has made plans that would actually be defeated if his people become too numerous or too powerful, because in such a case they would control the government and would have to dismantle it, ending its salutary effects. More fundamentally, this interpretation makes God contradictory on the subject of human punishments; in essence, it has him saying, "I don't want humans to punish one another, but I do want humans to punish one another." All this and more must follow if we conclude that all governmental punishment is sinful vengeance.

Hence, the more plausible interpretation is that punishment or "vengeance" is not sinful if it consists of punishment of wrongdoers by a dispassionate government. God has ordained governments—but not private individuals (Rom. 12:17, 19)—to act as his "servant[s] to execute wrath on the wrongdoer" (Rom. 13:4). It does not matter that these are pagan governments, like the Roman empire. As Paul noted in Romans 13, punishments administered by pagans may be reasonably just, even if not uniquely "Christian." In sum, while the final verses of Romans 12 forbid private vengeance, the first verses of Romans 13 strongly imply that such "vengeance" is legitimized when governments, the authorized agents of God, are applying it responsibly.

How far does this principle of legitimation extend? Will any and all otherwise sinful action be sanitized whenever the government is the actor? Can governments do no sin, by definition? That seems doubtful. In fact, in most contexts of wrongdoing, we should probably assume that the moral nature of an act does not change, no matter who the wrongdoer is. For example, the act of killing an innocent person for selfish reasons is a sinful act, whether the killer is acting in his private, individual capacity or in his capacity as ruler of a government. Likewise, treating one race of people as inferior to another is sinful, whether the discrimination is individual or governmental, for "God shows no partiality" (Acts 10:34). Denying justice to widows and poor people is sinful, whether one acts in his private capacity as a citizen or in the governmental office of judge or king (Jer. 22:15–17; Deut. 16:18–20; Exod. 22:22–23; Deut. 24:14–18). To put it another way, not all government "punishments" are approved by God. The acts of imprisoning someone for being a widow, or for worshiping Jesus Christ, are surely not divinely endorsed actions, and laws requiring such punishments are not approved by God.

For this reason Paul's statement should not be read to imply that every use of force by government is justifiable by definition. To say this would be to legitimate the Holocaust, the Crusades, and the persecution of Christians in ancient Rome, all of which involved acts of force performed by governments.

Each of these acts proceeded from wrong motives. And motive is an additional ground of moral distinction between permissible and impermissible punishment. Recall that in Romans 12, Paul is concerned with individual motives and attitudes surrounding vengeance. What makes private vengeance wrong is not only the lack of divine authority for it—the "government" versus "private" distinction—but the motives that often surround it. The central message of Rom. 12:17–21 is, "Do not repay evil for evil." To do so is to sin, whether one is a Christian or not. Paul is clearly concerned with our motives for punishment. When an individual punishes those who have wronged him, Paul suggests that the motive is often suspect. But the motive must be at least equally suspect when force is intentionally used to "punish" or harm those who have done no wrong. This is so whether the punisher is an individual or the government.

But with regard to government, Paul suggests that governmental punishments of those who do evil may typically proceed from different and better motives than those influencing the private vigilante. Usually, governments tend to be motivated by altruistic or utilitarian concerns like maintaining peace, protecting the weak, rehabilitating the wrongdoer, or assuring the greatest happiness for the greatest number, concerns very different from the sinful desires alluded to in Rom. 12:17, 19, to repay evil for evil or to make certain people suffer for their wrongs. Even if the government's motives are suspect in a particular case, the punishment (but not the motive) might well be supported from a Christian perspective if it truly constitutes government punishment of a wrongdoer, since this is the divinely ordained function of governments. However, with respect to the most commonly criminalized activities (murder, assault, theft), government motives for inflicting punishment normally are dispassionate—worlds apart from the sinful and passionate desires of private vigilantes. This general purity of motive should perhaps give us an extra reason to view the most common government punishments as permissible.

Hence, in Rom. 12:17–21 Paul is not condemning punishment as such, but the kind of punishment issuing from a bad attitude coupled with a lack of ostensible authority. Vigilante vengeance is wrong because its motivation is contrary to the Christian spirit of turning the other cheek and being willing to suffer wrong as Christ did. Vigilantism is also wrong because the vigilante has no authority, from God or man, to enact just punishment. Governments generally enact punishment dispassionately and with God's authority, and for those reasons such punishments are presumptively legitimate. This is so despite the occasional failings of individual judges or governments.

This leaves us with the following proposition: While God disapproves of punishment by private individuals carried out for the sake of revenge, many, but not all, of the punishments inflicted by governments are approved by God. In particular, where the government dispassionately punishes a "wrongdoer" (whatever that term might mean) in recompense for his wrongdoing, the punishment is presumptively legitimate; whereas when the government punishes or otherwise intentionally harms people who are not "wrongdoers," (for example, an innocent baby), the government has exceeded its divine mandate and is on no firmer moral ground than an individual who does the same thing. This interpretation is easy to reconcile with the text of Romans and also accords well with our moral intuitions.

So it makes sense that Paul could claim in Rom. 13:4: "[The ruler] is God's servant for your good . . . [and] the servant of God to execute wrath on the wrongdoer." This speaks to the divine purpose for government, and generally describes the actual activities of most governments as well. But for reasons already noted, Paul's descriptive statements about the things governments actually do should not be taken as an ironclad guarantee admitting of no exceptions. Romans 13 should not be taken to mean, for example, that Adolph Hitler's Nazi government faithfully fulfilled its charge as God's servant to reward the righteous and punish the evildoer when it perpetrated genocide. In the social context of Romans, in particular, Paul is surely not asserting, as an empirical matter, that Nero's government had never exceeded its divine authority and never would.

How then can we understand Paul? If he is making sense, he must not be making an absolute, unlimited kind of claim about what governments actually do. His descriptive claim must instead be understood as a generalization about what governments tend to do. This becomes even clearer when we examine the text of Romans in light of the prevailing policies of the government, by and large, at the time Paul was writing. In that light, Paul's statement about the actual conduct of rulers seems accurate enough, as long as it is understood to be a generalization. Nero's early reign seems to have been characterized, at least from a secular viewpoint, by generally sound public policies, orderly administration, vigorous suppression of theft and violent crime, and a prevailing optimism about the future.[2] But it seems highly unlikely that Paul intended to endorse each and every policy of Nero's government—for example, the public funding of idolatry.

To the extent Paul is describing actual governmental activity, then, his description is general. And this too seems supported by our own experiences. Most of the time, in first century Rome and the modern United States at any rate, criminal laws punish people for acts hurtful to others, which also happen to be sinful (although punishing "sin" is not likely to have been the state's primary motive in enacting the laws). However, one can easily imagine exceptions to these general observations, as when a government enacts laws that require the governed to sin or that persecute the righteous for loyalty to God. Unless Paul was woefully uninformed about the world in which he lived, he cannot have intended to disclaim any exceptions to his general statement about what governments actually do. In fact, the irony of his particular situation is that the very Roman government he was describing as God's agent of protection later became an exception to the generalization when Nero ordered the execution of a number of Christians in Rome, Paul likely among them.[3]

Considered then in its textual and social context, Rom. 12:14–13:7 appears to be saying, "Be willing to suffer quietly rather than insisting on the suffering of those who wrong you. Leave vengeance to God, who is just and will repay, one way or another. And by the way, one way he repays, even in this life, is through human governments, which he has ordained for just this purpose, and which generally fulfill this duty faithfully by punishing those who would harm others." On this understanding, the God-given purpose of governments is to punish victimizers, and governmental action of this sort is not sin, but rather a manifestation of the grace and justice of God.

This is not a new interpretation. We have noted in Chapter 2 that Augustine made this point as early as the fourth century, writing that governments are part of God's plan and exercise their limited authority on his behalf to minimize disorder and other harms that flow from private victimization. Thus, he taught that being a part of government—if a Christian is called by God to such a station—is not sinful, but can (like almost any other occupation in life) be seen as a service to God and others, if performed in the right way with the right motives.[4] In the course of this service, the government official (or voter) may be called upon to punish (or support punishment for) wrongdoers under law; but his motives and authority in punishment are far different from those of the private vigilante criticized in Romans 12. As Augustine and the earliest Church fathers uniformly held, governments are God's authorized method for societies to attain a certain level of peace and order as well as a limited amount of justice even before the hereafter.[5]

Judging Those Outside the Church

Some Christians have other reasons for doubting that human law has a place in God's plan. Some may be uncomfortable participating in human systems of justice because of the several passages in the New Testament alluding to the sinfulness of "judging" others. Jesus himself often warned against hypocritical judgment or condemnation of others. One of his most famous sayings is "Judge not, that ye be not judged" (Matt. 7:1, King James Version). Another important teaching regarding judgment is found in 1 Corinthians 5, especially verses 12 and 13, in which Paul tells the Corinthian church that it is none of their business to judge those outside the church—that is, unbelievers. Must Christians renounce punishments by governments because these punishments require us to judge others?

In the relevant part of his first letter to the Corinthians, Paul tells the church to expel from among them a man who was notoriously sleeping with his father's wife. In that context Paul writes:

> I wrote to you in my letter not to associate with sexually immoral persons—not at all meaning the immoral of this world, or the greedy and robbers, or idolaters, since you would then need to go out of the world. But now I am writing to you not to associate with anyone who bears the name of brother or sister who is sexually immoral or greedy, or is an idolater, reviler, drunkard, or robber. Do not even eat with such a one. For what have I to do with judging those outside? Is it not those who are inside that you are to judge? God will judge those outside. "Drive out the wicked person from among you." (1 Cor. 5:9–13, perhaps referring to Deut. 17:7; 19:19; 21:21; 22:21, 24; 24:7)

Does this indicate that Christians ought not participate in outlawing any behavior by those outside the church, instead leaving all such "judgment" to God?

Given the context, that seems a strained reading of the passage. First, it is no part of Paul's purpose here to give instructions about Christian participation in civil government, or indeed about civil government at all. That in itself makes this passage less authoritative on the subject than passages like Romans 13. Second, this passage from 1 Corinthians, taken in context, is intended most directly for a narrow audience, to instruct a particular church about how to deal with a particular problem with a particular person. To the extent it might be interpreted to give any broader instructions to other congregations, these would seem necessarily to involve: (1) situations of open and shameless sin by church members, and (2) to a lesser extent, relationships between church members and unbelievers. Issue #1, surely the primary issue in this passage, has nothing at all to do with whether Christians should support penal laws governing a mixed society of believers and unbelievers. Issue #2, regarding relations between believers and unbelievers, might at first appear relevant to penal laws, at least in the narrow situation where most Christians hold power and most unbelievers do not. But here too, Paul's instruction turns out to be uninstructive regarding Christian lawmaking, for two reasons.

The first reason is that the "judgment" Paul is talking about, of unbelievers by believers, cannot have involved any punishment except withholding fellowship. The Christians of Paul's day had no collective secular power, and thus had no means to "judge" those outside the church except by, as verses 9–11 indicate, refusing to "associate" or "eat" with such people. Paul sensibly instructs the Christians that they *cannot* in fact judge outsiders this way. It would be a physical and logistical impossibility, because Christians cannot remove themselves from the world. If Christians were to make it their policy never to eat or associate with anyone who was an idolater, swindler, and so forth, they would never be able to eat or associate with anyone except Christians—a logistical impossibility for most Christians in the first century, and an obstacle to evangelism as well. But believers were another matter. Christians *could* feasibly refuse to eat or associate with certain of their own number. The whole passage has to do with the procedure of withdrawing fellowship from a believer, and Paul is saying that *this* sort of punishment is not something Christians should be inflicting on unbelievers, because it would be impossible and because it would serve no purpose (since unbelievers may not care whether they associate with Christians or not). But Paul says nothing at all about other methods of punishing unbelievers.

The second reason is that the judgment to which Paul refers is in respect of sin, not unwise or antisocial acts in general. If Christians *had* been instructed in this context to judge those outside the church, the command would boil down to a mandate to punish the outsiders for their *sin*, in hopes that they will be caused to repent. This is what Paul says the procedure is designed to do with respect to believers. But directing the procedure to outsiders would be irrational in Paul's day since, as we have noted, outsiders generally would be unlikely to care whether they associated with Christians or not. Additionally, the goal of this command, inducing repentance from sin, is foreign to secular law. Secular law in fact punishes some acts that are not sinful, allows many acts that are sinful, and does not always punish for the benefit of the wrongdoer but rather for the benefit of others in society (as Romans 13 indicates). Christians are never told not to punish in *that* way. The "judgment" Christians must eschew, according to 1 Corinthians 5, is judgment and punishment of outsiders who *sin*, for the purpose of encouraging repentance.

It is interesting to note that in 1 Corinthians 6, immediately following the passage just discussed, Paul instructs the believers to take intra-church legal disputes before other believers rather than filing lawsuits in the civil law courts. This indicates that there are occasions when believers are to act as judges between other believers, at least, in temporal disputes. The rationale for this command is not that believers are only allowed to judge each other and should not exercise such judgment over unbelievers; quite to the contrary, Paul says: "Do you not know that the saints will judge the world? And if you are to judge the world, are you not competent to judge trivial cases? Do you not know that we will judge angels? How much more the things of this life!" (1 Cor. 6:2–3) (New International Version). Here is a clear statement of the competence of believers to judge nonbelievers as well as believers in temporal, legal-style disputes. It is quite doubtful, then, that Paul would have forbidden Christians in the first century from occupying the office of judge in the Roman law courts (had any of them been presented that opportunity). And if this is so, it is hard to see how his immediately previous instruction in 1 Corinthians 5 can be interpreted to ban all Christian involvement with penal laws—especially in light of all the other positions of secular power that the New Testament seemingly approves for Christians, positions such as tax collector and soldier.[6]

Mercy and Justice

Some Christian discomfort with the morality of human systems of law and justice probably stems from the importance of the doctrine of mercy in Christian teaching. Yet other biblical themes, like justice for those who are wronged, may help inform our understanding of mercy. A biblical study of both mercy and justice actually lends support to the practice of punishing offenders under human law, clarifying our understanding of God's nature as well as his desires for the civil state.

Mercy and justice can be understood as somewhat contradictory values. Mercy is the quality of giving someone else what they need or desire, regardless of what they deserve. For instance, a merciful business manager might not fire an insubordinate employee even after several infractions, and even though company policy clearly gives her the authority to terminate the employment under the circumstances. Justice, on the other hand, is the quality of impartially giving someone else exactly what they deserve, no more and no less, regardless of what they need or desire. So the umpire who is just will call a strike whenever a strike is thrown, regardless of how much the batter wants or even needs to get a hit. Mercy prioritizes human need, while justice prioritizes human desert.

Despite this tension between the two values, the Bible teaches, in numerous passages from both Testaments, that God's nature somehow blends justice and mercy in perfect fulness. He is somehow able to prioritize both simultaneously. He is perfectly merciful and perfectly just at the same time.

This dual nature of God is perhaps seen most clearly in the sacrifice of Jesus. Giving up his only son was an act of supreme, undeserved mercy toward humanity; but such a sacrifice was necessary because of God's justice. We often speak of Christ's death as the supreme example of mercy, and rightly so; but it is impossible to understand *why* Christ had to die until we gain an appreciation for God's sense of justice. The Scriptures teach that if God had been just without being merciful, or merciful without being just, there would have been no atonement and no need for one. Paul emphasizes the role played by mercy when he says that "God, who is rich in mercy, out of the great love with which he loved us even when we were dead through our trespasses, made us alive together with Christ . . . . For by grace you have been saved through faith, and this is not your own doing; it is the gift of God" (Eph. 2:4–5, 8). But Paul also says, "He did this to show his *righteousness*, because in his divine forbearance he had passed over the sins previously committed; it was to prove at the present time that he himself is *righteous* and that he *justifies* the one who has faith in Jesus" (Rom. 3:25–26, emphasis added). Even in the ultimate demonstration of mercy, God's justice shines forth.

Since God wants Christians to imitate his nature, he presumably wants us to incorporate and harmonize the principles of justice and mercy to the fullest possible extent in our own lives. In a well-known passage, Micah writes: "[God] has showed you, O man, what is good. And what does the Lord require of you? To act justly and to love mercy and to walk humbly with your God" (Mic. 6:8) (New International Version). Justice, mercy, and humility are to be blended in full measure in the nature of the godly person. Jesus' accusation of the Pharisees echoes Micah's concern for both justice and mercy: "Woe to you, scribes and Pharisees, hypocrites! For you tithe mint, dill, and cummin, and have neglected the weightier matters of the law: *justice* and *mercy* and *faith*. It is these you ought to have practiced without neglecting the others" (Matt. 23:23, emphasis added). In fact, the Old and New Testaments are full of directives and examples showing the need for justice and mercy in the lives of God's people.[7] Overall, it seems fair to say God strongly desires that our lives be characterized by both justice and mercy, to the fullest possible extent.

What might that mean in practice? What does it mean to blend justice and mercy as God does? This is a very difficult question, to be sure. But we can at least be sure that neither may be excluded; they must both be present in the lives of God's people. It would be contrary to God's nature to impose justice without any mercy; it would be equally contrary to his nature to grant mercy indiscriminately to the undeserving, denying justice to those who have been wronged by them. The Bible teaches that we are saved by God's mercy, and yet that a system of eternal reward and punishment has been fixed as well, set aside for the day at which God's justice will be revealed to those who have rejected him and mistreated their fellow man. In fact, the New Testament teaching about civil government itself indicates the divine drive to temper mercy for the wrongdoer with justice for the wronged (see again Rom. 13:1–4). Criminal justice systems are apparently established by God himself as part of a divine plan of justice, to give wrongdoers some of what they justly deserve even before the next life.

The indication from Scripture seems to be that God wants criminal justice systems to exist—that he himself desires some laws that provide human punishment for the lawbreaker. These desires become easier to understand once we recognize that God's mercy is never unconnected to his concerns for justice. Opposing all human laws that punish would seem to prioritize mercy to the complete exclusion of justice—and perhaps more importantly, to legitimize a disordered hell on earth which would seem anything but merciful to the righteous. On the other hand, knowing what we know about God, we can easily imagine that God would demand a human government in which justice has a place, perhaps even in order to provide a fuller mercy for those who are wronged, but does not reign supreme, being tempered by mercy for the wrongdoer in some individual cases. This kind of system, a system of merciful justice, seems more in keeping with God's nature than does anarchy.[8]

Conclusions About the Place of Law

From our examination of the New Testament thus far, it seems that there is a God-given place for secular law and for Christian involvement with it. The passages about mercy and justice, and those regarding the exercise of secular power by Christians, imply that God is not opposed to all human "punishment" or "judgment" of other humans. In fact, under the right circumstances, it seems to be God's will that human beings use government and laws to impose punishments on other human beings, regardless of whether the offender is a Christian, and regardless of whether the punisher is a Christian.

However, certain guidelines are suggested in Scripture for the acceptability of these punishments. In all legal punishments, whether of believers or unbelievers, Christians must eschew pride, hypocrisy, discrimination, bribery, harm for the sake of harm or vengeance, and selfishness. All such punishments should, like all our actions, be informed by mercy, and motivated by love and a sincere desire to serve others (which may include not just the offender, but real or potential victims as well). And interestingly, we have seen a strong indication from 1 Corinthians 5 and 6 that the punishments Christians support should not be in judgment of sin *as sin*, unless the perpetrator is herself a believer. All this suggests that while God supports human law, he does not want the realm of human law to be unbounded.

This should not surprise us. If it is true that God has fixed a place for law, it may also be true that he does not want law to exceed the boundaries he has set, due to the inherent limitations of human law. Thus, if Christians have a duty to help make law, they may also have a duty to help keep law in its proper place.

KEEPING LAW IN ITS PLACE

Two Different Kingdoms

As we consider the limitations of human law, it is worthwhile to recall Jesus' teaching about God's kingdom and Caesar's kingdom. We now revisit Luke 20:19-26,[9] which is arguably the only teaching of Jesus himself directly relating to civil government. The passage describes Jesus' response when he was asked whether it was right to pay taxes to Caesar. Jesus asked the questioners to look at a denarius, a common silver coin minted under Roman authority, and tell him whose portrait and inscription were on it. They affirmed, of course, that the portrait and inscription were Caesar's.[10] Jesus retorted, "Then give to Caesar what is Caesar's, and to God what is God's" (New International Version). In each of the three gospels' accounts of this event, the narrator tells us that the questioners were astounded by this answer.

What are we to make of this story, recorded by these first century biographers for their Christian audiences? At the most immediate level, as we noticed in Chapter 3, it seems to be an instruction to the early Church to pay Roman taxes without question. The principle would in fact logically extend to taxes imposed by any secular government, at any time. Despite questions the Christians may have had about how Rome was spending the money—questions, we have noted, that were very much on the minds of the Pharisees as well—the clear instruction to followers of Christ is to pay the tax.

This call to submit to taxation is reinforced by Jesus' teaching on another occasion, this time addressing the temple tax:

> When they reached Capernaum, the collectors of the temple tax came to Peter and said, "Does your teacher not pay the temple tax?" He said, "Yes, he does." And when he came home, Jesus spoke of it first, asking, "What do you think, Simon? From whom do kings of the earth take toll or tribute? From their children or from others?" When Peter said, "From others," Jesus said to him, "Then the children are free. However, so that we do not give offense to them, go to the sea and cast a hook; take the first fish that comes up; and when you open its mouth, you will find a coin; take that and give it to them for you and me." (Matt. 17:24–27)

The temple tax was a Jewish tax collected all over Palestine for the support and upkeep of the temple complex in Jerusalem. Jesus seems to distinguish this tax to some degree from Roman taxes paid into the coffers of Caesar. Perhaps Jesus viewed the temple tax as a "religious" tax rather than a "secular" one; or perhaps he was merely recognizing that this distinction between the two taxes was commonly accepted among the Jews. At any rate, Jesus claims that the temple tax, unlike the Roman tax (which he said belonged to Caesar, not God), was a tax imposed under the taxing authority of his own father, God. And since kings do not assess taxes on their own children, the true children of God were in some sense exempt from the temple tax. But in the end Jesus told Peter to pay the tax on behalf of them both, so that he and Peter would not "offend" the tax collectors. Once again, Christians are told to pay taxes, without regard to the identity of the taxing authority, the religious or secular purpose of the tax, or where the money goes. This message fits in perfectly with all the other New Testament passages about civic duty, instructing Christians to be model citizens, to work hard, and to obey the laws of the land.

Another message Jesus may have intended to convey in his teaching on the Roman tax was a lesson about materialism. Money is a human invention of merely temporary value. The "things that are Caesar's" would include coins and a few other worldly, perishable things, but the "things that are God's" are of infinitely greater worth—the heart, the soul, the mind.[11] To paraphrase Jesus here, one might say, "Who cares where your money goes? After all, it's just money. Don't obsess about it. Give God your heart and soul, and the rest will take care of itself." That message is quite consistent with his other sayings about wealth and the material world, and quite contrary to the prevailing spirit of his day—and ours.

Most importantly for this study, a third message cries out here: There is a distinction between the things of God and the things of Caesar. God's kingdom is simply not the secular state. Jesus was ever vigilant to distinguish between the two, in a context in which the Jews expected quite the opposite. In John 18:36, Jesus tells Pilate plainly, "My kingdom is not from this world. If my kingdom were from this world, my followers would be fighting to keep me from being handed over to the Jews. But as it is, my kingdom is not from here." In Luke 22:24–30, Jesus again contrasts his kingdom with that of a secular king. He tells his disciples that while the kings of the Gentiles strive for lordship over others, in the kingdom of God the disciples are not to be like that; instead, the "greatest" among them must be the servant of all.

And Jesus acted on this distinction, practicing what he preached. Besides offering his life as a sacrifice, besides living each day with the spirit of a slave of man, he rejected various attempts to make him out to be a secular ruler. In John 6:14–15, for example, we find him in hiding, withdrawing to a mountain by himself in order to avoid a Jewish crowd that intended to make him a king "by force." And in Matt. 4:8–10, he rejects the devil's offer to give him "all the kingdoms of the world." No matter the human government under which they live, Christians ultimately follow not an emperor or a president, but an impoverished Jewish rabbi who had so few friends in the halls of power that he was finally executed by the political establishment he decried.

Disciples of Jesus do not pledge ultimate allegiance to a flag, or to "the republic for which it stands," but to the Lord of a heavenly kingdom, a "meek and lowly" rescuer who consistently and decisively disclaimed pretensions to political power on earth.[12]

Jesus consistently set up a dichotomy between what belongs to the realm of Caesar—that is, the secular state—and what belongs to the realm of God. This is far from saying that God's will should have no influence on "secular life." Of course, there is a very real sense in which God's jurisdiction has no limit, in which his realm has no borders. There is no sphere of human activity outside the purview of God. But Jesus' words and ministry also challenge us to see the sense in which the realm of the secular state and the realm of the spiritual are mutually exclusive realms. We know from Paul's writings that Caesar is ordained by God to be God's agent in some way. Yet for Jesus' command about the Roman tax to make sense, there must be another sense in which Caesar and God are quite *distinct*, with different agendas and different priorities, so that to give Caesar what Caesar wants is *not* the same as giving God what God wants.

Assuming some kind of distinction between the spiritual realm and the secular state, then, what are we to make of it? How does it inform our understanding of God's will for governors (meaning voters, magistrates, legislators, or anyone else with political power)? The distinction would seem to mean at least that governors, even Christian ones, must not try to establish a theocratic legal system to bind unbelievers. They must not excessively mingle the secular state with the kingdom of God. If there really is a distinction in God's view between the "things that are Caesar's" and the "things that are God's," Christian governors should not begin their task with the presumption (even a rebuttable presumption) that God wants the secular state to punish sin and reward righteousness. The distinction between the kingdoms means the presumption must run in exactly the opposite direction. The concept of a "Christian nation," as used to denote some sort of thorough and intentional blending of religious doctrine and the force of law, has no place among the teachings of the New Testament; it is no more biblical than the concepts of a "Christian continent" or a "Christian hemisphere," and perhaps a good bit less biblical than the concept of a "Christian world." We have no authorization for claiming that our own government, more than others, is somehow approved by God. From all we are told, the realms of God and Caesar are distinct and are to remain so, with divine approval. Governments that ignore this distinction and exceed their divinely ordained sphere, even in God's name, may be asking their citizens to give to Caesar the things, like the heart and mind, that belong to God alone.

Imagine for a moment that Tiberius, the Roman emperor during Jesus' ministry, had been introduced to the God of the Jews. Imagine in fact that Tiberius had heard Jesus teach and had placed faith in him. Would Jesus' instruction about the Roman tax have been any different? It seems doubtful. There is still a distinction between a secular law, like the tax law, and God's law. When Jesus essentially says, "Caesar is not God," the point is not that the man currently holding the title of "Caesar" is himself unholy; rather, the point is that secular government is *neither holy nor unholy in itself*. It is in an important sense separate from issues of holiness, which belong to the realm of God. Even were Caesar a follower of Christ, he would not be God, his government would not be the kingdom of God, and his laws would not be God's laws.

Jesus said, "Caesar is not God," in the same sense he might say to an employee, "Your employer is not God." In each case, the listener owes a duty to another because of earthly bonds or secular convention. Jesus essentially says, "Give them what you owe them according to secular convention, but also be sure to give God what you owe him." That teaching makes sense. Of course, my employer may in fact be a Christian; but his expectations of me as an employee usually have nothing to do with religion. The duty I owe him is not a religious one. It could be performed by a Christian or a nonbeliever, just the same. It simply has no religious connection *per se*, one way or the other—it is separate from issues of righteousness.

In the same way, Jesus is apparently teaching that the requirements of secular law—the duties of citizens to Caesar—will usually be separate from issues of righteousness, and will be fulfilled by Christians and unbelievers alike, regardless of how godly or godless Caesar or his subjects happen to be. The concerns of the state are simply different from the concerns of God. This is not to say that the state is usually ungodly or is trying to require sin; it is just to say that the realms and interests of God are distinct from those of Caesar. Christians are bound as a religious matter to obey Caesar's laws as long as obedience does not conflict with God's will; but this is true whether or not Caesar is purporting to write "Christian laws." Obedience to human law is a religious matter only because God commands obedience, not because the nature of law is truly religious rather than secular. Human law is secular law, no matter which human makes it. And secular law does not define God's will, even if Caesar happens to be a believer. God defines God's will.

Of course, if secular law does require people to sin, Christians clearly must follow God's will instead, just as they should if their employers ask them to sin. But Jesus sees this situation as the exception, not the rule. Ordinarily, there should be no conflict between the expectations of God and Caesar, because Caesar's concern is not with men's souls. So in the ordinary case, Christians are to fulfill the expectations of both sovereigns, God and Caesar. But Jesus says there are two different sets of expectations, nevertheless. Again, he is doing more here than observing that the Roman state is in fact ungodly in A.D. 30. He is telling us something about the nature of civil governments in general. The expectations and concerns of Caesar are distinct from the expectations and concerns of God—not because Tiberius happens to be an unbeliever, but because the nature of civil government requires that it operate in a sphere separate from religion and its concern for the heart and soul.

Two Different Kinds of Wrongdoing

If this is true, what are we to make of Rom. 13:1–7, especially the assertion that civil governments are ordained by God for the purpose of punishing "the wrongdoer" (Rom. 13:4)? Is Paul saying that government is not limited to the "secular sphere" but should concern itself with the religious issue of wrongdoing? To answer this question, we must understand what Paul means by "wrongdoer" here. This will require reading this passage from Romans in light of its historical context, its textual context within the book of Romans, and other relevant biblical texts, including Jesus' comments about Caesar. If possible, we should want to interpret all the biblical texts in such a way that they will be consistent with one another and also make sense in their historical context.[13]

At first glance, without regard to these contexts, it may appear that "wrongdoer" in this passage refers to anyone who does what is sinful or "wrong." But this cannot be the meaning, for, as Paul notes in an earlier part of the Roman letter, "all have sinned and fall short of the glory of God" (Rom. 3:23). If "wrongdoer" means "sinner" and "wrong" means "sin," then the government exists to punish everyone. If this were so, the distinction Paul draws between "those who do wrong" and "those who do right" (Rom. 13:3) would disappear, because it is impossible for anyone to do only what is "right" in this sense.

Along these lines, it is important to recognize that the first century Roman government, as Paul must have known, did not legally forbid many things Christians would have regarded as sinful. To consider just two of many examples, the acts of prostitution (condemned at 1 Cor. 6:15–20) and abortion (generally considered by the early Church to be sinful) were apparently permitted by law in the early Roman empire.[14] Thus, whatever Paul meant when he said governments (including the Roman government) are established by God to "bring punishment on the wrongdoer," he could not have meant that governments are established by God for the purpose of outlawing all sin—or even most sin. The Roman government under which Paul lived surely did not outlaw most sin, and yet Paul said it was established by God, and that Caesar (probably Nero), the pagan, was generally a dependable servant of God to punish the wrongdoer. We must conclude, therefore, that "wrongdoing" in this passage cannot mean all sin. Whatever the government is designed to punish, it must not be every act that is sinful in God's sight. Which subset of sins or wrongs, then, qualify as "wrongdoing" as Paul is using that term?

Recall again Paul's words in their textual context:

> Bless those who persecute you; bless and do not curse them. Rejoice with those who rejoice, weep with those who weep. Live in harmony with one another; do not be haughty, but associate with the lowly; do not claim to be wiser than you are. Do not repay anyone evil for evil, but take thought for what is noble in the sight of all. If it is possible, so far as it depends on you, live peaceably with all. Beloved, never avenge yourselves, but leave room for the wrath of God; for it is written, "Vengeance is mine, I will repay, says the Lord." No, "if your enemies are hungry, feed them; if they are thirsty, give them something to drink; for by doing this you will heap burning coals on their heads." Do not be overcome by evil, but overcome evil with good.
>
> Let every person be subject to the governing authorities; for there is no authority except from God, and those authorities that exist have been instituted by God. Therefore whoever resists authority resists what God has appointed, and those who resist will incur judgment. For rulers are not a terror to good conduct, but to bad. Do you wish to have no fear of the authority? Then do what is good, and you will receive its approval; for it is God's servant for your good. But if you do what is wrong, you should be afraid, for the authority does not bear the sword in vain! It is the servant of God to execute wrath on the wrongdoer. Therefore one must be subject, not only because of wrath but also because of conscience. For the same reason you also pay taxes, for the authorities are God's servants, busy with this very thing. Pay to all what is due them—taxes to whom taxes are due, revenue to whom revenue is due, respect to whom respect is due, honor to whom honor is due. (Rom. 12:14–13:7)

In this part of Romans, Paul first tells the Christians, "Bless those who persecute you; bless and do not curse them" (Rom. 12:14). He then instructs his readers not to seek revenge against those who harm them, but instead to do good to their persecutors and to leave room for "the *wrath* of God" (Rom. 12:19) (emphasis added).

It is crucial to note that the Greek word ὀργή (*orgē*) from Rom. 12:19, usually translated in English versions as "wrath" or "anger," is the same word used in Rom. 13:4: "But if you do what is wrong, you should be afraid, for the authority does not bear the sword in vain! It is the servant of God to execute *wrath* on the wrongdoer" (emphasis added). The "wrath" (*orgē*) government brings on "the wrongdoer" is brought upon him by God's agent as part of God's ordained plan and is thus presumably God's wrath, the same "wrath" (*orgē*) that Christians were just instructed to wait for.

So who is "the wrongdoer"? It seems to be *the one who harms others*, for this is who the Christians would otherwise seek vengeance against. But as it is, they are instructed to wait for "the wrath of God" as exercised upon such people by the civil government. What "wrong" then is the civil government punishing? Not wrong or sin generally, but the particular wrong of *harming others*. Whatever sins the Roman state actually did punish at the time Paul wrote, the vast majority of them must have been of this nature.

So in Romans 13 Paul states a general truth. Generally speaking, it is true that governments punish wrongdoers—that is, those that harm others—while protecting and vindicating the innocent. To that extent and for that purpose they are established by God and serve his will. Of course it should be clear by now that not all governments fulfill God's purpose or do his will. While Paul is firm on the subject of what governments are *supposed* to do, there are obviously exceptions to Paul's general claim about what governments *actually* do. There have in fact been governments that failed to punish some of those who harm others, just as there have been governments that punished some people who were not harming others. Paul is not denying it, nor is he placing God's stamp of approval on such governments. He is merely stating a general truth about what governments tend to do, while simultaneously justifying them to the extent they do it.

But that means this justification is limited in two important ways. Paul is not legitimating any and all duly enacted laws. And just as certainly, he is far from saying that governments ought to punish sin generally, wherever they find it. The agency divinely bestowed on government is apparently of a more limited sort. Governments are God's agents of wrath to punish those who victimize or persecute others. This is the agency God had granted Nero's government, and this is the agency Paul says Nero was generally fulfilling.

So the point Paul makes in Romans 13 is not inconsistent with Jesus' teaching about Caesar; to the contrary, Paul reinforces our understanding of that teaching. Paul essentially says: "It is generally true that the government and its officials are fulfilling functions established for them by God, and pursuant to God's plan, generally their laws end up punishing those who sin against others and protecting those who are sinned against. Therefore Christians should always do good to others, pay their taxes, and be good citizens, fulfilling their own legal obligations and giving public officials the honor due their positions." But Paul, like Jesus, stops short of claiming that Caesar ought to act like God's agent for all purposes.

Likewise, Jesus' distinction between the spiritual realm and the secular state would seem to reinforce our understanding of Paul's teaching: The realms and concerns of God and Caesar are distinct. Although governors are agents of God, their agency is not unlimited, even if they happen to be Christians. When Paul says government is authorized by God to punish the wrongdoer, the authorization to which he refers is simply to punish those who harm others. Paul is silent as to government authority to punish sin generally, and the silence is important. In light of Jesus' teaching on the separate realms of God and Caesar, Paul may plausibly be read to suggest that the state is not authorized to criminalize all "wrongdoing" or sin. Nor could any human government have any hope of accomplishing this. Rather, the sphere of Caesar's legitimate agency is limited to avenging and deterring wrongs that are directly harmful to others. Both Jesus and Paul consistently affirm that the divine purpose for Caesar's authority is distinct from God's redemptive purpose among mankind.

While Christians ought to use every opportunity and position of power with which they have been blessed to do God's will, we must make sure we understand what God's will is for the exercise of those particular powers, especially if we are told God has ordained a certain position of power for a unique purpose. While Christians ought to use common sense to apply biblical principles to all areas of life, including public policy, we ignore at our peril such direct biblical guidance about the limited purpose of governments under the New Covenant. Christian voters and rulers should be reluctant to begin their task with the presumption that God wants the secular state to witness for him in every way we can imagine. More specifically, in light of the New Testament passages about governments, Christians should be reluctant to assume that anything a Christian evangelist might properly say or do to induce the repentance of an unbelieving drug addict, or that a parent might properly say or do in rearing his own child, is a proper thing for law to say or do in governing all of us.

Certainly God wants more individuals in every society to be righteous. If this occurs on a broad scale, the society may be said to be a righteous society. A whole nation may even become, in this sense, a "righteous nation," which would surely please God. But all this says nothing at all, necessarily, about governments and laws. In fact, it seems that God has carefully circumscribed the role of government and law in bringing about righteousness. Perhaps we cannot know precisely why; but some of the possible reasons for this are discussed in the following chapter.

BECOMING SERIOUS ABOUT LIMITING LAW

When assessing current governments and laws in the United States, evangelicals as a group tend to be quick to characterize them as failing to fulfill their divine mandate. When we see our government-run schools and city halls refuse to explicitly acknowledge the authority of the one true God, we take this as evidence for our claim that our governments have forsaken God and his will. We find additional evidence in the government's refusal to outlaw homosexual practice, as well as its refusal to pass judgment on the homosexual lifestyle. If our governments were suddenly to widely legalize prostitution, and to legalize abortions at any stage of pregnancy for any reason, we would doubtless cite these developments as further proof that our unholy governments have violated God's will.

And yet each of these policies was in place under Nero's government, at the time Paul wrote Romans. The governing authorities during the reign of Nero not only refused to explicitly acknowledge the authority of the one true God, but they explicitly encouraged the worship of false gods. In addition, the laws freely permitted abortions,[15] various types of homosexual conduct, and prostitution, all of which were frequently and openly practiced in the culture.[16] Yet when Paul had opportunity to express his views about that government, he claimed that the governing authority of his day was "God's servant to do you good" and held "no terror for those who do right, but for those who do wrong." Paul did not wail about the wickedness of his government and the secular humanists and pagans who controlled it; rather, he boldly characterized the government of his day, ruled by unholy men, as generally fulfilling God's will, citing it as an example of a government acting on God's behalf to benefit mankind. Somewhere along the line, we have misunderstood God's will for governments.

In short, there is no indication from the New Testament that law is or ought to be designed so as to proclaim God's reign, offer thanksgiving to God, reward righteousness, or punish sin in general. To the extent the New Testament addresses propriety in government at all, it suggests that government is divinely ordained as God's limited agent of vengeance, not his missionary society or his executive branch on earth. It suggests that human law ought to be (and generally is) designed for a purpose that satisfies even secular concerns: to punish and prevent victimization, the kind of sin or "wrong" for which victims might be tempted to try to get revenge. Human law is not ordained to induce people to comply with all of God's will.

But if God wants people to come to know him and to comply with his will, why wouldn't he want every available tool to be used to induce such a result? To answer this question, one must consider the nature of human law. Because conforming to God's law invariably involves free choice and a right heart, and the secular law cannot police the heart or force people to "freely choose" what is good, secular law may be *incapable* of ensuring conformity with God's law. If so, this unfitness of law in the realm of the heart provides an extra reason not to use it for that purpose. The next chapter explores this argument more fully.

NOTES

1. The discussion which follows regarding vengeance is adapted from my article, "Government as God's Agent: A Reconsideration of Romans 12 and 13," *Stone-Campbell Journal* 8, no. 2 (Oct. 2005): 190–94.

2. Stephen Benko and John J. O'Rourke, *The Catacombs and the Colosseum* (Valley Forge, Pa.: Judson Press, 1971), 56; James S. Jeffers, *The Greco-Roman World of the New Testament Era* (Downers Grove, Ill.: Intervarsity Press, 1999), 318; Richard J. Cassidy, *Paul in Chains* (New York: Crossroad Publishing Co., 2001), 13, 26, 34–35; Michael Grant, *Nero: Emperor in Revolt* (New York: American Heritage Press, 1970), 57–60.

3. F. J. Foakes-Jackson, *The Life of St. Paul* (New York: Boni & Liveright, 1926), 231–40; Jerome Murphy-O'Connor, *Paul: A Critical Life* (New York: Oxford University Press, 1996), 368–71.

4. Herbert A. Deane, *The Political and Social Ideas of St. Augustine* (1963; 2d printing, New York: Columbia University Press, 1966), 130, 142, 224 (citing, for example, Augustine, *Contra Faustum Manichaeum* 22.58; Augustine, *Epistula* 151.14; Augustine, *Epistula* 138.2.14). See also Augustine, *City of God* 5.24.

5. For the thought of Augustine, see Deane, *St. Augustine*, 10–11, 116–17, 137, 142. Regarding the attitudes of the early Church and the Ante-Nicene Fathers toward the Roman state, see T.M. Parker, *Christianity & the State in the Light of History* (London: Adam and Charles Black, 1955), 35–40; J. Philip Wogaman, *Christian Perspectives on Politics*, rev. ed. (Louisville, Ky.: Westminster John Knox Press, 2000), 35–38.

6. Regarding the position of tax collector, see Luke 19:1–10; Luke 3:12–13. Regarding the position of soldier, see Luke 3:14; Matt. 8:5–13; Acts 10; Acts 16:22–34. Notwithstanding these texts, evangelicals of the past have sometimes argued that Christians should have nothing to do with penal laws or positions of political power. For a brief historical survey of evangelical attitudes in this area, see Mark Noll, "The Scandal of Evangelical Political Reflection," in *Being Christian Today: An American Conversation*, ed. Richard John Neuhaus and George Weigel (Washington, D.C.: Ethics and Public Policy Center, 1992), 74–82.

7. These passages make beneficial reading. Among others, the following passages address the ideal of justice: Deut. 16:18–20; Exod. 23:1–3, 6–8; 1 Kings 3:5–12; Isa. 5:22–23; Jer. 21:12; Amos 5:11–15; Luke 11:42; and Col. 4:1. The ideal of mercy is emphasized in, for example: Hos. 6:6; Jonah 3 and 4; Matt. 5:7; Matt. 18:21–35; Luke 10:30–37; James 2:12–13; Luke 6:35–36; and Col. 3:13.

8. One is reminded of Paul's description of God in 1 Cor. 14:33: "God is a God not of disorder but of peace."

9. Again, parallel accounts are found at Matt. 22:15–22 and Mark 12:13–17.

10. A denarius of that day was a Roman silver coin that carried the value of about a day's wage for a typical unskilled laborer. During the ministry of Jesus, a denarius would have been imprinted with a portrait of the current emperor, Tiberius, with a

laurel on his head, along with the Latin inscription "TI(berius) CAESAR DIVI AVG(ustus) F(ilius) AVGVSTVS, PONTIF(ex) MAXIM(us)," meaning "Tiberius Caesar, son of Augustus the God, Augustus, and chief priest." See R.A.G. Carson, *Coins of the World* (New York: Harper & Brothers, 1962), 128–29, plate 16; Larry J. Kreitzer, *Striking New Images: Roman Imperial Coinage and the New Testament World* (Sheffield, England: Sheffield Academic Press, 1996), 17–18; H. Noel Humphreys, *The Coin Collector's Manual*, vol. 1 (London: H.G. Bohn, 1853), 317–18; James S. Jeffers, *The Greco-Roman World of the New Testament Era* (Downers Grove, Ill.: Intervarsity Press, 1999), 151. The religious claims in the inscription are striking. Tiberius claimed to be the son of a god (or might we say "the son of god"?). The "god" was Caesar Augustus, the previous emperor, who had adopted Tiberius as his son and heir. The inscription also gives Tiberius the title of chief priest of the state religion of Rome, which involved the worship of various deities of the Roman Pantheon. Jesus, however, would have none of this. Caesar's kingdom, to Jesus, was completely separate from religion, the divine, or the supernatural, regardless of all Caesar's claims to the contrary. Caesar's government simply had no special connection to religion or the divine, and no inscription on a coin could change that fact. The application to the government of the United States, with its coinage bearing the inscription "In God We Trust," is worth pondering.

11. See Jesus' teaching at Matt. 22:37 ("Love the Lord your God with all your heart and with all your soul and with all your mind"), strongly endorsing the similar Torah command found at Deut. 6:5.

12. The "meek and lowly" language comes from Jesus' characterization of himself. See Matt. 11:29 (King James Version). Coming from the mouth of the son of God, such humility cannot fail to impress, and it is reflected in many other biblical descriptions of him. See, for example, Isa. 53:1–9; Luke 2:1–7; 2 Cor. 10:1; Phil. 2:5–8. See also Rev. 5 (Jesus depicted as a lamb that appeared to have been slaughtered).

13. The discussion which follows is an extension of my argument in "Government as God's Agent: A Reconsideration of Romans 12 and 13," *Stone-Campbell Journal* 8, no. 2 (Oct. 2005): 195–97.

14. Regarding prostitution, see Benko and O'Rourke, *Catacombs*, 180–82. Regarding abortion, see Michael J. Gorman, *Abortion & the Early Church* (Downers Grove, Ill.: InterVarsity Press, 1982), 30, 47–62.

15. More specifically, first century Roman law does not seem to have penalized the act of abortion *per se*. If any legal penalty attached to abortion, it was only in situations where a wife had obtained an abortion, contrary to her husband's wishes. Where abortion laws existed, they protected the interests of husbands in having children, but not the child's interest in being born. In any event, the weight of evidence suggests that even the laws protecting husbands were not yet in place as Paul wrote the book of Romans; instead, abortions were completely unregulated by law. See Gorman, *Abortion*, 30–32.

16. By listing abortion alongside homosexuality and prostitution, I do not mean to discount the possibility that there are important differences between these activities. Many, perhaps most, of those who oppose abortion on moral grounds would charac-

terize an unborn child, at any stage of development after the egg is fertilized, as a person. If they are correct, then abortion (but not contraception) harms other persons in a very significant way, a way that prostitution and homosexuality do not, and therefore governments that do not ban abortions are failing to fulfill their divine mandate to protect the innocent from wrongdoers. In other words, Romans 13 would be read to suggest that governments should punish those who perform or request abortions, although the law might well allow prostitution and homosexual conduct because those activities do not involve wrongdoing that necessarily harms other persons. Following this line of reasoning, one could conclude that notwithstanding the limited agency of governments, Christian voters should oppose abortion rights and support laws against abortion.

This argument is of course founded on the hotly contested supposition that personhood begins at a particular time before birth. I do not mean here to express any opinion as to when personhood begins; I would merely reiterate that the determination that personhood begins at a particular point before birth is crucial to concluding that abortion harms other persons, and this determination in turn is necessary in order to legitimate laws against abortion in light of Romans 12 and 13. To say this another way, the above argument for the government's duty to protect other persons by outlawing abortion "after stage X of pregnancy" (stage X being conception, implantation, viability, or whatever stage is chosen) must be premised on the assumption that from God's point of view, "stage X" is the precise beginning of personhood. Such assumptions are discussed further in Chapter 10.

Chapter Six

Freedom from Law: The "Heart" of the Matter

The story is told of a young boy who was sent to the principal's office for discipline. The unfortunate grade-schooler had been discovered reading a comic book when he should have been listening to his teacher. The principal asked the boy to be seated and proceeded to discuss at length the various rules of behavior enforced by the school, expounding the merits of each. The youngster listened attentively. The master went on to note that rules are part and parcel of life. "You see, my boy," the good man explained, "society could not exist without rules, for rules are the source of freedom. This is their purpose, to give birth to freedom. From the days of Solon to our own, systems of rules have assured human freedom, so that indeed wherever we find freedom we find rules. Rules have given us freedom to think, to speak, and to pursue our dreams, to become whatever in life we wish. Now tell me, what is it that you wish for yourself?" The boy paused a moment, looking a bit perplexed, and then ventured, "Well, sir, right now I wish I didn't have quite so much freedom."

This story encourages us to examine the ideas of "freedom" and "law" more closely. What is the relationship between them? Does law enhance freedom, as the principal held? Or was the boy correct to be perplexed by this claim? Or were they both right? Before turning to Scripture, it might be useful to explore briefly the ideas of "freedom" and "law" from a secular perspective.

FREEDOM AND LAW: THE ENLIGHTENMENT VIEW

In a sense the principal must be right. Law must be freedom-enhancing, for without law, the freedom of the weak majority would be severely limited by the whims of the mighty few. Laws prohibiting murder, kidnapping, theft, and the like can assure freedom by providing security for the weak members of society against certain forms of private coercion that would otherwise reduce freedom.

This understanding of law runs strongly through the writings of the Enlightenment, the intellectual movement so influential on American political thought. The view of law as freedom-enhancing may be seen in the writings of both Thomas Hobbes and John Locke, two important influences on Enlightenment thought, who separately argued in the seventeenth century that law was necessary to provide greater degrees of freedom. Both men imagined that anarchy would be a miserable situation because human beings would continually fight each other for access to power and scarce resources. Hobbes argued that law is instituted to avoid the problems of anarchy by allowing people "to live peaceably amongst themselves, and be protected against other men."[1] Similarly, Locke argued that law's purpose is to protect a set of natural rights from violation by other people,[2] so that "*the end of Law* is not to abolish or restrain, but *to preserve and enlarge Freedom:* For in all the states of created beings capable of Laws, *where there is no Law, there is no Freedom.*"[3] Thus, by preventing and punishing victimizing behaviors, law brings freedom—freedom to farm, produce, hoard, labor, and generally live as one chooses, without interference from other people.

But law can also be understood as freedom-limiting. Law is the power of the government to control individual behavior by threatening the force of the government as punishment for disobedience. If a particular act is outlawed, the law, in an important sense, deprives individuals of the freedom to perform that act. Of course, depending on the act, I might be physically able to perform the act despite its illegality; but my freedom to choose to perform it has been limited by the threat that I will be detected and punished by the state. Even laws against murder are freedom-limiting in this sense, for they limit the range of choices otherwise available to would-be murderers. Some laws (like murder laws) limit freedom a little, for justifiable reasons, while other laws limit freedom much more and may not be justifiable; but every law limits freedom somewhat in an individual case, or else there would be no need to make a *law*. Law is nothing if not coercive.

Hobbes and Locke recognized this as well. Ideally governments will make laws enhancing freedom, but every law reduces freedom a little along the way. Law always involves tradeoffs. Hobbes and Locke both asserted that these tradeoffs had generally been recognized by societies as worthwhile, and for that reason societies had voluntarily created governments. Both argued that, under some theory of social contract, the governed had surrendered certain of their preexisting freedoms to the state.[4] Thus both agreed that the government has the authority, derived from the mutual consent of the governed, to make laws depriving its people of freedom. According to Hobbes and Locke, the governed made this sacrifice in order to free themselves of the most egregious forms of private coercion. But however that may be, no one can doubt that governments make laws and that those laws coerce people. Particular laws may or may not prevent private coercion, but they will always be in some sense coercive themselves. Good laws may indeed prevent private coercion, but they do so at the cost of public coercion.

Many laws are justifiable because they are worth this tradeoff, but there is some point, as Locke well understood,[5] at which the scope of public coercion becomes so great, and overall freedom becomes so limited, that the governed would be at least as well off without any law at all. A small amount of law is certainly justified to prevent coercion and enhance overall freedom, but as the scope of law expands to impose more and more public coercion, law reaches some critical mass at which it begins to reduce rather than expand overall freedom. Law would then, in a sense, become an irreconcilable opposite of freedom. Law and freedom would become inversely related, so that to expand law further is to limit freedom overall.

Locke's view of law became pervasive during the Enlightenment. From the viewpoint of secular Enlightenment thought, at any rate, law was necessary to freedom but also dangerous to it, and the danger was not to be dismissed lightly. Law always limits freedom in individual cases and sometimes in the aggregate, although good law may be said to increase freedom in the aggregate.

FREEDOM AND LAW: THE BIBLICAL VIEW

Of course the Bible speaks frequently of "law," and not always in positive terms; but it may be surprising to some that the Bible has much to say in praise of "freedom." In the Scriptures, the word "freedom" means different things in different contexts and often does not refer to freedom from secular restraints on personal liberty. But occasionally the Bible does speak of "freedom" in exactly that sense. Since this kind of freedom is precisely our concern here, we should consider such passages closely.

One of the more interesting of these is found at 1 Cor. 7:21–23. Writing to those who were slaves when they became Christians, Paul says:

> Were you called while a slave? Do not worry about it; but if you are able also to become free, rather do that. For he who was called in the Lord while a slave, is the Lord's freedman; likewise he who was called while free, is Christ's slave. You were bought with a price; do not become slaves of men.[6]

Paul's instructions seem to show that God, or at least Paul, places some value on "liberty" in the sense that Thomas Jefferson or John Stuart Mill would have used that term. God's will is that we accept the station in life in which we are called—at least, that was his will for the Corinthians in the first century—but it is also his will that we be free of human bondage. If the law allows, we should go out of our way to achieve freedom and preserve it.

Probably the most significant biblical discourse on law and freedom comes from the book of Galatians, particularly chapters 3-5. These chapters deserve exploration in some depth, with a view toward trying to understand how God views law and freedom.

The first thing to notice is that the term "law" as used in these chapters denotes the law of Moses, the Jewish Torah, not the secular law of the Roman state. This is clear from the context. Paul is writing to oppose those who would bind Jewish customs and "laws" (such as circumcision) onto Gentile Christians. Similarly, as we noted earlier, the term "freedom" as used here does not always signify freedom from all authority, secular or divine; rather, in this context the term denotes, variously, freedom from sin, freedom to do right, or freedom from the regulations of the Torah. Still, it is noteworthy that Paul continually presents "freedom" and "law" in inverse relationship to one another. As law's scope is increased, freedom is reduced, and vice versa.

In view of the length of these three chapters, it might be useful to summarize them. At the risk of unintentionally glossing over or even distorting some of the meaning in this passage, which is always a possibility with summaries, I present here a short summary of these three chapters. Consider what they may say about God's view of the purpose and limitations of law and the inherent value of freedom.

> Salvation and the Holy Spirit come through faith, not through observing the law. The law is fulfilled by outward behavior, but faith is a matter of the heart. God made a gracious promise to Abraham that through Jesus, his blood descendent, all the nations of earth would be blessed. That promise was not set aside by the law of Moses; rather, it has been fulfilled in the sacrifice of Jesus, and is being fulfilled even now as Gentiles and Jews alike accept God's grace through faith. Thus there is no conflict between the Mosaic law and God's gracious promise, extended to Abraham and fulfilled in Jesus. The promise was that God would provide a means by which all people could attain righteousness and freedom from sin, but the law was powerless to bring this about.
>
> So why did God give us the Mosaic law? It was enacted because of transgressions, to supervise us until Jesus came, like a guardian or trustee for us in our infancy, to lead us to faith in him. But now that Jesus has come, the law has fulfilled its purpose and no longer governs us. Those of us who have accepted Jesus through baptism are now spiritual heirs of Abraham because of God's earlier

promise, and we benefit from the promise as heirs benefit from an inheritance after they have reached the age of majority. We have moved from the status of "slave" or "minor"—a status in which we merely follow orders and have no free choice—into the status of "sons" and "heirs".

And yet it appears that some of you want to turn back to your former status, in which your decisions are made for you by rules (in this case, the Torah) and outward behavior is the measure of success. Don't you realize what the Torah says about the difference between slavery and freedom? It says, in a figurative way involving the stories of Abraham, Hagar, and Sarah, that the child bound by the law (Ishmael, born to Hagar) is a slave, while the child born pursuant to God's promise (Isaac, born to Sarah) is an heir and is free. Today, the children of the law, the slaves, are those Jews who say Christians must obey the Mosaic law in order to obtain salvation. The children who are free heirs of the promise are those Christians, Jew or Gentile, whose citizenship is in the heavenly kingdom; and that citizenship is established through faith—it does not come by race or gender or position of earthly power, and certainly not by observing the law.

In fact, Jesus' intent in his sacrifice was to set us free from the Mosaic law. Thus, if you submit to even one regulation of the law, you are making the sacrifice of Jesus worthless. Whoever thinks his salvation depends on obeying the law is apart from Jesus and has fallen away from grace. The legal regulations of Moses are void now—the only thing that counts is faith expressing itself through love. Who has deceived you on this issue? I wish whoever is requiring circumcision would go the whole way and emasculate themselves! You were called to be free of legal rules.

But that doesn't mean you should live according to your sinful nature—instead, live according to the Holy Spirit voluntarily. Make your holiness spring from within. It must be much more than a matter of outward behavioral conformity with a list of rules. The only "rule" to follow is to love your neighbor as yourself. But if you still wonder what behaviors will characterize the Spirit-led life versus the life led by sinful nature, let me tell you what behaviors each spirit results in, respectively. [Paul then lists the "fruits" of the sinful nature and the "fruits" of the Spirit.]

What do these chapters tell us about how God views freedom and law? A few observations seem especially pertinent for our purposes.

First: Law is fulfilled by outward behavior, but faith is a matter of the heart (Gal. 3:12). Paul is drawing a clear distinction between the purview of law and the purview of righteousness. Law concerns itself with outward behavior, while righteousness comes from within.

Second: Observance of law cannot make one righteous (Gal. 3:21).[7] This is a rational deduction from the earlier point that righteousness comes from the heart, not outward acts. Since law can only regulate outward acts and not the heart, law cannot control that which influences righteousness.

Third: Jesus saved us with the intent of freeing us from legalistic requirements, of the Torah or of any other source (Gal. 3:10–13; 3:23–25; 3:29–4:11; 5:1–2). This makes sense, for mere obedience to behavioral rules, as we have seen, cannot make one righteous, and Jesus' aim was no less than to provide sinful men the opportunity to be righteous.

So again, we see the idea of law presented in opposition to freedom. Righteousness, salvation, relationship with God—these do not come from the observance of legal rules, but rather from faith in Jesus, the Promised One. Knowing this, Jesus intended, by his sacrifice, to free us from rules designed or touted as "righteousness-enhancing."[8] Of course, this does not mean that Jesus intended to free us from all laws; some laws, after all, are *not* generally designed or touted as "righteousness-enhancing." But it does suggest that any laws which *are* primarily intended or advocated to enhance righteousness are fatally flawed in God's sight. In fact, Jesus intended to rescue us from such laws. They cannot possibly accomplish their objective.

The godly ideal of "Christian freedom" seems to be summed up in Gal. 5:13: "For you were called to freedom, brothers and sisters; only do not use your freedom as an opportunity for self-indulgence, but through love become slaves to one another." This is such a simple concept, and yet Christians through the ages have had such difficulty internalizing it! Paul is not calling for moral relativism here; on the contrary, he is calling for a moral purity derived from moral absolutes—but a moral purity that is internal and entirely divorced from law, a moral purity springing instead from *freedom*. No one is made righteous by observing behavioral rules, and thus no Christian should feel bound by any in order to please God. And certainly no Christian should try to bind such rules on anyone else to bring those others closer to God.[9] On the other hand, Paul is no moral relativist. This freedom for which Jesus died is not a license to gratify the sinful nature, to commit sinful acts, or to do whatever is right in your own eyes. Far from it. It is instead a call to inner purity. It is a call to abandon a life of rule-following for a free, voluntarily chosen life led by the Holy Spirit.[10] True righteousness, then, must be free and freely chosen. Paul is making a strong claim that freedom of choice is essential to righteousness, but that law now has no place in producing righteousness.[11]

This teaching, this stress on the ineffectiveness of rules and laws, is no passing concern for Paul. It is, in fact, one of the central themes of his writings. Over and over, he tells Christians in various locations that rules are useless in producing righteousness. Consider his strong words to the Colossians:

> See to it that no one takes you captive through philosophy and empty deceit, according to human tradition, according to the elemental spirits of the universe,

> and not according to Christ. For in him the whole fulness of deity dwells bodily, and you have come to fulness in him, who is the head of every ruler and authority. In him also you were circumcised with a spiritual circumcision, by putting off the body of the flesh in the circumcision of Christ; when you were buried with him in baptism, you were also raised with him through faith in the power of God, who raised him from the dead. And when you were dead in trespasses and the uncircumcision of your flesh, God made you alive together with him, when he forgave us all our trespasses, erasing the record that stood against us with its legal demands. He set this aside, nailing it to the cross. He disarmed the rulers and authorities and made a public example of them, triumphing over them in it.
>
> Therefore do not let anyone condemn you in matters of food or drink or of observing festivals, new moons, or sabbaths. These are only a shadow of what is to come, but the substance belongs to Christ. Do not let anyone disqualify you, insisting on self-abasement and worship of angels, dwelling on visions, puffed up without cause by a human way of thinking, and not holding fast to the head, from whom the whole body, nourished and held together by its ligaments and sinews, grows with a growth that is from God.
>
> If with Christ you died to the elemental spirits of the universe, why do you live as if you still belonged to the world? Why do you submit to regulations, "Do not handle, Do not taste, Do not touch"? All these regulations refer to things that perish with use; they are simply human commands and teachings. They have indeed an appearance of wisdom in promoting self-imposed piety, humility, and severe treatment of the body, but they are of no value in checking self-indulgence. (Col. 2:8–23)

What is Paul's point about regulations? In other passages, he lists specifically a number of sinful acts to be avoided by Christians. In fact, he makes two such lists in this same letter, just a few verses later, in Col. 3:5–10. If he is being consistent, he cannot mean that there is no such thing as a forbidden, sinful outward act. But his focus here is on the difference between the earthly and the heavenly. That focus continues into chapter 3, where Paul lists the things "in you" which are "earthly" and must on that account be "put to death" (Col. 3:5). Paul's point in chapter 2 seems to be that "regulations" are in themselves "earthly." An interlinear word-for-word translation of Col. 2:20 is instructive: "If you died with Christ from the elements of the world, why as living in world are you being decreed to?"[12] Paul seems to say that "being decreed to" in order to attain holiness is a worldly idea, not a Christian one. The world believes righteousness can be attained by submitting to human regulations like "don't taste" or "don't touch," but Christians know better. True righteousness comes from the heart and through being connected to Jesus, the head. Refusing to taste some particular food, or refusing to fornicate for that matter, can no more make one righteous before God than refusing to enlist in the army makes one a pacifist, or refusing to curse Grandma makes one a member of Grandma's family. Regulations of outward conduct are powerless to produce what is most necessary for pacifism or kinship—or righteousness. As Paul said, righteousness means checking self-indulgence, and regulations "are of no value in checking self-indulgence" (Col. 2:23).

He says much the same thing in Romans 14 and also in 1 Corinthians 8. In both of these passages Paul is addressing the question whether it is permissible for Christians to eat certain kinds of foods. The Pharisees and other strict Jews tried to abstain, as a matter of conscience, from a long list of foods they considered "unclean"; while some Gentile Christians apparently had conscientious scruples about eating meat that had been made available for public consumption after having previously been offered to a god or goddess in a pagan temple ritual. The apostles and elders of the Jerusalem church, at some point after Paul's first missionary journey, advised the Gentile Christians to abstain from meat that had been offered to idols, although they did not bind the Jewish food regulations on the Gentiles (Acts 15:20, 28–9). Paul himself, however, compares regulations about foods (whether pork or idol meat) to regulations about holy days, the kinds of rules that are worldly and perishable (Rom. 14:2, 5; see also Col. 2:16). The truth is that "'Food will not bring us close to God.' We are no worse off if we do not eat, and no better off if we do" (1 Cor. 8:8). Christians who understand this are free, then, to eat "unclean" foods or to eat meat sacrificed to idols—but not if that liberty becomes "a stumbling block to the weak," that is, to those Christians who do not understand the freedom Christians have with regard to food. Better to avoid meat altogether, says Paul to the Corinthians, than to cause someone else to fall away, perhaps by influencing her to eat meat in violation of her own conscience (1 Cor. 8:13). Nevertheless, the truth remains, for those who are enlightened, that "nothing is unclean in itself . . . [for] the kingdom of God is not food and drink but righteousness and peace and joy in the Holy Spirit" (Rom. 14:17). The elements of God's kingdom—righteousness, peace, and joy—are matters of the heart. And rules about what to eat, like all other rules regulating outward acts, cannot produce them.

The teaching that rules can produce righteousness was not just an incorrect opinion; to Paul, it was an ungodly heresy that threatened to devalue the sacrifice of Jesus and reorient Christianity toward the flesh and away from the spirit. It looked too much like a return to the "legal demands" of the Old Covenant, which Christ had nailed to the cross (Col. 2:14). Here is how Paul describes the heresy to Timothy:

> Now the Spirit expressly says that in later times some will renounce the faith by paying attention to deceitful spirits and teachings of demons, through the

> hypocrisy of liars whose consciences are seared with a hot iron. They forbid marriage and demand abstinence from foods, which God created to be received with thanksgiving by those who believe and know the truth. For everything created by God is good, and nothing is to be rejected, provided it is received with thanksgiving; for it is sanctified by God's word and by prayer. (1 Tim. 4:1–5)

Paul obviously takes this false teaching very seriously. He strongly implies that it originates with "deceitful spirits" and "demons" and that its teachers are hypocritical liars with no conscience. What is there in this teaching that is so terrible, so ungodly? Are the teachers telling Christians to do some unspeakable outward act? No. Are they denying the existence of God? Hardly. They are teaching Christians to feel bound by conduct regulations that God has not established. There is nothing sinful, of course, about doing the things they were requiring—remaining unmarried or abstaining from certain foods. The sin is in believing and teaching others that we *must* do these things in order to please God. The doctrine is sinful because it is hypocritical (1 Tim. 4:2); because it robs God of his proper praise for the wonderful and pleasurable things he has created for people to enjoy (1 Tim. 4:4–5); and also because it robs Christians of their freedom in Christ, deceiving them into believing that God's kingdom is a matter of outward acts rather than the inner spirit (1 Tim. 4:1; Gal. 5:1; Rom. 14:17; Eph. 2:8–9; Col. 2:20–23).

The truth to which we keep returning, to which Scripture leads us again and again, is that God places some value on human freedom. Certainly freedom can be used in an ungodly way, to commit sin; but just as certainly freedom can be used by a Christian for righteousness, and Paul repeatedly insists on Christian freedom as a God-ordained good in itself. In fact, Paul says freedom, and not law, is the *source of true righteousness*, and the *divine motivation behind our salvation*. That is monumental. Whatever else God may value, it is a twisting of the New Testament text to pretend that human freedom is valueless to him—that he mainly wants us to follow the right rules of behavior, and cares little what range of options we have available. That understanding of God is not to be found in the New Testament. Judging by the 1 Timothy text, for example, God apparently wants Christians to choose for themselves whether to marry and what kinds of food to eat. It is not just that he doesn't care what we choose in these areas. *He wants us to be able to choose*. Why? Is marriage or food so important in itself? Or can it be that God simply enjoys giving us the pleasure of choosing for ourselves, of enjoying the variety of his creation for its own sake and praising him for it? God has of course fixed limits to permissible choices; but to see him purely as choice-limiter is never to have encountered the Creator of infinite pleasurable variety, the divine choice-expander who inserted humans into a creation infinitely more diverse, enjoyable, and interesting than the formless void which preceded his miraculous handiwork. In fact, 1 Timothy 4 suggests that praising God fully may demand the exercise of freedom of choice in experiencing a variety of his pleasurable creations.

The fact is, God does not save us so that we can follow his rules, or anyone else's. He saves us so that we can experience freedom. "It was for freedom that Christ set us free" (Gal. 5:1, New American Standard Bible).

PRIORITIZING CHOICE ON PRINCIPLE

The Choice (or autonomy) that Paul emphasizes seems central to the Christian gospel. Unfortunately, the importance of Choice seems to elude many well-meaning moral absolutists—politically conservative Christians in particular—who often seem to equate Choice with Evil.[13] From this group one often hears comments like these: "A few people in this country still care about righteousness, but these days more and more people are insisting on their right to choose." "For too long, our culture has prized personal autonomy instead of God." "I'm not pro-choice; I'm pro-God." The implicit assumption in statements like these, of course, is that conceptually, righteousness and autonomy are opposites. Choice necessarily excludes God. When we insist on the right to choose, we are acting pridefully, sinfully exalting our own will above God's.

This viewpoint is forcefully expressed in F. LaGard Smith's book *When Choice Becomes God*. Although most of the book is an argument against abortion and its legalization, the underlying theme, as the title suggests, is much larger: the antagonism between Choice and God. Smith cites various examples to prove an American cultural revolution which he claims has caused the mainstream increasingly to value tolerance over moral imperatives, individualism over community, diversity over unity, moral relativism over absolute truth, and secular humanism over religious faith. In his view, these changes can be summarized as a cultural adoption of consumerism, or Choice, as the ultimate good. In adopting this attitude, our culture has blasphemously placed "the individual" upon God's throne and has attempted to give each human being the authority of God. "Consumerism is America's new religion," Smith writes. "From *Choice*, the god of consumerism, comes the First Commandment of Choice written in stone: 'Thou shalt have no other gods.' And the Second is like unto it: 'Thou shalt have the right to choose.'"[14] For Smith, the key question is: "Which God shall we choose? . . . Is God to be our God, or is Choice to be our God?"[15]

But Smith's "choice" of rhetoric is unfortunate, for this supposed dichotomy between Choice and God is a false dichotomy. It is confusing

Choice with bad choices. There is absolutely no conflict, ever, between righteousness and the right to choose. In fact, the right to choose is what makes righteousness possible. Choice and God's will are not opposites, nor does it make sense to speak of the elevation of freedom of choice over God's will. To put it simply, God's will *is* freedom of choice. It always has been. As we just noted, it is why God saved us. It is why he established a New Covenant and abolished the conduct regulations of the Old. Worrying that some people "make Choice their God" is akin to worrying that some people make "the atonement of Christ" their God. The statements are nonsensical. Of course, it makes sense to say that some people make "selfish desires" their God,[16] or that some people place their own preferences above God's, or that some people believe that the only moral code that rightfully governs them is the one they choose for themselves; but it does *not* make sense to say that a certain person values his *freedom to choose* above God's will, any more than saying that a certain person values his eternal soul above God's will. Both Choice and the soul are part of God's deep desire for every human being, and it is God's will that we retain them both, in full measure.

Importantly, Choice is necessary to accomplish God's will. Choice is not just like any other talent or opportunity we possess, like wealth or singing ability. Choice is different, and of a higher order, than our other talents and opportunities, because Choice is a necessary precondition for righteousness, for every person. No act is good, no thought is good, unless freely chosen. The capacity for Choice makes us God-like (and, incidentally, Satan-like). And God made it that way.

Lest I be misunderstood, I hasten to add that I share Professor Smith's concerns about the current fad of non-judgmentalism writ large. We have noted in Chapter 1 that American culture has tended increasingly toward moral toleration of impurity. Smith is right to chide Christians for acquiescing. Christians are called to avoid placing themselves in God's role of perfect judge, but this does not imply that we are to ignore the sin around us—otherwise how could we evangelize? If others are not living according to God's will (as I understand it), there is no indication from Scripture that I must "tolerate" that, if "tolerate" means keeping quiet about it. In fact, Scripture seems to indicate the opposite: After I have honestly checked myself for hypocrisy, love demands that I involve myself in those people's lives to try to convince them to make different choices. The prophets and the apostles (to say nothing of Jesus himself) certainly were not shy about decrying evil in God's name. Christians must never cave in to creeping moral tolerance.

Nevertheless, there is an important difference between *moral* tolerance and *legal* tolerance, a difference we may forget if we continue to speak of them as if they are the same thing. The extent of a Christian's own *moral* tolerance should be derived from an understanding of God's will for how human beings ought to live their lives—what particular choices they should make or not make each day. But a Christian's decision about the proper extent of a society's *legal* tolerance need not essentially depend on his understanding of God's will for how other human beings ought to live their lives; instead, it represents a more complex judgment, based on (among other things) his evaluation of the power of human law to influence a particular human behavior, and his understanding of God's intentions for government. One way to capture this distinction might be to say that for the Christian, the proper extent of *moral* tolerance must depend on God's will for *individual* action, while the proper extent of *legal* tolerance must depend on God's will for *collective* action through civil government.

Putting the issue this way makes it clear that Christians who stand strongly against creeping *moral* tolerance are not necessarily engaged in hypocrisy or cognitive dissonance when they simultaneously support a large degree of *legal* tolerance. They are not simply following God's will in most aspects of life and then ignoring his concerns in the political arena. Rather, a conscientious Christian could rationally conclude that God has somewhat different desires for collective governmental action than he has for individual action. It is not unthinkable, in light of Scripture, that God prefers collective legal tolerance rather than collective legal enforcement of his will—or, in practice, that God prefers collective legal tolerance to collective legal enforcement of *some person's understanding* of his will. If vocal Christians continue to blur this distinction by demonizing Choice as a characteristic of our sinfully selfish culture, speaking as if human autonomy is ungodly and all sorts of toleration are the same, Christians may come to forget (or even disbelieve) that matters may be somewhat more complex from God's point of view.

We would do well to remember that God's way, at least since the advent of the New Covenant, has never been to limit Choice in order to assure our obedience to some litany of divine desires for us. In fact, such a scheme is inherently illogical, since God's desire for us is that we *choose* the good. Obedience requires Choice that is significantly unfettered. We also know that God desires that everyone choose the good.[17] Why, then, would we assume that God wants us to deprive others of the freedom of choice necessary for them to choose what is good?[18]

The insight Smith and certain other moral absolutists overlook is that a legal regime which protects and expands Choice is not automatically ungodly, but may actually be understood as fulfilling the will of God. Of course, if humans choose wrongly, God is displeased; but perhaps the solution is not to legally limit or forbid Choice itself, but rather to follow the biblical model of trying to persuade people, non-coercively, to make good choices. Freedom of choice is not contrary to God's will. Conscientious Christians may rationally and honestly oppose laws that restrict overall Choice.

But if that is true, what law could a conscientious Christian support? Doesn't *every* law restrict Choice? Not at all. Every law restricts some *particular* choice, but as we noted at the beginning of this chapter, some such restrictions are necessary in order to preserve or expand total Choice—that is, the sum total of autonomy. Murder laws are an obvious example of the kind of legal restriction of Choice that is necessary to protect Choice in general. If murder were not forbidden by law, murderers could, without fear, take away our most significant and fundamental opportunities to choose, with the result that overall Choice would be severely limited, even though some of the choices available to murderers would be marginally expanded.[19] Murder laws may limit some of the choices available to a few individuals, but they expand Choice. Certainly there is room for many such laws, even in a Choice-protecting environment.

Some may respond that laws do not and cannot deprive humans of "Choice" as I have defined that term here, since every mentally healthy adult can choose to do right, or wrong, no matter what the law says. Of course there is a sense in which this is true. But will anyone seriously argue that the freedom to choose is unaffected by law? Laws and other exercises of force, public or private, clearly influence one's range of realistically possible choices. Surely the robber who holds a gun to his victim's head and offers the option "Your money or your life" has not allowed his victim true freedom of choice, despite the physical possibility of refusing the robber's demand for money. The law limits freedom of choice in much the same way. For example, when the law forbids Christian religious practices upon pain of imprisonment, it may not be saying "Your money or your life," but it *is*, in a very real sense, saying, "Your religion or your physical freedom." Of course, the Christian in this situation could (and should) risk imprisonment to do God's will; but claiming that he has true "freedom of choice" is simply making that concept a nullity. If this person is said to have freedom of choice, who does not? On that theory, no mentally competent adult could ever be denied freedom, by definition, until death. But in fact, people have been denied "freedom of choice" (as we commonly use that term) since time began, and it insults their memories and degrades their suffering to claim that they really had "freedom of choice" all along.

Paul himself speaks of freedom in the common way, contrasting it with life under the law of Moses. Recall that Paul in the Galatian letter describes the law as having "imprisoned" people before the coming of Christ (Gal. 3:23), but now "Christ has set us free. Stand firm, therefore, and do not submit again to a yoke of slavery" (Gal. 5:1). Again, in an extended analogy in

Galatians 3–4, he calls anyone who is bound to the law a "child of the slave" (Gal. 4:23, 31) and contrasts him with the "child of the free woman" (Gal. 4:23, 30), a person who is saved by faith apart from law. Quite directly, Paul claims that the law of Moses enslaves people and is to be distinguished from the voluntary faith that sets us free. Although one could formulate a technical argument that slaves have just as much "freedom of choice" as anyone else (inasmuch as they may choose to refuse their masters and suffer the consequences), the truth is that slaves do not have true freedom of choice. Slaves have no Choice. And as Paul understands, neither do those who are bound by the Torah's list of behavioral rules. Those who are bound by law to observe "special days, and months, and seasons, and years" (Gal. 4:10) as commanded by Moses, for example, are "no better than slaves" (Gal. 4:1). Surely such people can still "choose" to disobey the law and suffer what they conceive to be the spiritual consequences; but Paul understands this to be no choice at all. Laws do indeed deprive humans of freedom of choice in a sense that is morally important.

Consider another illustration. If a law harshly penalized people for worshiping Jesus, many people who now call themselves Christians would perhaps change religions or abandon religion altogether. Certainly that would be the influence of such a law at the margins of belief. But despite the law, God wants people to choose to worship Jesus. The effect of this law would undoubtedly be that fewer people would do that. By making such a law, then, we have discouraged a set of beliefs and acts that are pleasing to God. Of course, people are still capable of "choosing" to violate the law and worship anyway (and in fact the Bible teaches that they ought to do so), but the law has made that good choice less possible, practically speaking, and also less likely. To that extent the law has reduced freedom of choice. Probably most Christians would agree that this type of law would be displeasing to God, and thus a Christian should not support it. I think we might also widely agree that the reason it would be displeasing to God is that this law, by limiting freedom of choice, discourages righteousness among those it governs.

Now consider a law that penalizes anyone who does *not* worship Jesus. If I "worship" Jesus as the law dictates, but only because of the law (as most unbelievers probably would), I am not worshiping in spirit and truth, as God wishes.[20] By making such a law, we have again discouraged a set of beliefs and acts that are pleasing to God. Of course, the worshiper is still capable of "choosing" to worship for the right reasons even if we enact the law, but again, the law has probably made that good choice less likely. Those who worshiped according to God's will before the law was enacted may be likely to continue doing so, but unbelievers who only worship because of the law are further from God's will than ever[21] and are unlikely to be as receptive to evangelism (which must necessarily be at the hands of the legally "privileged") as they might have been without the law.[22] Moreover, God's will is for people to *voluntarily* worship Jesus; in what sense can *anyone* (even "true believers") do that, when the government punishes every other choice? Thus, this type of law arguably would, like the first law, be displeasing to God, and a Christian should not support it either. The reason this law would be displeasing to God is the same reason the first law displeased him: This law, by limiting freedom of choice, discourages righteousness among those it governs.

But all this is not to say that Christians should stop trying to shape government policy in light of God's will. In fact, for the Christian, what higher standard could there be for assessing government policy? We should recognize, however, that God's purpose for government may be a very narrow one—one which does not include coercing virtue in order to produce righteous citizens. Government can influence our environment in many ways, and we must be open to the possibility that the environment most conducive to righteousness is not necessarily the most coercive one. What would a righteousness-encouraging environment look like? It would contain a maximum amount of the raw materials necessary for human beings to be righteous. But Choice is one of the necessary raw materials. One cannot be righteous without freedom of choice. We may surmise, for example, that Paul would have disapproved if Caesar had enacted laws requiring all his subjects to observe Jewish regulations about unclean foods and holy days; Paul would have viewed such laws as interfering with righteousness. True, an environment that protects and expands Choice may result in either good or evil choices. But if we use the law to limit or eliminate overall Choice in particular areas, we correspondingly limit or eliminate our prospects for good choices. This is why, as a matter of principle, Christians can rationally believe they should favor government policy that maximizes Choice rather than laws that limit overall Choice in the name of reducing sin, benefitting a certain disadvantaged group, or praising God.

PRIORITIZING CHOICE FOR PRAGMATIC REASONS

Apart from arguments of principle, there are also practical reasons Christians ought to reject legal moralism. These reasons become clearest when we consider the two main types of political arguments raised by legal moralists: the "policy argument" and the "character argument."

First, in what I am calling the "policy argument," advocates claim that we should support policies (or candidates who support policies) that discourage "immorality" and encourage "morality." Second, in what I am calling the "character argument," the claim is that moral voters should support candidates who are themselves "moral."[23] This position particularly has gained ground among evangelicals in the wake of the Clinton/Lewinsky scandal. But reflecting on these two arguments should cause us to realize that they both present several serious practical problems.[24]

Let us begin with the character argument. One practical problem of this argument in particular is that it is impossible to assure "good" (or "orthodox") character during the entirety of any officeholder's tenure. Indeed, as power is increased, character usually declines.[25] The problems this poses in dictatorships and other autocratic systems are obvious. But the same phenomenon occurs in democracies; once a person of bad character has assumed power, the people will not often be able to rid themselves of him until the next election, at best—and this assumes that they recognize the problem, gather enough votes to correct it at election time, and make a wise evaluation of the characters of the potential successors to the office. Additionally, virtue is of course no guarantee of experience or expertise. Even if they choose a person of good character, he may support unwise policies. In fact, persons of good character may easily turn out to be less effective than their immoral opponents in fostering our public policy preferences, be those liberal or conservative, religious or secular.

So there are significant practical difficulties inherent in choosing government officials based primarily on their reputation for (or self-promoting claims of) godliness. This is not to suggest, of course, that we should be completely apathetic about the character or virtue of our elected officials; a reputation for honesty, for example, seems desirable in any political candidate, even from a purely secular point of view. It is merely to suggest that political conservatives, and Christians generally, may be unlikely in practice to reach their goals for government by trying to elect people who are the godliest—or worse, who best fit some preconceived mold of religious orthodoxy. In other words, there are several good reasons for evangelicals not to make a candidate's evangelical credentials or professions of faith a primary consideration as we vote.

Another practical problem, inherent in both the "policy" and "character" arguments, is that even mature, devout Christians don't always know sin when they see it. After all, each of us sins sometimes out of ignorance, or even out of a wilful failure to recognize sin for what it is. We ought to think twice before assuming that we know all of God's will perfectly and apply it inerrantly.[26] I am not arguing here that there is no absolute standard of right and wrong, or that if there is, we cannot know the standard at all. Rather, I am arguing that, in our limited human wisdom, we cannot know the standard as

God does, perfectly and completely—a claim which must surely be unobjectionable to most Christians. If we recognize that we could be wrong about some things we think we are right about, that becomes an extra reason for refusing to make "orthodox morality" an issue in voting or policy preferences. Each Christian must admit, in all humility, that he may misunderstand God's true opinion regarding many different issues which might otherwise form topics for legislation. This practical consideration alone urges the Christian to be extremely cautious in any attempt to outlaw sin or vote against sinful candidates.

Moreover, even if we could always be sure we were right about what is sin and what is not, we cannot realistically hope to reach a critical mass of societal consensus on such issues. While societal consensus is completely irrelevant to God's law (God is God, after all), some level of consensus is usually essential for *man's* law to function effectively. The secular law that is widely disapproved and widely ignored by the masses is completely useless—or worse. And yet realistically, we can never hope to build consensus throughout American society on biblical values. In fact, the Bible promises that such an effort would be doomed from the beginning.[27] And even if we could build such a consensus, enacting laws on this basis is a recipe for evils like another Inquisition, or religious wars and persecutions of the kind experienced in Europe in the 16th and 17th centuries. This is true despite the best intentions of the founders of such a movement, who may well have been righteous people with good motives. History teaches that movements to legislate morality often get co-opted by those with selfish or ignorant motives, with results that the founders hardly anticipated or approved.

Since we cannot hope to control a government (or a critical mass of society) comprised of "orthodox" Christians (meaning Christians who share our own moral precepts on every subject law might touch), we must ask the pragmatic question of how we can most effectively live and work with others who have very different values from ours. Perhaps the answer lies in allowing the law to tolerate much that we dislike in order to create an environment of freedom and diverse options, while we vigorously advocate a change of heart among individual unbelievers. An environment of Choice allows true religion to thrive. And the sanctity of Choice is a unifying idea, a principle around which both moral absolutists and tolerationists can conscientiously build a consensus.

Even if we could be sure we know good from bad perfectly, and even if we could build a substantial consensus of opinion around our orthodoxy, we face another practical problem in pursuing the policy argument: sin legislation is impossible to enforce consistently. Of course, if "sin" is merely defined as a certain outward action, as we have a tendency to do, then banning that act is as easy as banning any other—although even here, many "sins" that do not harm others are done privately (sexual immorality, for example) under circumstances where no one who knows of them will report them, and such sins will therefore be quite difficult to police. But if "sin" is defined from a more biblical perspective, in such a way that in many cases we cannot be sure it is occurring without knowing a person's "heart" or motives, then it becomes very difficult to say with certainty when someone else has sinned, or to define sin in the law before it is committed. In fact, many sins may be committed in the absence of any outward act at all. "Pride" is a perfect example of a sin of this type. Such sins are obviously impossible to outlaw, because they cannot be accurately defined in the law or detected in life.

This leads us to another huge practical and philosophical weakness in the policy argument: the unwillingness of that view's proponents to advocate it consistently. Deep down, *no one* really wants to outlaw *all* sin. Intuition tells us not to go to that extreme. Even the most conservative Christians do not propose to outlaw gluttony, gossip, or lying, across the board, despite the fact that these sins, unlike pride, involve outward actions and are often detectable.

What is it that makes us unwilling to outlaw *these* sins? Or perhaps more to the point, what is it about *other* sins that makes us think they *should* be outlawed? Is there some principled basis upon which we could think we ought to outlaw some sins but not others? If we wish to outlaw murder but not gluttony, surely it is not because one is sinful and the other is not, or because one can be detected and the other cannot. In other words, our reason for wanting to outlaw murder must be something besides the fact that murder is a detectable sin. Perhaps the unifying principle here, the principle that leads to results that best comport with our intuitions as well as the text of the New Testament, is that we want to outlaw murder because murder is a victimizing activity that deprives others of Choice. The New Testament suggests that laws should protect individual freedom of choice and forbid only those acts that deprive others of it. That is a consistent and understandable principle to limit government. And again, this principle is easier to enforce and easier to build consensus around, thus solving two of the huge practical problems of the legal moralists' position at once.

The Choice regime would be easier to enforce because the things we would outlaw under this regime are not thoughts or feelings, but victimizing actions that are outward and verifiable. For example, assault and forgery,[28] as outward verifiable actions, are easier to accurately detect than sins like pride or sloth. And the Choice regime would be easier to build consensus around because the secular moral tolerationists constantly advocate freedom of choice and are already infatuated by the concept. As we noted in Chapter 1, they see themselves as the protectors of Choice against the intolerant moral absolutists. If moral absolutists like us likewise adopt a legal regime of Choice, as

I am suggesting, there is a great opportunity for consensus, cooperation, and cultural healing, not to mention evangelism. And all this could be achieved consistent with the moral absolutist stance that truth and righteousness are absolute, invariable, and significantly knowable. The Choice regime is not moral relativism in disguise, but an uncompromising moral absolutism that, in the tradition of Roger Williams, defines freedom of choice as a moral absolute.

Both of the legal moralists' arguments—the policy argument and the character argument—are, in the end, premised upon the same basic assumption: that public policy ought to be determined according to God's will. It is easy to agree with that assumption. But moral absolutists need not agree that governments ought to punish sin and reward righteousness. Both principle and pragmatism suggest reasons for thinking that Christian "lawmakers" should prioritize *freedom of choice* as they decide how to legislate or how to vote. Choice, and not coercion, seems to be God's will for mankind, and so it is difficult to understand where Christians would derive the authority for the impractical, un-God-like task of coercing righteousness through the secular law.

THE CHOICE PRINCIPLE

In the first part of Chapter 5, we determined that human governments and their legal restrictions have a proper place in God's plan. We have now suggested that this place has boundaries, beyond which government should not stray. Romans 12 and 13 indicate that the divine purpose of governments is to punish "wrongdoing," but not all sorts of wrongdoing. Instead, governments are to punish the kind of wrongdoing that directly victimizes others, the kind of wrongdoing for which victims might be tempted to take revenge on the wrongdoer. The kind of activity to be banned, in other words, is Choice-limiting activity. In this chapter we have seen the high value God places on the freedom of human beings to make their own choices, from within as wide a range of options as possible. Human governments seem to be part of his plan to provide an environment which maximizes freedom of choice and minimizes unjust limitations of Choice, thereby providing his creatures maximal opportunities for righteousness, as well as some level of peace and security.

What kinds of legal restrictions, then, would be justifiable in God's sight? If possible, we should want to derive a principle for lawmaking, a rule of thumb, that will embody God's will, allowing a respected place for government but constraining it to its proper sphere. At a minimum, the principle would say that criminal laws should punish and prevent victimizing activities, but should not punish people for acts that do not directly harm others in some way (at least in the absence of some explicit biblical authority for such a law).[29] So the goal of criminal law should be to deter and punish particular acts of wrongdoing so as to expand total Choice in the society, but with the side constraint that even in the name of expanding total Choice, no criminal law should punish or restrict those who are not (within the meaning of Romans 12–13) "wrongdoers"—that is to say, no law should criminalize those who have not directly limited the Choice of others. Perhaps our principle could be expanded beyond the realm of criminal law to apply to most civil law as well; however, criminal law is the sphere in which government self-consciously undertakes to "punish wrongdoing," and so if our principle applies anywhere, it should apply to criminal law.

Thus we are led to a principle I will call the Choice Principle, which represents an attempt to capture the essence of God's will for governors. The Choice Principle may be stated as follows: In the absence of explicit New Testament instruction regarding the type of law being considered, a Christian should favor only those criminal laws which restrict acts directly victimizing others and which are necessary to increase overall human Choice. A corollary to the Choice Principle would be: Christians should *not* support any law just because it restricts a behavior God views as sinful, or promotes a behavior or result God views as righteous (as if a mere behavior or result could be "righteous" in itself, regardless of individual motives). We might even say that for a Christian, the only legitimate justification for a secular law is a secular justification.

This may sound like a paradox, but again, I want to stress that this is not some sneaky kind of hypocrisy. Committed Christians can affirm and act on these principles without leaving their Christianity behind. In fact, if the preceding arguments are correct, then these principles are not only consistent with committed Christianity, but may be affirmatively required by it. In any event, I wish to contend strongly that the Choice Principle reflects an understanding of God's will for Christians and government that is at least as reasonable, sincere, and biblical as any other understanding.

NOTES

1. Thomas Hobbes, *Leviathan*, ed. Michael Oakeshott (London: Crowell-Collier, 1962), chap. 18, par. 1.

2. John Locke, *Two Treatises of Government*, ed. Peter Laslett (1960; reprint with amendments, New York: Cambridge University Press, 1963), bk. 2, chap. 9, secs. 123, 124.

3. Locke, *Two Treatises*, bk. 2, chap. 6, sec. 57 (emphasis in original).

4. Hobbes contended that the contract was amongst the governed alone, that the sovereign was never a party to it and thus could not violate it, and that the governed had surrendered all of their alienable freedoms. Hobbes, *Leviathan*, chap. 17, 18. Locke, however, argued that the contract was between the governed on the one hand and the sovereign on the other, that the sovereign might sometimes violate the contract and be legitimately punished by the governed, and that the contract had bound the governed to surrender only their freedoms to punish crimes and to preserve themselves and others in ways consistent with the law of nature. Locke, *Two Treatises*, bk. 2, chap. 9, secs. 128–31; ibid, bk. 2, chap. 13, sec. 155.

5. See, e.g., Locke, *Two Treatises*, bk. 2, chap. 11, sec. 137; ibid., chap. 18, sec. 202; ibid., chap. 19, sec. 222.

6. Quotation taken from New American Standard Bible. I am aware that there are some significantly differing translations of verse 21. An interlinear word for word translation from the Greek renders the verse as follows: "Slave were you called, not to you let be care; but if also you are able free to become, more use." Paul R. McReynolds, ed. and trans., *Word Study Greek-English New Testament* (Wheaton, Ill.: Tyndale House Publishers, 1998). The meaning of the Greek word for "use" (χρῆσαι) at the end of the verse is apparently open to some debate, since sometimes in the New Testament it means "use," and sometimes "obtain" or "take measures" or "act." Is Paul telling the slaves, "If you are able to become free, take measures to do so"? Or is he telling them, "If you are able to become free, use your current slave status even more"? The New International Version and the Revised Standard Version, along with the New American Standard Bible, render this verse in such a way that Paul is instructing the slaves to "take measures," to gain their freedom if they have opportunity (although the RSV does mention in a footnote the possibility of a different interpretation). The King James Version arguably conveys this meaning as well: "Art thou called being a servant? Care not for it: but if thou mayest be made free, use it rather." The New Revised Standard Version, however, renders this verse as follows: "Were you a slave when called? Do not be concerned about it. Even if you can gain your freedom, make use of your present condition now more than ever." Obviously, this would be a much different message to the slaves. A footnote mentions that the verse can also bear the interpretation of an instruction to gain freedom if possible. I do not claim any expertise in ancient Greek, but in light of the textual context, it seems to me the best translation in this case is the more common one, instructing the slaves to gain their freedom as they have legal opportunity and to use that freedom for good. Just two verses later, in verse 23, Paul unquestionably says, "Do not become slaves of men." Yet Paul's overall purpose is to tell the Christians to remain in whatever state they were in when called. Remembering that context, and knowing from verse 23 that Paul would prefer that Christians not be "slaves of men," it seems natural for him to instruct the *slaves* that the command to remain in one's "original state" applies to them in a *special* way. The uncircumcised are not to become circumcised, and the circumcised are not to seek to remove the marks of circumcision. And "in view of the impending crisis" (verse 26), unmarried people are to stay unmarried, and married people are to stay married. But if this rule were applied exactly to *slaves*, it would result in the strange teaching that slaves were to remain slaves and not ever to

become free, even if given opportunity. Given Paul's distaste for slavery (verse 23) and the social attitude toward slavery as something to be avoided at all costs, that teaching would be strange indeed—although the teachings to obey one's master and not to run away are perfectly understandable and consistent with Paul's other teachings on submission to authority. To clear up any misunderstanding, then, Paul might well have said to the slaves: "Obey your masters, don't run away, and don't worry about being a slave, for you are no less valuable in Christ's kingdom than any free person; but of course, I am not telling you never to become free, like I told the married people never to divorce or the uncircumcised people never to be circumcised." Thus, it would seem to me that the most natural rendering of: "But if also you are able free to become, more use," would be: "But if you are also able to become free, use *that* opportunity all the more."

7. There are a number of passages in the book of Romans that reinforce this point. See Rom. 8:3 ("For what the law was powerless to do ... God did by sending his own Son in the likeness of sinful man to be a sin offering") (New International Version); Rom. 3:20 ("No one will be declared righteous in his sight by observing the law") (New International Version); Rom. 3:28 ("We hold that a person is justified by faith apart from works prescribed by the law"). Although the "law" referred to in these passages is obviously the Torah, the point would seem to apply to *any* set of legal rules and regulations—observance of these cannot make anyone righteous. In this regard, see also Col. 2:16–17, 20–23, where Paul expands the point to say that observance of *any earthly regulations*, whether Jewish, pagan, or gnostic, cannot make one righteous.

8. These would certainly include, as chapters 4 and 5 of Galatians indicate, circumcision (Gal. 5:2–6) and the observance of "special days, and months, and seasons, and years" (Gal. 4:10).

9. See Gal. 5:12 ("I wish those who unsettle you [i.e., those who try to force all Christians to be circumcised according to the Torah] would castrate themselves!").

10. Along the same lines as this passage from Galatians 5, see 1 Pet. 2:16 (While submitting to established secular authority, Christians are to "live as free people, yet do not use your freedom as a pretext for evil").

11. I am aware that some strains of Christian thought view the role of human free will as, at most, a minimal component of righteousness. In fact, some Christians would no doubt claim, along with secular behaviorists like B.F. Skinner, that human freedom of choice, as we normally think of it, does not exist—that humans have no more capacity for choice than do trees or rocks. But I respectfully submit that both these views are fraught with great philosophical and biblical difficulties, not the least of which is this section of Paul's letter to the Galatians. A fuller critique of behaviorism or determinism is beyond the scope of this book, but many respectable sources offer such critiques. For the casual reader, a good introduction and criticism of behaviorism is found in Steve Wilkins, *Beyond Bumper Sticker Ethics: An Introduction to Theories of Right and Wrong* (Downers Grove, Ill.: InterVarsity Press, 1995), 63–81. A more in-depth argument against behaviorism (and other forms of determinism), written from a Christian viewpoint, is Austin Farrer, *The Freedom of the Will* (New York: Charles Scribner's Sons, 1958). Probably the most famous opponent of

Calvinistic determinism was James Arminius, who raised a number of classic arguments against it. See generally James Arminius, *The Works of James Arminius*, 3 vols., ed. James Nichols (vols. 1 and 2) and W.R. Bagnall (vol. 3) (Auburn, N.Y.: Derby, Miller & Orton, 1853). More recent critiques of determinism include M.R. Ayers, *The Refutation of Determinism* (London: Methuen & Co., 1968); Alvin Plantinga, *God, Freedom, and Evil* (New York: Harper & Row, 1974); Robert Shank, *Elect in the Son* (Springfield, Mo.: Westcott, 1970; reprint, Minneapolis: Bethany House, 1989); and Norman L. Geisler, *Chosen But Free* (Minneapolis: Bethany House, 1999).

12. Col. 2:20, in McReynolds, *Greek-English New Testament*.

13. Undoubtedly, the national debate over abortion rights, which has been cast as a "pro-life vs. pro-choice" debate, has contributed to this attitude, at least within the pro-life camp.

14. F. LaGard Smith, *When Choice Becomes God* (Eugene, Oreg.: Harvest House Publishers, 1990), 22 (emphasis in original).

15. Smith, *When Choice*, 20.

16. See Phil. 3:19 ("their God is the belly"); Rom. 16:18 ("such people do not serve our Lord Christ, but their own appetites").

17. See, for example, 2 Pet. 3:9; Acts 17:30.

18. See also, for example, Col. 2:20–23 (regulations are of "no value in checking self-indulgence"); Luke 22:24–27 (do not use power selfishly, as "benefactors"); Luke 9:51–56 (do not bid fire to come down from heaven to consume unbelievers); 2 Cor. 9:6–15 (moral value of giving is in the free choice).

19. For a fuller explication of this point, see Chapter 9.

20. See John 4:23–24.

21. See, for example, Matt. 25:25–28; 1 Cor. 13:1–3; Gal. 3:1–5, 10–11; Matt. 7:21; Isa. 29:13; 1 John 4:20.

22. See Thomas Aquinas, *Summa Theologiae*, II-II, q. 10, a. 11, in Paul E. Sigmund, trans. and ed., *St. Thomas Aquinas on Politics and Ethics* (New York: W.W. Norton & Co., 1988), 63 (arguing that the rites of unbelievers should be legally tolerated if necessary to avoid "some interference with the salvation of those who if they are tolerated will gradually be converted to the faith").

23. See, for example, William Bennett, *The Death of Outrage* (New York: Free Press, 1998); Mike Huckabee, *Character is the Issue* (Nashville, Tenn.: Broadman & Holman, 1997).

24. My insights here are not new. See generally John Locke, *A Letter Concerning Toleration*, ed. J.W. Gough (Oxford: Oxford University Press, 1976).

25. See John Emerich Edward Dalberg-Acton, First Baron Acton, "Letter from Lord Acton to Mandell Creighton dated April 5, 1887," in *Essays on Freedom and Power*, ed. Gertrude Himmelfarb (Glencoe, Ill.: The Free Press, 1949), 364. Here the illustrious historian Lord Acton writes: "I cannot accept your canon that we are to judge Pope and King unlike other men, with a favourable presumption that they did no wrong. If there is any presumption it is the other way against holders of power, increasing as the power increases. . . . Power tends to corrupt and absolute power corrupts absolutely. Great men are almost always bad men, even when they exercise in-

fluence and not authority: still more when you superadd the tendency or the certainty of corruption by authority."

26. See, for example, Isa. 55:8–9; Rom. 3:22–24; Job 40:1–42:6; Rom. 9:20; 1 Cor. 1:20, 25; Isa. 66:1–2; 1 Pet. 5:5–6; Matt. 7:3–5; 1 Cor. 10:11–12.

27. See, e.g., Matt. 7:13; Matt. 10:17–25; Luke 13:22–30.

28. For more on force and fraud, see Chapter 9.

29. It may be that tax laws, which punish intentional tax evasion, should be regarded as one of these exceptional "victimless crime" laws having direct authorization in Scripture, at least if the money so collected is used to fund government activity that is otherwise consistent with God's will. See, for example, Rom. 13:6–7; Luke 20:20–25. But these passages cannot, in my view, be used to justify *every* conceivable tax—say, a special tax gathered to fund persecutions of Christians. Of course, we understand that governments may sometimes undertake activities (like religious persecution) that are not consistent with God's will. In such circumstances, the above passages make clear, I think, that Christians are still obliged to pay whatever taxes have been established by law, even if the money is used to fund ungodly government policies. But the questions we are currently considering are what taxes *should* be established by law, and what policies should be funded. I am merely claiming that taxation itself, even though it compels those who have not directly harmed others, does not seem to be contrary to God's will—although surely some *particular* taxes *can* be, depending on the circumstances.

Chapter Seven

Common Objections

I am fully aware that the Choice Principle is not something most people (Christian or Non-Christian) would associate with the tenets of evangelical Christianity. I am continually amazed, however, at how counterintuitive legal toleration at first seems to many evangelicals. In the interest of further explaining and defending the Choice Principle, particularly to evangelicals, I wish here to explore some of the most common objections to it.

"EVERYONE LEGISLATES MORALITY!"

When confronted with the argument for legal toleration, perhaps the most common objection voiced by evangelicals is: "You can't say that we shouldn't write our own moral views into the law, because *everyone* legislates morality, even the choice-oriented tolerationists. It's just a question of *whose* morality will dominate the law. Everyone wants their own conception of the good to be enacted into law. Christians should vote so as to make the law prioritize *Christian* conceptions of the good rather than worldly conceptions of the good, such as autonomy." The implication is that the maximization of Choice is itself a "morality" that is being "forced" upon the governed when we enact tolerant laws (or, more accurately, when we refuse to enact restrictive laws).

I recognize that this argument has some force. But if one person can conclude that Choice is just another conception of the good, someone else can just as easily conclude that anyone's particular conception of the good is just another choice. Of course it is true that legal toleration, the decision to structure law so as to allow others to abide by their own values, embodies the values of the person who made that decision. If that's all it takes to constitute a "conception of the good" or a "morality," then legal toleration is indeed founded on a particular conception of the good. On this understanding, protecting other people's right to choose is just another morality, and everyone truly wants to enact their own morality into law. But that is a weakened use of "morality." Using "choice" in a similarly weakened way, it might fairly be said that legal moralism is merely another *choice* made by one or more individuals, and every law reflects a desire to allow someone to choose. One who wants the law to impose a particular conception of the good is simply saying he wants *the power to choose* what he and others will be allowed to do.

From that point of view, one might respond to the objector, "You can't say that we shouldn't prioritize freedom of choice, because *everyone* does, even the intolerant legal moralist. It's just a question of whether you want to allow the same freedom of choice to others that you covet for yourself." The assertion, "Every law embodies morality, because legal toleration itself is just another morality," can be met with, "Every law embodies freedom of choice, because legal moralism itself is just another free choice."

Why do we seem to be talking past each other? Because to say "legislating freedom of choice is just prioritizing your morality" is using the term "morality" more broadly than is common (and is also playing fast and loose with the idea of "legislation," which usually connotes some form of coercion). The justifiable response is to broaden the definition of the word "choice," as in: "Well, everyone prioritizes personal choice too, because legislating your version of morality is just prioritizing your personal choice over that of others." This kind of debate gets us nowhere.

It is understandable that the Choice Principle might initially be seen as just another conception of the good—after all, the Choice Principle, like the views of its opponents, arises out of a particular moral understanding of what good government looks like. But the Choice Principle embodies a morality different in kind from all others, because it opposes on principle the legal enforcement of anyone's positive morality.

Consider the activity of eating apples. I can imagine someone who likes to eat apples, and I can imagine someone who hates to eat apples (two particular conceptions of the good). I can also imagine someone who believes she knows whether it is good for other people to eat apples (a conception of the good which might, in her view, give her a justification for trying to make laws prioritizing that positive morality). It is more difficult, however, to imagine someone who prefers to be disallowed from choosing for herself whether to eat apples. And if we posit an unsympathetic authority doing the choosing for her—say an authority that may sometimes want to hurt her or an authority that occasionally may not know or care what is best for her—it becomes almost impossible to imagine someone who knows this and yet prefers not to make the choice about apples herself. The need for personal choice, if it is merely a conception of the good, is unique because it is apparently a conception of the good we all share.

So if I have power over Joe, but I decide to allow Joe to choose for himself whether he will eat apples, is my decision just the manifestation of another particular conception of the good? Is my decision not fundamentally different from the decision to force Joe to eat apples, or the decision to forbid Joe to eat apples? Have I forced my morality on Joe (or on Fred, who thinks I should make Joe eat apples)? Perhaps some wish to define their terms in such a way that freedom is just another value one can "impose" on someone else. Perhaps they would also say that allowing someone else a choice is really "coercive." It is perhaps possible to define terms this way; but these are certainly strange and counterintuitive definitions, and they cheapen the ideas underlying the words. It is as if I said to someone, "I am now going to force my value system on you. My value system is that my value system can never be forced on you." In what sense am I really "forcing" my values on him? Does it make sense to refer to this as "coercion" on my part? And exactly who among the "coerced" would complain under such a "tyranny"?

Now consider a government that decides not to make laws restricting the consumption of apples (or, for that matter, alcoholic beverages). How would we describe that government with regard to its apple (or alcohol) policies? We would say the government allows individuals the freedom to consume the product if they so choose, or to abstain from consumption if they wish. The government does not somehow "coerce" anyone, restrict freedom, or "force" on anyone (even "the larger society") a particular conception of the good. The government has simply not acted at all. It has done nothing. If Sally's immoral conduct offends me, and the law does not prohibit Sally's conduct, that surely does not prove that the law has "acted" and "forced" me to endure offense. *Sally* is the one who has acted immorally, not the government. Both politically liberal and politically conservative Christians would do well to acknowledge this distinction, rather than castigating inactive governments for "creating" an unjust society, or for fiendishly corrupting our morals.[1] When government inaction is labeled a form of government action, and freedom is said to be a type of coercion, we have truly entered the era of Orwellian Newspeak.[2]

We have great reason to believe that Choice is unique in God's sight. Unlike most virtues, Choice is not a product of righteousness. Righteousness is a product of Choice. Freedom of choice is not just another virtue; instead, Choice is a necessary precondition for virtue. Choice is an indicator, not of righteousness, but of human-ness. Humans alone, out of all God's creation, seem to be given the capacity to choose between right and wrong. Thus humans alone are given the capacity for good and for evil—a capacity that varies according to the range of choices reasonably available to them. Sometimes humans limit the range of choices available to other humans. But God has chosen not to do this. At the Creation, God could have made us all robots, without the capacity for Choice. Or he could have created the Garden of Eden without a Tree of Knowledge, thus limiting our range of available choices. By making us robots, or by disallowing tempting options to exist, he would have completely denied us Choice. God could thereby have eliminated sin. But this would have eliminated righteousness as well. Alternatively, he could later have taken a lesser step: he could have reduced our range of available choices by leaving us under the penal laws of Moses, which would be to deny us Choice at the margins of life. But he knew that no act can be righteous unless it is freely chosen. Hence, Choice is a necessary precondition for righteousness and virtue, in a way other values and conceptions of the good are not. And when we limit overall human Choice, by law or otherwise, we restrict righteousness, in a way that might well displease the one who gave us all a wide range of Choice.

If the Choice Principle is a "morality," it is a unique one. For that reason it doesn't matter, I think, whether we call it a "morality" or not. Its critics can gain no mileage from that characterization. Even if prioritizing Choice in the law represents a particular conception of the good, it is a unique and minimal one and differs in important ways from any other particular conception of the good that might be enacted into law. It is simply not true that prioritizing the Choice of others is just another way to legislate, or force upon others, a particular morality.

"WE MUST BRING THIS NATION BACK TO GOD!"

Another objection commonly voiced goes something like this: "Our nation is reaching a moral crisis point. Christians must vote and be politically active before it's too late, so we can make our voices heard above the voices of our depraved culture—then maybe we can bring this nation back to God." One scripture that seems especially popular with those calling for this sort of national revival is Prov. 14:34: "Righteousness exalts a nation, but sin is a reproach to any people." As we noted in Chapter 1, this text and others are used by some evangelicals to support a nationalistic diatribe against sinful popular culture and a call to make the United States a "Christian Nation." The call often employs a strong element of nationalism or patriotism. The "culture" around us is portrayed as the enemy, and government is viewed, somewhat cynically, as nothing more than a convenient tool for the mighty to use to shape society and culture in whatever way they wish, without limitation by natural law, the Constitution, or any other source. For too long, the argument goes, secular humanists and pagan opportunists have been "the mighty" and have controlled the government for their own ends—isn't it high time Christians gained control instead? After all, Christians are a majority in this country. So we should recognize our opportunity to oust the current leaders, shift the policies, and control the government ourselves, for God's glory.

For reasons we have already examined, Christian political involvement is probably not sinful in itself. And of course it is a noble aspiration to bring a large group of people "back to God," whether they are from our nation, another nation, or many different nations. Whether government and law can accomplish this is a separate question. It is interesting, however, that in recent years evangelicals seem to be calling "our nation" back much more often than they are calling back other groups of people for whom Christ died—for example, "our country club" or "our state" or "our corporation" or "our ethnic group." Might it be that the call to "bring our *nation* back to God" has more to do with nationalistic pride than with a genuine concern for the souls of all the lost? If our concern is actually to bring *people* to God, why not say that instead?

In fact, the call to "bring this nation back to God" almost seems to hinge on an understanding of "this nation" itself as a special moral agent, with a special purpose in God's redemptive plan, and not just as a large group of individual moral agents who happen to live under a government that calls itself the United States of America. It is as if God loves "this nation," pleads with "this nation" to repent, will someday judge "this nation," and ultimately "this nation" will either be condemned to hell or granted eternal life in heaven. Likewise, "this nation" is presumably commanded to love its enemies, to pray, to give to the poor, and to spread the gospel. From these assumptions flow also a whole set of public policy preferences: "God will punish this nation if we do not stand against Iraq" (or drugs, or homosexuality, or poverty, or what have you). The call to moral purity and the calls to patriotism and political activism intertwine and become so interdependent that it is impossible to tell them apart.

But in contrast to the call for a "godly nation," the biblical view seems to be that groups do not have a soul or free will and are therefore not separate moral agents. Yes, there are references to righteous and sinful nations, and to God's love for groups (in particular, the Jewish race) throughout the Bible. But since the advent of the New Covenant, God has never given any indication that his salvation will be extended on the basis of nationality, or that there is anything particularly special about an entire nation accepting him (as opposed to many individuals from different nations doing the same). In fact, the indication in the New Testament is quite to the contrary. And while there are many scriptures indicating that Jesus died for "the nations" or something to that effect, a fair reading of the New Testament as a whole indicates that these scriptures are referring to Jesus' salvation of individuals, not nations. It is quite difficult to conclude that "nations" and "peoples" have their own independent moral standing before God, just as it is difficult to find Scriptural support for the notion that the United States has some special place in God's heart. At least under the New Covenant, God wants a relationship, not with a nation, but with the individuals who comprise it.

To illustrate, let us suppose that every individual U.S. citizen except one were in a saved condition in God's sight and were even exhibiting the fruits of a Spirit-filled life. Under almost any definition one can reasonably concoct, the U.S. would be a "Christian nation." Would God then be satisfied, because our nation had finally achieved this status? Or would he instead focus all his attention and longing upon the single lost *individual*, upon whom he places *infinite* value? To pose the question is to answer it. Recall, for example, Matt. 18:12–14, where Jesus asks: "If a shepherd has a hundred sheep, and one of them has gone astray, does he not leave the ninety-nine on the mountains and go in search of the one that went astray? And if he finds it . . . he rejoices over it more than over the ninety-nine that never went astray." God cares nothing about the status of a "nation" as such, only the human beings who comprise it. Our God is a God of individual salvation, not collective salvation.

It is not surprising that we should find many passages in the Old Testament to the effect that righteousness exalts a nation, that sin destroys a nation, that God loves a certain nation or hates another nation, that a nation ought to adopt the Lord as its God, and so on. These passages are largely poetic, employing hyperbole and personifying nonhuman things, as poets have commonly done for millennia. In any event such passages might easily be understood as general truths referring merely to the majority of individuals within a nation, or perhaps to the character of the individuals in control of it. But there is no biblical indication that converting these people would be more important to God than converting an equal number of other people. Individual repentance, not "collective repentance" (whatever that might mean), is what God craves. Moreover, God had very different dealings with people under the Old Covenant than he does under the New, and of course this was true with the Hebrew nation particularly. But when the New Covenant came, the biblical message seems to be that these dealings would and did change. If salvation had ever been a collective matter before, the New Testament ushered in a decidedly individualistic relationship between man and God, in which membership in the Jewish nation (or any other particular nation) was no longer relevant to a right relationship with God.[3]

The fact is that Christ died, not to save nations as such, but to save individuals. From all we are told, it is irrelevant to God whether those individuals are from Nation A or Nation B.[4] Thus, for example, if exactly 300 million people in the world are going to truly give their lives to God as he desires, God doesn't care whether 300 million Americans give their lives to him or, instead, whether 200 million Chinese and 75 million Indians and 25 million Americans do it. This is true even though a "whole nation" would be coming to him in the first instance but only minorities of three different nations in the second. So it is largely unintelligible to talk about "bringing this nation to God" or "making this a Christian nation," as if that goal were more important than, or separate from, evangelism generally. God's desire is to save people, not nations.

So what does it mean to say, "Righteousness exalts a nation, but sin is a disgrace to any people"? If "nations" and "peoples" are not separate moral agents in God's sight, the verse must be referring to the righteousness or sin of individuals within a nation. We can all agree that righteousness exalts a person, and sin is a reproach to any person. When we say a *group* of people (a "nation," for example) is righteous, or is exalted through righteousness, we are referring to the persons comprising the group. We are not saying that the group itself can *sin* or *be righteous*. Nations *can* in a sense be exalted or disgraced, but the righteousness or sin that accomplishes this must originate with individuals, not with the nation itself. And those individuals' responses to the gospel are valued no more or less by God whether they live in one country or one hundred.

A separate problem with the "defeat evil culture and save our nation" objection is its call to "bring this nation *back* to God." The call implies that "this nation" was "with God" to begin with, at some prior time. This is a common assumption among many evangelicals, and in fact (as we noticed in Chapter 1) much evangelical literature explicitly claims a history of moral purity for this Christian nation which has only recently been denigrated, defiled, or revised.[5] Even putting aside the question (just discussed) of how a "nation" itself can be considered righteous or unrighteous given that it is a moral nonentity, these historical claims will be difficult to prove.

The difficulty stems partly from the fact that it is very unclear just what the term "Christian nation" is supposed to mean. It is rhetoric that undoubtedly packs an emotional punch. But is it a claim about our people or about our laws? If it is simply a claim that our laws have historically required or supported religious practices to a greater extent than they do today, it somewhat misses the point. Perhaps those laws were mostly supported on secular rather than religious grounds. Or perhaps such laws were as unholy in God's sight as laws prohibiting Negro suffrage. If legal history teaches anything, it is that a law's pedigree is no guarantee of either its wisdom or its moral validity. In any event, our country's history in this area is certainly a mixed bag; one can likely find as many laws historically supported by our people for purely secular reasons as for purely religious ones, and at least as many famous American warnings *against* a legal code too influenced by religion, as calls for religious revival through legal enactments.

But in fact, I believe the proponents of the "Christian heritage" thesis are not primarily arguing that our country's *laws* have always been somehow "Christian." I think they are making what is in some ways an even stronger claim, a claim about our people. One kind of claim about our people is that a large majority of them have always professed to be Christians. This is a claim that surely no one will dispute. But this kind of claim is very weak, for it says exactly nothing about our people's actual moral values or actions in history—much less their beliefs about ideal government. I imagine, then, that those who say America was founded as a "Christian nation" have in mind some stronger historical claim about the actual beliefs of our people in times past—not that our people were sinless, but at least the kind of historical claim about early American moral attitudes that supports their current desire to "return to our moral roots." Note that even if this stronger claim is true, it does not by itself show that these values were encoded into law, or that it was a good thing if they were.

But to support this stronger claim it will not do, of course, to show merely that some government officials have at some prior time publicly talked about God, claimed to be religious, claimed to make laws based on their religious views, or indeed claimed that America is a "Christian nation." To show that America was truly at some past time a "Christian nation" or a "godly nation," presumably the proof would have to consist of, at a minimum, some evidence that at some prior time, a majority of Americans, or at least a majority of our high government officials, were in a *saved condition before God*. But one would of course be hard pressed to point out a given year or even a given hour of our national history in which this was true. Nor will the exploits of our governments (local or national) over the years aid in the proof. If anything, the record of such ignoble governmental adventures as our institutionalized slavery and racial discrimination, our governmental dealings with Native Americans, our imperialism overseas, and our long history of governmental corruption and scandals at home, should rather lead one to presume (until proven wrong) that "our nation" was decidedly *not* Christ-like during *any* of its history, regardless of the religious-sounding rhetoric of some of its leaders (who, whether influenced by baser self-interest or not, cannot have failed to notice that religious-sounding rhetoric does not usually hurt one's standing with his constituents—at least not in a nation in which overwhelming majorities of the people profess to be Christian).

A final problem with the objection, and in many ways its central problem, is its call to use *government and law* to "bring this nation back to God." We have noted that God has not ordained government for this purpose. And we have seen that using law to make people righteous appears to be both ungodly and impractical. Laws cannot change hearts. For this reason, the law is incapable of bringing anyone back to God. Laws may control behavior, but they cannot bring about righteousness—righteousness is a matter of the heart. And to the extent that laws limit or eliminate Choice, they likewise limit our capacity for righteousness, since Choice is always necessary for righteousness. In short, changing the legal system will *not* "bring this nation back to God." Only individual conversion and renewal will bring Americans (or anyone else) to God.

"WE SHOULDN'T SEND THE WRONG MESSAGE!"

A third common objection to legal toleration is that refusing to outlaw a sin is a form of condoning that sin, of sending a message to the world that "we" (again, usually a society, a community, or a nation) don't care whether someone engages in this activity or not. This objection is founded on an assumption that part of the purpose of criminal law is to send messages about societal norms and moral expectations, and that this by itself is a sufficient justification for outlawing some immoral practices.

The problem is that our laws do not in fact function as moral messengers. If this were part of the purpose of our criminal laws, we would surely criminalize a lot more of what most of us find to be immoral. Refusing to outlaw a sin is simply *not* the same as condoning that sin, and most people in our society seem to understand the difference. There are many acts and vices which are considered morally wrong in all situations by a majority of Americans but which are not usually punished by law. Examples might include adultery, or making racist or sexist remarks privately.[6] The law does not usually forbid these activities; but the law's silence hasn't spawned a general assumption that no one cares whether people do these things. On the contrary, there seems to be a widespread understanding among Americans that these acts, to the extent they become known by others, will bring reproach upon a person. Our society generally disrespects its philandering husbands and its Archie Bunkers, at least to the extent it recognizes them. Still, there seems to be very little support among Americans for outlawing these sorts of vices.[7] The law is not, and is not perceived by most people in our society to be, a definitive statement of all our society's moral values. As most Americans intuitively understand, the law has a much different job to do.

Moreover, "messenger" (as opposed to "protector") is not a role in which the law typically excels. The message is often lost in transit. Many factors, such as discriminatory enforcement or unenforceability, can alter, jumble, or destroy the intended message.

Regarding discriminatory enforcement, consider, for example, the laws that used to exist prohibiting certain sex acts between consenting adults in private. In 2003, the U.S. Supreme Court overturned a 1986 precedent and held that such laws are unconstitutional.[8] But here was a realm of law, if there ever was one, where it seems the intended "message" of the law, whatever it was, had been completely lost on most people. Just before the 2003 case was decided, at least thirteen states still had laws on the books banning oral and/or anal sex between consenting adults. Four of these states limited the prohibition to same sex conduct; among the other states, some presumably banned such conduct even between a husband and wife in the privacy of their own bedroom.[9] As one might imagine, these laws were rarely enforced. But when they were, the recorded court cases indicate that they were enforced disproportionately against homosexuals. This may well have been the result of anti-homosexual discrimination by police officers, since survey evidence indicates that the prohibited activity occurred in a far greater number of instances between people of opposite genders than between people of the same gender.[10] So what "message" was being received by society as a result of such laws? Was the message, "Oral and anal sex are wrong"? Or was the message, "*Homosexual* oral and anal sex are wrong"?[11] Or perhaps, "*Homosexuality* is wrong"? What if someone had discovered that 85% of the people who were convicted of this crime were black—what would have been the message of the law then? Or what if only .01% of the people who committed this crime ever got caught—what is the message of the law under those circumstances? What if it could be shown that majorities of Americans do not see anything wrong with oral or anal sex between consenting married couples in private, and that majorities of Americans also understand that most Americans agree about this? What message would the law have carried then, if it were applied to a consenting married couple?

Messages in the law get lost if there are enforcement problems. And when enforcement is very difficult, as it is with bans of private sexual conduct and many other "morals" laws, discriminatory enforcement becomes both more likely and more extreme. We can safely predict that laws which are very difficult to enforce fairly will almost always fail to send the intended message to society.

But even if our message to society takes the form of a law that will be enforced vigorously and evenhandedly, that message is susceptible to distortion at many points down the line. Sending messages is a more or less precise task, while law is a blunt instrument that cannot be wielded with precision. Those who specialize in sending important messages to a society, such as advertisers, image consultants, and journalists, spend untold hours precisely crafting words, symbols, and actions designed to convey precisely the right message to the receivers. While writing laws usually requires lots of time and effort, laws are not usually crafted with the intention that they even be read and understood by the wider public, much less that they persuade anyone of anything. (Try reading the U.S. Code sometime.) What society sees are the results of our laws, and only the highly publicized results at that (perhaps, say, a prison sentence imposed for violation of the securities laws in a notorious "insider trading" case). If we are trying to accomplish a delicate task like communicating a precise moral message to society, imprisoning someone (for example) is a rather indelicate and imprecise way of going about it. (Try asking ten average Americans why Martha Stewart's insider trading activities were morally worse than the daily activities of any well-informed institutional investor. Did people get the message?) Society may or may not know who the prisoner is, that she went to prison, why she's being punished, what the law really says, or a whole host of other things they ought to know if the message is to be accurately communicated. And of course, as noted earlier, people may not believe the law is representative of community mores even if they do understand it.

We should also bear in mind that even if the law were a perfect messenger of societal expectations, the costs of using law to send a message are enormous. The costs of restrictive laws, of course, are borne most directly by those accused of violating them. One might say a "message" to society that costs a particular individual a year in prison carries a fairly hefty price tag. That message had better be extremely important to the receivers. The fact that most of the receivers do not themselves bear this cost does not justify our overlooking the cost in our calculations of the costs and benefits of using restrictive laws to send messages. It seems unfair to make one person suffer just so that the rest of us can tell ourselves that we all think some activity is morally unacceptable.

But besides this type of cost, there is also a larger societal cost. We all run a certain risk when our government enacts more and more restrictive laws, because the government thereby sets a precedent that the state may legitimately make us pursue values that we may not share. The state that may curtail my liberty to privately view *Playboy* because it is offensive to societal moral standards, may logically also curtail my liberty to privately read anything else the state or society finds offensive—say, J.D. Salinger's *The Catcher in the Rye*. To give the government our tacit assent to exercise this type of power over *any* materials is to run the risk in practice, if not in theory, that eventually the government will assume the same type of power over *all* materials.

And any fine theoretical distinction limiting the state's power over one type of material and not the other—even if such a distinction can be rationally defended—is likely to be lost on a majority of the governed. Perhaps we imagine we can craft a detailed legal rule explaining how to distinguish between protected classics and proscribed smut. But even if we can, who will read and understand our new rule? Who will be able to apply it accurately in advance, to themselves, so as to avoid falling afoul of it? How many people are likely to agree with it in all its details? If a majority of the governed do not understand or agree with the law, the law will probably be an unclear messenger of societal mores; but more to the present point, people who do not agree with a law or understand its prohibitions are not likely to be persuaded by its "message," even if the message is understood clearly. And besides all this, governments may more easily exceed their proper powers when the masses do not understand what the government thinks the difference is between a "proper" law and an "improper" one. In short, there are likely to be high and perhaps unintended costs to all of us when we enact laws for the purpose of sending messages.

It should be obvious that there are other effective ways to send a persuasive social message without using the law. Perhaps the most effective method is by living and speaking counterculturally. Today, as in the first century, the world cannot help noticing those who are different, and God is still powerful enough to change hearts through our differences—through our words and our example and our love. If we are trying to persuade, these are powerful ways to do it. We know this works, because we have seen the results. And this option will always be open to us, no matter how little power we may have to influence law. Why then must *law* be our messenger?

"DOING SOMETHING IS BETTER THAN DOING NOTHING!"

While recognizing the weaknesses inherent in the above objections, some would nevertheless object to legal toleration by asserting that since Christians have a civic duty to vote and participate in government to make it the best it can be, and since Christians know certain sins when they see them, Christians ought to use their political power to try to outlaw at least the most clearly obvious and practically detectable sins. After all, doing something is better than doing nothing.

But the truth is, doing something is often *worse* than doing nothing. Even if Christians have a civic duty to participate in governing, and even if Christians do know certain sins when they see them, that is far from showing that Christians ought to use their political power to outlaw some particular sin. In fact, if the Choice Principle is correct, the rational conclusion flowing from these premises would be exactly the opposite—having the duties we have and knowing what we know, Christians should use the law to maximize individual Choice, not to limit Choice by outlawing sins or coercing virtue. If this is true, doing something (through government) is decidedly not better than doing nothing.

But to respond more directly to this particular objection, I would suggest that when pressed, few Christians will endorse it. Most Christians would have a hard time consistently outlawing the most obvious and detectable sins. In our list of "most obvious" sins that we must outlaw, we could include the usual suspects, like prostitution and drug abuse. Perhaps Christians on the political Left would want to outlaw other obvious sins like usury or environmental degradation. But if we are going to be consistent, we will also have to list other "obvious and detectable" sins, things like public blasphemy and idolatrous pagan worship rituals. Are we willing to go that far? If detectability is the standard for deciding which sins should be outlawed, why are we not willing to outlaw *all* the detectable sins?

I anticipate the response might be something like, "Well, detectability is not the only standard. Our inability to outlaw *all* the obvious and detectable sins shouldn't keep us from outlawing some of them. We can't save the whole world, but doing a little good is better than doing none at all." But at this point the criticism loses its force, for the critic has not announced any method for distinguishing between the obvious and detectable sins that *should* be outlawed and those that *shouldn't*. If we don't want to outlaw all detectable sins, how should we choose which of the detectable ones to outlaw? For example, how did we choose prostitution and not idolatry? If the sole and sufficient justification for outlawing prostitution is that prostitution is an "obvious and detectable" sin, then why isn't the same justification also sufficient for outlawing Hindu idol worship? If we conclude that Hindu rituals should not be outlawed, then detectability was not a sufficient reason to outlaw them; this may suggest that we need some other justification for outlawing prostitution, as well. Christians who want to outlaw merely a subclass of all the obvious and detectable sins must state how they will define that subclass and why—and which Scriptures led them to these conclusions. So far, such thoughtful theology seems to have been conspicuously absent from the political arguments of the most vocal legal moralists.

"SOME THINGS JUST SHOULDN'T BE DONE!"

Among Christians on the political Right especially, the objections to legal toleration may be founded on some core assumptions having little to do with religious faith, after all. These assumptions may well be shared by many evangelicals, due less perhaps to their common religious beliefs than to similarities in culture, upbringing, and political ideology within this group. I suspect the reason many evangelicals want to outlaw some particular sins and not others is not because these people want to reduce sin generally, or even because they really believe, after careful examination, that God desires such laws. Rather, they wish to outlaw certain behaviors because they believe "some things just shouldn't be done." In other words, they believe society is better off, from a secular viewpoint, if those particular behaviors (which also happen to be sinful) are prohibited. Thus they do not wish to outlaw all sins, just some. They wish to outlaw prostitution (for example), not really because prostitution is sinful (although they believe it is), and not to help would-be prostitutes and their clients to become more godly, but because they believe society as a whole is made worse off, from a secular standpoint, when more of its members engage in prostitution. Perhaps they cannot say the same for certain other obviously sinful behaviors, like rituals of Vishnu worship, and thus they do not advocate outlawing those.

The first thing to notice about this view is that it must depend entirely upon secular, as opposed to religious, understandings—particularly, secular understandings of what it means to make society "better off." Indeed, some conscientious atheists might agree with this argument for outlawing prostitution, and for the same reasons. By the same token, however, all conscientious Christians need *not* agree with it. It must be supported, if at all, entirely apart from the text of the Bible and entirely apart from one's faith in God. For purposes of this objection, it will not do to claim that prostitution is bad for society because prostitution is sinful or leads us away from God. Rather, one must show, through appeal to exclusively non-religious sources and values, that "society" is "better off" when certain sinful behaviors (like prostitution) are minimized.

The first problem one confronts in taking up this burden of proof is that it is very difficult for Christians to define "better off" without reference to the moral standards set by Christianity. Again, for the purposes of this argument, "better off" cannot mean less sinful or more moral; it must mean something else. In assessing the harms posed by prostitution, then, we will want to take account of real "secular" costs like disease and family destabilization; but by the same token, we cannot discount real secular *benefits* like personal liberty and free markets. Freedom is not worthless even from a religious point of view, much less from a secular one. Suppose it were well documented that reducing prostitution also marginally reduces the instances of certain diseases in the population. We cannot for that reason alone outlaw prostitution, unless we determine that the value of the freedom to engage in prostitution is outweighed by the value of preventing disease. As difficult as this evaluation is, and as many disagreements as we might have over the correct quantification of the respective values, it will not do to ignore the value of freedom in the calculation, or to pretend that such freedom is worthless from a secular viewpoint. If we must proceed from a secular foundation, we cannot automatically assume that personal liberty doesn't benefit anyone.

Or consider another example. Although we could certainly prevent a great number of deaths annually by outlawing cars, I am not aware of any Christian who supports such a Draconian measure. Why shouldn't we outlaw cars, if doing so would save lives? Aren't life and health more important to a society than freedom (in this case the freedom to drive a car)? The answer, as we all apparently agree, is no. Freedom does indeed have value, and in this case the freedom to drive a car in fact outweighs the competing values of life and health. That is not to say that no restrictions on freedom would ever be justifiable in order to prevent deaths; it is just to say that we all agree that *some* restrictions of freedom surely would *not* be justifiable on that basis. Freedom has value.

How then should we decide which freedoms should be limited, and which protected, in order to benefit society? One possible standard is the Choice Principle, which can be defended on either purely Christian or purely secular grounds. Those who wish to reject the Choice Principle, but also wish to outlaw certain acts because of the secular harms they cause, will need some other secularly justifiable standard for deciding which sins to outlaw. It is difficult to imagine what such an alternative standard would say. If there is some other non-religious standard for deciding which freedoms are worth limiting in the name of societal benefit, a standard that would require outlawing prostitution as unsafe while permitting cars in the name of freedom, I have not heard it.

I have certainly not heard it from evangelicals on the political Right. To support the full legislative agenda of that group, one presumably would have to support the continued legality of unwed motherhood, and speech advocating divorce or espousing female inferiority, on the ground that allowing such behavior or speech is on balance harmless or even beneficial to society in secular terms; while simultaneously, one would have to support laws against gambling and the publication of pornography on the ground that these activities are overall detriments to society from a secular viewpoint. The societal harms demonstrably imposed by gambling and pornography seem (at most) no worse than the societal harms posed by unwed motherhood, divorce, and misogyny. One wonders, then, why the freedom to contract to gamble is automatically worth less than the freedom to become an unwed mother or to publicly say women are inferior to men. Perhaps one must conclude that some within the Christian Right, like the political Right generally, have devalued individual freedom itself, instead prioritizing values like unity and order. Perhaps some evangelicals have accepted a measure of right and wrong, and of societal benefit, based more on the mores of secular conservative subculture than on an honest and informed interpretation of God's will.[12]

The most common objections to a Choice-oriented legal regime thus seem flawed for one reason or another. Choice, if it is a conception of the good, is indeed different from competing conceptions of the good. For one thing, it is highly valued by God as a necessary precondition for every righteous act. We cannot "bring this nation back to God" without protecting Choice. And although it is true that "some things just shouldn't be done," Christians should carefully consider the possibility that our selective lists of those forbidden acts, as well as our strategies for reducing their occurrence, may be based more on secular influences like our culture, bias, and upbringing than on an objective assessment of God's will.

NOTES

1. As a group, politically conservative Christians probably have much less trouble recognizing the distinction between government action and government inaction in some other contexts—for example, when someone claims racial discrimination in violation of the Fourteenth Amendment.

2. It is perhaps interesting to note in this connection that according to George Orwell's novel *Nineteen Eighty-four*, one of the three slogans of the Party, emblazoned on the Ministry of Truth building, was "Freedom is Slavery." George Orwell, *Nineteen Eighty-four* (1949; reprint, New York: New American Library, 1984), 7.

3. See especially Jer. 31:27–30; Joel 2:28–32; Matt. 28:18–20; John 4:21–24; 1 Pet. 2:9; Rom. 9:6–8, 22–26; Rom. 10:9–17; Gal. 4:21–28; Eph. 2:11–18; Col. 3:11; Heb. 7:18–25; Heb. 10:11–22; Heb. 6:10–11; Phil. 2:12; Rev. 5:9–10.

4. See, for example, Gal. 3:26–29.

5. See, for example, Gary DeMar, *America's Christian History: The Untold Story*, 2d ed. (1995; reprint, Atlanta: American Vision, 1995); Tim LaHaye, *Faith of Our Founding Fathers*, 2d printing (Green Forest, Ark.: Master Books, 1996); Jerry Falwell, *Listen, America!* (Garden City, N.Y.: Doubleday, 1980).

6. See question #7 and accompanying answers, in "Washington Post/Henry J. Kaiser Family Foundation/Harvard University Value Study," 4 Oct. 1998, <http://www.washingtonpost.com/wp-srv/politics/polls/vault/stories/data100498.htm> (31 Oct. 2005). In this nationwide poll of 2,025 adults, 88% of respondents said that they believed "a married person having an affair" is always morally unacceptable regardless of circumstances; 82% said "making a racist remark in a private conversation" is always morally unacceptable regardless of circumstances; and 67% said "making a sexist remark in a private conversation" is always morally unacceptable regardless of circumstances. Subsequent polls show similar results. See, for example, George H. Gallup, Jr., Gallup Poll Monthly 113, 1 June 2003 (available on WESTLAW

at 2003 WLNR 11072826) (finding that 93% of Americans consider "the extramarital affair" to be "morally wrong").

7. See, for example, AP poll, Roper Center for Public Opinion Research, June 1997, Question ID: USAP.923M Q3 (available on WESTLAW). In this 1997 poll of 1,016 adults nationwide, 74% of respondents said they thought adultery should not be punished as a crime.

8. *Lawrence v. Texas*, 539 U.S. 558 (2003), overturning *Bowers v. Hardwick*, 478 U.S. 186 (1986).

9. See *Lawrence*, 539 U.S. at 573. It is somewhat unclear exactly which of these states' laws would have applied to consenting married couples acting in private—which is just one example of the confusion that surrounded these laws. Alabama (by statute) and Idaho (by state court interpretation of a state statute) allowed a clear exception for any married couple. See Ala. Code § 13A-6-65; *State v. Holden*, 890 P.2d 341 (Idaho Ct. App. 1995). Other states provided statutory or judicially created exemptions for all heterosexual contact. See Mo. Rev. Stat. § 566.090; Okla. Stat. tit. 21, § 886; *Post v. State*, 715 P.2d 1105 (Okla. Crim. App. 1986); Tex. Penal Code Ann. § 21.06. But even so, heterosexual married couples that engaged in consensual oral or anal sex in the privacy of their own bedrooms, with no one else present or watching, were arguably violating the law in at least eight states: Florida, Louisiana, Massachusetts, Mississippi, North Carolina, South Carolina, Utah, and Virginia. Such couples were also apparently violating the law in Michigan if the contact involved the anus of either party. Of course, notwithstanding the laws, prosecutions were almost never brought against married couples acting privately and consensually. The relevant state statutes were: Fla. Stat. ch. 800.02; La. Rev. Stat. Ann. tit. 14, § 89; Mass. Gen. Laws ch. 272, § 34; Mich. Comp. Laws § 750.158; Miss. Code Ann. § 97-29-59; N.C. Gen. Stat. § 14-177; S.C. Code Ann. § 16-15-120; Utah Code Ann. § 76-5-403; Va. Code Ann. § 18.2-361. With respect to the Virginia statute, it should be noted that the U.S. Court of Appeals for the Fourth Circuit once said in dictum that the statute could not constitutionally be applied to a heterosexual married couple acting consensually, in private, with no onlookers. See *Lovisi v. Slayton*, 539 F.2d 349 (4th Cir. 1976), *cert. denied*, *Lovisi v. Zahradnick*, 429 U.S. 977 (1976). But before *Lawrence*, that conclusion was open to serious doubt, given that: (1) it was dictum; (2) it was rendered by a federal court interpreting state law, with no state court's statutory interpretation to support it; and (3) it was explicitly based on an interpretation of then-current U.S. Supreme Court jurisprudence surrounding the constitutional right of privacy, a jurisprudence that predated *Bowers v. Hardwick* (the landmark U.S. Supreme Court case that upheld a Georgia sodomy statute similar to Virginia's, in which the Court specifically *rejected* a claim that the statute violated the constitutional right of privacy).

10. For example, 1972 survey data published by Morton Hunt in his landmark study of American sexuality showed that at least 56% of all married heterosexuals in America claimed to participate in cunnilingus with their spouse on an ongoing basis. Morton Hunt, *Sexual Behavior in the 1970's* (New York: Dell Publishing Co., 1975), as reported in William H. Masters, Virginia E. Johnson, and Robert C. Kolodny, *Human Sexuality*, 4th ed. (New York: HarperCollins, 1992), 372. As of 1995, about 116 million American adults were married heterosexuals. U.S. Bureau of the Census,

Marital Status and Living Arrangements: March 1995 (Washington, D.C.: Government Printing Office, 1997), as reported in John W. Wright, ed., *The New York Times 1998 Almanac* (New York: Penguin, 1997), 280. So if Hunt's 1972 percentage was still roughly accurate in 1995, at least 65 million heterosexual adults in this country participated in at least one form of oral or anal sex on an ongoing basis with a partner of the opposite sex. (This number is actually quite conservative because it excludes all *unmarried* heterosexual adults, excludes incidents of fellatio and anal sex altogether, and is not adjusted for probable underreporting among the married group.) On the other hand, consider how many *homosexual* adults were engaging in oral or anal sex during the same period. According to data from the 1996 General Social Survey conducted by the National Opinion Research Center at the University of Chicago, only about 3.5% of American men and 2.1% of American women report that they are homosexual. (National Opinion Research Center (NORC), *General Social Survey*, 1996, as reported in Wright, ed., *Times 1998 Almanac*, 300.) It seems likely that there might be substantial underreporting of homosexual preferences even in an anonymous survey; in addition, we want to account also for bisexuality and for sex conduct rather than preference (to the extent that some people engaged in regular homosexual relations might not have homosexual preferences). So to be quite generous, let us double the reported percentages and assume, for the sake of argument, that in 1996 fully 6% of American adults regularly had sexual relations with a partner of their own gender. There were approximately 196 million adults in America in 1996. (U.S. Bureau of the Census, Population Division, April 21, 1997, as reported in Wright, ed., *Times 1998 Almanac*, 277.) Therefore, under our generous assumption, there were then a total of perhaps 12 million American adults who regularly engaged in oral or anal sex with a partner of their own gender. Even so, the total number of *same-sex* participants was only 12 million, a far lesser number than the (extremely conservative estimate of) 65 million *heterosexual* adults engaged in the activity a year earlier. While it is still possible that same-sex encounters accounted for more *total incidents* than opposite sex encounters, this and similar data (as well as a mountain of anecdotal evidence) strongly suggest otherwise. See also Gary D. Allison, "Sanctioning Sodomy: The Supreme Court Liberates Gay Sex and Limits State Power to Vindicate the Moral Sentiments of the People," Tulsa L. Rev. 39 (2003): 97 (reporting results of a 1994 U.S. study showing that approximately 80 percent of Caucasian men, 75 percent of Caucasian women, 72 percent of Hispanic men, 61 percent of Hispanic women, 50 percent of African-American men, and 35 percent of African-American women perform oral sex).

11. This is apparently the message the U.S. Supreme Court understood these laws to be communicating. See *Bowers*, 478 U.S. at 191, in which the U.S. Supreme Court upheld a Georgia sodomy statute, which would have applied by its terms to both heterosexual and homosexual activities, on the sole ground that the U.S. Constitution does not protect "a fundamental right to engage in *homosexual* sodomy" (emphasis added). As noted earlier, the *Lawrence* court overturned *Bowers*, repudiating in particular the *Bowers* characterization of the right that is at stake when the state bans sodomy. *Lawrence*, 539 U.S. at 566–67.

12. Along these lines, it is interesting (and somewhat distressing) to note the apparent double standards of evangelicals on the political Right in certain of their

well-publicized battles with the culture around them. To mention just one of these battles, in the late 1990s the Christian Right mounted a campaign against the prime-time television show "Ellen" for favorably depicting its star character as a lesbian. But of course, many prime-time shows have portrayed major characters in a way that winks at their sinful lifestyles—consider such television staples as "M*A*S*H" (Hawkeye the lovable womanizer), "I Love Lucy" (Lucy the lovable gossip), and "The Andy Griffith Show" (Otis the lovable drunkard), for example. Fornication, slander, and drunkenness are undoubtedly just as sinful as homosexuality (see, for example, 1 Cor. 6:9–10), but as far as I know, the Christian Right to this day has never mounted a single organized protest against "M*A*S*H," "I Love Lucy," or "The Andy Griffith Show," which are still widely televised in syndication. (In fact, during a stroll through a Christian bookstore a few years ago I noticed a series of evangelical Sunday School/Bible study materials which purport to actually *study* episodes of "The Andy Griffith Show" as moral exemplars, on the premise that the show contains many great biblical truths. It is difficult to imagine the authors creating a similar series based on "Ellen." But I did notice that the character of Otis did not feature prominently in the Andy Griffith materials.)

Such inconsistencies prompt an obvious question: Is it possible that the Christian Right's agenda regarding television programming is due less to biblical teachings than to the influence of secular conservative subculture, which reserves its most virulent condemnation for homosexuality?

Chapter Eight

Making Men Moral

Some Christians have made highly sophisticated arguments in favor of legal moralism. These more refined arguments recognize and attempt to solve some of the problems we have noted in preceding chapters. A fine example in this vein is Robert George's book *Making Men Moral*.[1] Professor George has set forth his claims with academic rigor, and he makes a forceful and scholarly case for legal moralism. His book represents some of the best the other side of the argument has to offer, and as an example of this scholarship it is worthy of extended consideration here.

Robert George is a legal moralist. Very much in the tradition of Aristotle and Aquinas, George argues that the law should be used to promote virtue. Laws should be made to eliminate some (but *only* some) otherwise available opportunities to choose to do wrong. In other words, Professor George believes lawmakers should make laws outlawing certain carefully-selected wrongful acts on the basis of the acts' moral wrongness. These laws are made not for the purpose of preventing sin or wrong altogether, but to create what George calls a "good moral ecology"—an environment conducive to virtue. In essence, the lawmaker should make law so as to reduce the total amount of *temptation* in a society, for the good of the governed. But upon what basis should he pick and choose which wrongful acts or temptations to outlaw?

The answer, predictably, is quite complex, and requires some background analysis. Professor George astutely recognizes, as we have recognized in Chapters 6 and 7, that righteousness requires free choice as a precondition; therefore he explicitly rejects the idea that laws can make people good *directly*. In other words, a person who refuses to do a bad act only because it is illegal is still sinning, notwithstanding his nonparticipation in the bad act. However, George contends that certain "anti-vice" laws have a role to play in making people good *indirectly*, or (as he puts it) "helping people to *make themselves* moral,"[2] as long as the laws correctly prioritize true good over true evil. George argues that moral good and evil are objectively fixed and knowable, and that religious faith is one way (though not the only way) of knowing them. Once the enlightened statesman (or voter) distinguishes true good from true evil, he will know which acts are truly good and which are truly evil. Then he may outlaw a carefully selected set of the truly evil ones.

Although George does not advocate outlawing all truly evil acts, he proposes the following test for determining, on a case-by-case basis, whether a particular behavior should be outlawed as impermissible vice:

A behavior should be outlawed if:

1. The behavior is truly "wrong" according to the objective moral code, and
2. There are no countervailing prudential considerations that militate against adopting the law. For these purposes, "prudential considerations" could include things like unenforceability, unfairness (such as discriminatory enforcement), or anticipated widespread resentment or rebellion toward the law.

In George's view, as long as we accurately define "right" and "wrong," and properly list and weigh the prudential considerations, legislation meeting his criteria is justifiable, and such laws can help in shaping a society that will provide an environment friendly to virtue and hostile to some of the most seductive and harmful vices. That environment, in turn, will protect people from some moral harm, at least at the margins, because over time, their characters will become stronger and more virtuous than otherwise as a result of their (unwillingly) refraining from the outlawed vices.

I think a great number of Christians today might agree with at least the fundamentals of Professor George's position, although they perhaps would not frame the argument as clearly as he has. It is indeed an attractive argument, the more so because few particular moral absolutes and prudential considerations have been specified. Its paternalistic appeal might win many adherents on the Left as well as the Right, at least until a particular list of moral absolutes becomes an explicit part of the package. But despite the elegance of George's argument, I believe his prescription suffers from several defects, which I have organized around three critical questions: (1) Is the prescription workable in practice? (2) Will the prescription in fact lead to "better" or "more virtuous" people? and most importantly for the Christian, (3) Is the prescription reconcilable with God's will?

1. IS THE PRESCRIPTION WORKABLE IN PRACTICE?

Liberals in the Lockean tradition have long warned of the practical difficulties inherent in any attempt to legally ban evil—which, to be honest, is exactly what George proposes to do, albeit to an admittedly limited extent. These are the sorts of practical dangers that lay persons will often mention when they express doubt about whether the law should be used to help create a more moral society. Academics may have a tendency to discount such "obvious" answers, preferring instead to search for some deeper truth. But sometimes the truth *is* obvious. The common sense approach is sometimes the best. This might be a good time to remind ourselves of these obvious practical obstacles, already discussed in Chapter 6, because George's prescription is not exempt from them.

First, no human being can know good from evil perfectly, or apply that knowledge inerrantly. We don't even know the scope of what we don't know. Any project that depends (as George's does) on a policy maker's ability to judge good from evil *for each behavior presented* is guaranteed to write our human misconceptions into the law, in ways that we will not be able to detect even if we mean well. And the narrower the class of conduct at issue, the less likely that our moral judgment about that conduct is accurate. Humility counsels against outlawing specific types of behavior just because we deem them to be immoral.

Second, setting up a framework for banning evil is particularly dangerous because "we" may not always control the government, and those who do may not always "mean well." Nor should we expect them to be as enlightened as we are.[3] Majoritarian democracy does not provide any assurance that a particular group or moral code will always control the government. Unless the government is limited beforehand, by constitution or some other mechanism, we must expect majorities to trample minority rights from time to time in any democracy. And the winds of culture have always blown the untethered mores of the majority hither and yon. Each rising generation is enchanted by new moral fads. Once one realizes that one's own current moral preferences may not always command majority support, it becomes easy for each of us to see the need for some preset limits on the legal entrenchment of someone's particularized conceptions of the good life.[4]

Third, even if we always control the government and always ban only what is truly evil, we cannot assume those who are governed by our laws will generally agree that they are good laws. We cannot hope to reach a societal consensus on every vice law we pass. While we might hope, for the reasons just considered, to reach a consensus on the need for constitutional limits on legal moralism, we cannot realistically expect to reach a critical mass of societal consensus on any particular moral code for legal enactment, especially as regards "victimless crimes." And we need some degree of societal consensus if our laws are to be effective. The secular law that is widely disapproved and widely ignored by the masses is completely useless—or worse. Thus, a prescription for banning evil is a recipe for other evils, like divisiveness, discontent, and disrespect for law, that may well infect society because of our efforts.

So much for the classical liberal response to proposals for outlawing vice. But George's particular prescription poses additional practical difficulties in implementation. These further problems stem from the fact that George has provided a number of exceptions, which he terms "prudential considerations," to his general rule that truly wrong acts should be outlawed. These exceptions are not defined in detail, but they at least seem to be quite broad.[5] If George did not intend them to be broad, they seem useless and his prescription Draconian; but if they are in fact as broad as they seem, they will be likely to defeat his purpose. One of his prudential considerations in particular merits critical analysis: Like Aquinas, he opposes laws that are contrary to "the customs of the country," even when those laws would forbid truly immoral acts. In granting this concession, George may have created an exception so wide as to swallow his rule, in the process nearly embracing the fallacy that he accuses Patrick Devlin of embracing.

George vs. Devlin

As we have noted, George attempts to soften the blow of his prescription by providing numerous exceptions to the general rule that wrong acts should be outlawed. He calls these exceptions "prudential considerations," and they include, notably, the need to "tailor the criminal law to the character of the people and the moral state of their society in order to avoid the likely bad consequences of imposing on people burdens they cannot bear."[6] In another passage he states this exception as follows: Vice should not be prohibited "where, given the condition of the people, the prohibition is likely to be futile or, worse yet, productive of more serious vices or wrongs. ... [L]aws, if they are to serve the common good of leading the people to virtue, must be 'according to the customs of the country', and 'adapted to place and time.' "[7] This is all very reminiscent of Aquinas.

But George is unwilling to allow the moral code undergirding his morals legislation to be completely determined by community consensus. He criticizes Patrick Devlin for arguing in *The Enforcement of Morals*[8] that morals laws are legitimate exactly to the extent they are necessary to preserve social cohesion or integration in a given community. George argues, to the contrary, that "a concern for social cohesion *per se* is not a sufficient ground for enforcing moral obligations."[9] It becomes a sufficient ground "only if that morality is true."[10] After all, communities can cohere around *immoral* values, George asserts, and such communities have no moral claim even to preservation, much less integration and cohesion. Therefore, the bare fact that a society has reached a consensus that an act is immoral should not, by itself, justify banning that act, even if failing to ban the act leads that society to lose its cohesion.[11]

Thus, George at first seems somewhat contradictory on this point. On the one hand he argues against Devlin by claiming that *societal consensus* on morality should *not* affect morals legislation—only the "true" morality should—but on the other hand he claims, following Aquinas, that societal consensus *should* count as a possible reason *not* to enact a particular morals law. If George is being consistent, he must be saying that if a societal consensus supports an inaccurate moral view, that fact should never count *in favor of*, but should sometimes count *against*, morals legislation. In other words, his view would be: We should never outlaw a morally permissible act just because there is a societal consensus that the act is immoral, but sometimes we should *legalize* a truly *immoral* act just because society thinks it is *not* immoral. So in George's view, societal consensus about morality should cause us to *legalize* some *immoral* acts, but not to *outlaw* any *morally permissible* acts. But why should this be true? Why should the presumption run in only one direction—the direction of *liberty*? Is it possible that George is recognizing some *inherent* value in liberty, even the liberty to act immorally?

However we answer that question, it is clear that George is no libertarian, even where moral considerations are not involved. In fact, he advocates outlawing some acts that are not truly immoral and do not lead to immorality—for example, practicing accounting without a license—because the acts are "dangerous" to society.[12] So according to George, it would seem that legitimate regulatory laws must satisfy two independent criteria: (1) There must be no good (or "prudential") reasons *not* to ban the act in question; and (2) the act in question must be either truly immoral or dangerous to the public. This indicates that there is a substantial two-pronged burden of proof on anyone who claims an act should be outlawed; the default rule is "legalize everything." Again, this seems to suggest a priority on liberty.

But importantly, the "public danger" justification for law, found in George's second criterion above, must necessarily be defined in terms of *societal consensus* rather than an objective standard. There is simply no possible objective standard for measuring "dangerousness." If a morally permissible act is "truly dangerous" to the public, George clearly believes the lawmaker is entitled to ban it—but how shall the lawmaker know whether it is "truly dangerous" or not? And how shall he quantify the extent of the danger? How shall a lawmaker decide, for example, whether the morally permissible act of driving a car is "truly dangerous" to society? Are there any objective standards for him to follow in answering this question?

"Danger" would seem to be more like "ugliness" than like "wrongness." Even if "wrongness" can be objectively determined, *danger*, like beauty and ugliness, is in the eye of the beholder. Moreover, "dangerous" and "safe" are only two of the discrete points along a whole continuum of "dangerousness"—not (like "right," "wrong," and "neither right nor wrong") a complete set of all possible points. In other words, a lampshade can be "somewhat attractive" and an activity can be "slightly dangerous," but a behavior cannot be "somewhat morally wrong." Although it is possible in theory to construct a rational, objective test for deciding whether a given act is morally wrong, there is no conceivable objective standard for deciding what "truly dangerous" means, much less for deciding which acts fall into that category. At most, we could quantify "risks" of certain events occurring as a result of a certain act—but where knowledge of a given risk might make one person conclude that the act is "dangerous," the same information might lead another person to conclude the opposite about that same act, and there is no objective standard by which to judge who is "right." So when George says public officials can outlaw acts that are "dangerous" to the public, there is no way to give "dangerous" an objective content or meaning, outside of its meaning to particular individuals.

Thus when George says "dangerous" acts may be outlawed, he is simply saying public officials can outlaw whatever acts are determined by *societal consensus* to be dangerous to the public.[13] We don't wish to outlaw everything that some wise person regards as dangerous; we only outlaw "dangers" that *most of us perceive* as dangerous.

But now George's position about "societal consensus" is even more unclear. It seems that under George's prescription, societal consensus actually *should* cause us to outlaw some morally permissible acts—as long as that societal consensus is about the *dangerousness* of the act rather than its *immorality*. George seems to be saying that although "a concern for social cohesion *per se* is not a sufficient ground for enforcing moral obligations," such a concern may nevertheless be a sufficient ground for enforcing *other* obligations, required by criminal laws motivated by something besides morality.

Now whatever the fine distinction might be between the legal enforcement of "moral obligations" and the legal enforcement of criminal laws generally, the person convicted of violating a criminal law prohibiting some act he viewed as safe and morally permissible is not likely to appreciate it. In fact, if a certain act is to be outlawed, it matters little whether the justification stems from societal moral views or societal perceptions of danger. Either way, the act is criminalized because of societal opinions contrary to the opinions of the actor. Either way, minority views have been devalued, and minority rights have perhaps been trampled, by the tyranny of the majority—which is presumably the very result George wishes to avoid by disallowing popularly supported morals legislation when the forbidden acts are in fact morally permissible.

It seems, then, that George is not so far from Devlin's position as George would have us believe. Devlin claimed that no criminal law should be made without societal consensus to support it. George seems to agree completely. Devlin further claimed that if a societal consensus exists that a certain act should be outlawed, then a due concern for social cohesion demands that the act be outlawed. George seemingly agrees with this rule too, except in situations where society views the act as *immoral* (specifically, if society *wrongly* views the act as immoral, or if society *rightly* views the act as immoral but there are prudential reasons why the law will not likely accomplish its goal). In such cases George would oppose the law that Devlin would support; but otherwise, George would support the law, and for the same reasons as Devlin.

This insight opens up a whole range of distasteful and even irrational legislative possibilities that would be justified by George's prescription, in full agreement with Devlin's theory. For example, suppose a societal consensus develops that allowing blacks and whites to mingle in public, or in public accommodations, would pose a danger to public safety.[14] George's prescription, like Devlin's, seems to require the enlightened lawmaker to pass a law requiring racial segregation in public places or accommodations, even if he knows that in fact racial integration is morally permissible and poses no "real danger" to public safety. However, according to George and contrary to Devlin, he should *not* have passed the same law if a societal consensus had developed that racial mixing is "merely" *immoral* and not necessarily dangerous. But because society decided that racial mixing is "dangerous," he must ban it even if it is not. This seems silly, and not at all what we (or George?) want our enlightened lawmaker to be considering as he decides what to ban.

The Wide Exception of "Widespread Acceptance"

However one interprets George's views of Devlin, it is at least clear that George would *not* favor outlawing immoral acts that are accepted by societal consensus to be morally permissible, or acts that "average people in the society [cannot] generally abstain from committing."[15] Thus, whenever a particular vice is widely accepted and practiced in the society, that vice should not be outlawed, no matter how immoral it is (at least, if the vice is not the type of vice, like murder, that *must* be "forbidden in every society, for the simple reason that social life is impossible unless [it is] prohibited").[16]

That is a wide exception indeed, and one which might produce some very distasteful results. For example, in racist societies, surely "social life" is not made "impossible" by societal adoption of race-based slavery. On this basis an enlightened statesman following George's prescription in such a society could actually conclude that he should not legally forbid race-based slavery as immoral. George's exception for societal consensus is so wide, in fact, as to make his rule (that government should sometimes legislate for purely moral reasons) largely meaningless. In what sense can the government legislate a "good moral ecology" if it cannot even legally forbid widespread slavery? Isn't this sort of situation the very reason why we might *want* a government that legislates for moral reasons?

Other "Prudential Considerations"

Even putting aside the prudential consideration about societal consensus, George's prescription remains unworkable, because his other "prudential considerations" are just as broad. According to George, these other considerations, concerns that could defeat an impulse to ban a certain vice, would include such things as the need to avoid placing too much power in the hands of governments likely to abuse it; the need to direct limited attention and resources to the worst offenses; the need for enforceable law; and the danger that criminalizing certain vices may strengthen organized crime and make the vices more widespread, dangerous, or expensive to society.[17] These considerations may be interpreted very broadly or very narrowly, depending on who is in charge of enforcing George's prescription. In any case, they must somehow be weighed against the enormity of the wrong one is seeking to prohibit. Presumably, the greater the wrongfulness of the vice, the more likely it should be banned, regardless of these prudential considerations.

But how shall we perform this weighing? More specifically, should it matter for our calculation how many people are tempted by the vice, or should we consider only how qualitatively "bad" the vice is? If it matters how many people are affected by the vice, then how many people in the community must be tempted by a certain vice before it rises to the level of a temptation that lawmakers ought legally to prohibit? One person? One hundred? Ten thousand? A certain percentage of the community population? And with regard to qualitative rankings of vices, how shall we decide which vices are the most evil? The sale of alcohol may tempt some to be drunk; the sale of beauty magazines may tempt others to focus improper attention on external appearance; the sale of television sets may tempt still others to be materialistic and covetous, or lustful. These are real, widespread vices, and they are deadly (at least from a Christian perspective).

Of course, in a first effort to describe a theory of this sort, Professor George should not be expected to resolve all the practical difficulties inherent in particular applications of it. Still, if the theory obviously presents numerous practical problems and gives us no hint how they might be resolved, we are at some point entitled to conclude that the theory is unworkable. George in fact recognizes that he needs a rational standard to distinguish the temptations posed by, say, the sale of pornography, from the temptations posed by, say, the sale of fashion magazines. In the arena of speech and the press, then, he proposes the following standard:

There should be no content-based restrictions on speech unless:

1. the speech to be restricted is not the sort of speech that makes for true communication and cooperation, but rather, is something else, such as gratuitous abuse (false advertising, oral hate speech insulting the live audience, etc.); or
2. the cooperation made possible by the speech in question is for manifestly evil ends (negotiations surrounding criminal conspiracies, etc.); or
3. the speech in question is likely to result in serious harms or injustices, or prevent the realization of important goods (revealing national security secrets, incitement to riot, etc.).[18]

But at this point one is prompted to ask, again, how this test could be workable in practice. For the purposes of applying each prong of this test, how are we to distinguish pornography, or even obscenity, from fashion magazines? For that matter, how are we to distinguish between speech that results in "true communication and cooperation" and speech that results in hatred and division? "Trust me—I know it when I see it" is not a very convincing answer, especially when given by a government official with censorship powers. Perhaps this difficulty is a "prudential consideration" that, according to George, would be powerful enough to militate against any prohibition of either fashion magazines or obscene expression (after all, he does say that usually neo-Nazi publications should be permitted due to such prudential considerations).[19] But it seems unlikely that George would interpret his prudential considerations that broadly, for he seemingly favors banning at least the grosser forms of obscene pictures and words.[20] Under George's test, if obscenity is to be banned, it must be because obscenity either does not make for "true communication and cooperation" or is "likely to result in serious harms and injustices." In practice, it is the enlightened lawmaker who must have reached this conclusion in order to ban particular pictures or words. Thus, the practical effect of George's prescription is to entrust government officials (or perhaps a majority of voters) with the power to decide, case by case, whether a given sort of picture or idea is "not the sort of speech that makes for true communication and cooperation" or is "likely to result in serious harms and injustices."

That kind of standard invites the lawmaker to forbid whatever speech he believes to be divisive or unjust. This is just the type of ad hoc decision the anti-majoritarian First Amendment, and our political ideals, have attempted to place beyond the powers of government legislators and executives, and indeed the voting public. Currently our courts do not interpret the First Amendment to forbid all legislation banning gross obscenity and incitements to violence; nevertheless, the courts have required such laws to satisfy rigorous tests in order to assure that they are not grounded merely in subjective evaluations of the sort George is proposing—for example, determinations that the speech is "unjust" or "does not promote true communication and cooperation." In allowing lawmakers to decide which speech is too unjust or divisive to be heard, George seems to be narrowing freedom of speech, trusting lawmakers and the majoritarian process to make only reasonable restrictions of speech. This represents a significant shift, for American political theory has never been so trusting of either government officials or voters.

Of course, every theory of policymaking must admit the possibility of differing interpretations of that theory's general standards. (Regarding the Choice Principle, for example, there will necessarily be somewhat differing interpretations of the standard "maximize overall Choice.") But the wiggle room provided by George's "prudential considerations" may be so large as to make the prescription unimaginable in concrete cases.[21] This example only addresses the "speech" aspect of George's prescription, but his theory would suffer the same practical difficulties in the context of other proposed bans as well.

2. WILL THE PRESCRIPTION LEAD TO "BETTER" OR "MORE VIRTUOUS" PEOPLE?

George argues that his prescription will lead to a "better society," by which he means a more virtuous one. Let us evaluate whether he is correct on either claim.

Will the Prescription Lead to a "Better" Society?

George assumes, without explicitly endorsing any particular religious or ethical beliefs, that a "better" (or preferable) society is a more virtuous one. But without reference to particular religious or ethical standards, it is not obvious that a more virtuous society is always preferable to societies having other advantages. For example, a society which follows George's prescription and bans only selected vices, choosing those vices not because they are most evil but on the morally arbitrary grounds of enforceability or the like, might end up forbidding a host of minuscule and victimless vices while allowing some of the most egregious evils to go unpunished for practical reasons. Such a legal framework might be so internally inconsistent (or even discriminatory?) as to be unjust and morally inferior to the laws of a society where no acts are banned solely on the basis of their moral wrongness. The ethical principle underlying such an evaluation would be that it is inherently unjust to be so *inconsistent* in banning wrong.

Or to take another example, imagine two communities. One is an Amish community, providing its members what George would call a "good moral ecology." The laws of this community strictly forbid most vice while also providing lots of training in virtues (like unselfishness). But in this community, there are very few real alternatives to the Amish lifestyle and very little knowledge of any. The other community is a secular community which provides its members what George might call a "bad moral ecology," a community in which vice as such is virtually unlimited by law (say, a slightly more extreme version of Las Vegas, Nevada). In this community people have lots of incentives to be selfish and many opportunities to do wrong, but also lots of opportunities to do good and lots of knowledge of the alternatives. There is also much diversity and freedom in the second community, and people may choose among many different paths claiming to lead to goodness. How does one show, without reference to particular religious or ethical standards, that the Amish community is "better" than Las Vegas? To say the Amish community is "better," one must systematically discount values like autonomy and diversity in favor of other values such as unselfishness. And from a secular perspective, there is no obvious justification for devaluing autonomy this way across the board. From a secular perspective, often it is better to be free than self-sacrificial.

The problem is that, in declaring autonomy to be (merely) an "instrumental" good,[22] George implicitly devalues autonomy in favor of a list of intrinsic moral virtues, without explicitly endorsing any religious worldview at all. He essentially assumes, presumably through some theory of natural law, that even atheists will rationally conclude that unselfishness, temperance, and the like are more valuable than autonomy or diversity. I doubt that this conclusion would be a rational one for an atheist to reach, just as I doubt that many atheists would in fact embrace it. Without reference to particular religious teachings, George will have difficulty showing that a more virtuous society is always preferable to other societies.

Will the Prescription Lead to a More Virtuous Society?

Notwithstanding George's particular approach, Christian faith might easily lead us to agree that more virtuous societies (defined as those in which more people do God's will more often) are preferable to less virtuous societies.[23] After all, the Christian may appeal to his own faith and a set of assumptions about God's will for man that George never explicitly endorses. But even if we conclude in this way that virtuous societies are preferable to sinful ones, and thus that freedom is only valuable because it leads to virtue, we need not also conclude that limiting freedom through George's prescription leads to a more virtuous society.

George claims that more people will be more virtuous, at least in the long run, when laws eliminate their ability to choose certain bad behaviors today, and that this is so regardless of their current wrongful desires to engage in the prohibited conduct. If his claim is true, however, it must be because one of the following is true: Either (1) the long-time *desire* to do a bad act, a desire George admits is wrong in itself, is generally *less* wrong, *less* character-weakening, *less* corrupting, than a long history of actually *doing* the bad act; or else (2) a legal prohibition of the act will cause people's desire for that act to fade in the long run, so that eventually, they will not only abstain from the bad act, but will do so *willingly*, thus making a virtuous choice.

Let us consider the first possibility first. Is the longstanding desire to do a bad act somehow less wrong or less corrupting than a long history of actually doing the bad act? George admits that "laws . . . cannot compel the internal acts of reason and will which make an act of external conformity to the requirements of morality a moral act."[24] So how can vice laws lend anyone moral aid? He explains, "It is not that the person deterred solely by the law from wrongdoing realizes a moral good by not engaging in the vice. . . . Rather, it is that he avoids, albeit unwillingly, the bad impact of (further) involvement in the vice on his character."[25] Apparently, then, George means to distinguish "failing to realize a moral good" from "a bad impact upon one's character." He is claiming that although the person fails to realize a moral good, he unwillingly avoids a bad impact on his character.

But what is that "bad impact," exactly? If a person longs to participate in a vice, it is not self-evident that involvement (or "further involvement") in it has an additional bad impact on the person's character. Maybe the question boils down to this: Will people really become more morally corrupted, in the long run, by sleeping with a prostitute ten times, than by "merely" sinfully desiring ten times to sleep with one? This is an empirical question whose answer is not immediately obvious. George seems to be answering in the affirmative, but he certainly gives no empirical evidence to support this answer.

Instead of citing empirical evidence, George supports his view that bad acts corrupt by broadly claiming that "people become morally bad by yielding to vice."[26] But he has already admitted that these people are already morally bad for merely *desiring* to engage in the vice. In what sense do they become *more* "morally bad" by actually behaving the way they already want to behave?

More directly, the assertion that "people become morally bad by yielding to vice" represents a complex and contentious theological claim. Although it is unclear exactly what George means by "morally bad," such a claim might well be rejected by many traditions of Christian thought. Questions about what constitutes moral depravity or a choice to sin have been debated for millennia. While some philosophers through the ages undoubtedly have asserted that *bad acts* are the cause or beginning of moral depravity, many Christian thinkers have concluded that a person becomes morally bad (or morally corrupted) at an earlier point: the point he chooses to yield to temptation by *desiring* or *meditating upon* the wrong, whether or not he actually "yields to vice" by performing any sinful outward act.[27] Indeed, George himself admits that people are morally bad (or at least make a morally bad choice) when they merely *desire* to do a bad act—this is why laws can never make men moral directly. In any event, it would seem reasonable to assume that a chosen habit of bad *thoughts* can, in the long run, be at least as damaging to one's moral character as a habit of bad *deeds*. (Consider that a lifetime of bad *deeds*—and painful memories of them—has probably caused many to repent when a history of bad thoughts alone would not have impelled them to it.) How is it, then, that people who already desire the bad "become morally bad" (morally worse?) by engaging in bad behavior?

If people with evil thoughts do *not* become morally worse by engaging in bad behavior, George must be arguing that the legal prohibition of an act will cause people's desire for that act to fade in the long run, such that eventually, they will abstain from that act *willingly*, and thus make a virtuous choice. But is this true? This, again, is an empirical assertion that is not necessarily confirmed by intuition or evidence. George has not shown that it is even possible (not to mention likely) for the legal prohibition of any act to result in a long-term decrease in people's desire to commit that act. In fact, our intuition might lead us to suspect the opposite, under the theory that forbidden fruit always appears more desirable. Why then does George assume that people's desires for a vice will fade when they are denied access to it?

The answer may lie in George's view of the nature of vice. He seems to assume, without exactly saying so, that all vice is like the vice of drug abuse in important ways. In his view, since vice is so bad and harmful, people who choose to engage in vice, of any kind, are behaving irrationally. (Again one is reminded of Aquinas.) And since no one would be "irrational" willingly, the wrongdoers must be essentially addicted to those bad behaviors "against their will," in the way most hard drug addicts presumably are addicted to drugs "against their will." They are "out of their minds." Thus, if the opportunity to engage in a particular bad behavior is removed so that people are now unable to engage in it, all (or most of) the people who used to desire to engage in it will be forced to wean themselves off of it, at which point they will become rational again and stop desiring to engage in it. George's legal prescription, then, is essentially a "detox program" for vice.

Making George's assumptions explicit, as he does not, raises difficult questions. In what sense can anyone desire anything "against his will"? Even more importantly, as an empirical matter, do most people desire to commit evil acts only because they continue to commit them? (If so, what explains their desire to engage in the behavior *for the first time*?) Are most vices as habit-forming and reason-defeating as drug abuse? Or are choices to engage in them more occasional and less logic-overriding, more akin to a choice at one particular meal to eat chicken instead of fish? These, again, are empirical questions whose answers are not self-evident—but George seems to assume, without empirical proof, particular answers for each question.

Of course George's assumptions may be empirically correct as to some particular vices, like drug abuse itself; but even if a ban on some particular act might cause people's desire for that act to fade in the long run, the legal prohibition of an act is incapable, by definition, of causing people to abstain from that act *willingly*. And it is willing abstention, not mere absence of desire, that is virtuous.

Virtue (or "morality") is, in George's own words, "above all an internal matter, a matter of rectitude in choosing: one becomes morally good precisely, and only, by doing the right thing for the right reason."[28] So willing abstention from a vice is a virtuous choice, but lack of desire to commit it is not. George is surely correct about this. (How virtuous is it of me, for example, to "willingly" abstain from drug abuse, when I have no desire to abuse drugs?) But in order for any choice to be made willingly, it must also be made in an environment of available alternative options. In order for a choice of abstinence to be made willingly, then, it must, at a minimum, be made under circumstances in which the rejected act is both physically possible and legal. In other words, refusing to abuse heroin, for example, under circumstances where possession of heroin is illegal or where I have no access to heroin, is not a truly free choice, and therefore such a "choice" cannot be said to be either willing or virtuous to any significant extent.

Or to take another example, imagine a concentration camp inmate who is unjustly persecuted by a guard at the camp. He may choose, during his imprisonment, to hate the guard (an understandable choice, but surely not a virtuous one), or he may choose to love and forgive the guard (an extremely virtuous choice). We say he may choose because he has real options, and for the same reason we can call one of the choices "virtuous." But in what sense can the prisoner "choose" to abstain from imprisoning the guard? If he claimed he had "chosen" not to imprison the guard, would we believe him? Would we call this "virtuous choice"? Of course not. Imprisoning the guard was impossible for him.

Similarly, if a particular vice is prohibited by law, most of us do not truly "choose" to abstain from it, for we have no realistic option besides abstention. For that reason such a "choice" would not be, in any real sense, "virtuous." For example, in American society today, the "choice" to abstain from theft or murder is not deemed to be particularly virtuous, or voluntary. Murder and theft are forbidden by laws which are reliably enforced, so there is no real freedom to murder or steal. Under those circumstances, abstinence is not significantly voluntary, and for that reason it cannot be deemed significantly virtuous. All this raises grave doubts about the potential for George's prescription to produce more virtuous people through legal prohibitions.

In continuing to consider whether George's prescription leads to a more virtuous society, perhaps we can step back and rephrase the question in a more common-sense way: Assuming that our goal should be to reduce the overall quantity of sin or evil in the society, why should we believe that laws against a few temptations are likely to do this? Everyone (including George) agrees that we cannot remove all temptations, through law or any other mechanism, and that people can and will sin regardless of whether they are able to engage in bad outward behaviors. Temptation will always be with us, and so will sin—it's just a question of how much. George is essentially claiming that his prescription will reduce the total quantity of sin in the long run. But will the removal of a subset of temptations (opportunities to engage in bad acts) really do this, or not? Empirical uncertainties persist: If a particular vice is outlawed, will an unpredicted "black market" form for that good or service or behavior, so that those who used to be tempted will still engage in the vice, and continue to sin just as much as before? Will those people instead merely select different vices, ones that we were not able or willing to outlaw, and continue to sin just as much as before? Will they now sinfully *desire* to commit bad acts rather than sinfully engaging in them, and thus continue to sin just as much as before? Once again, these are empirical questions whose answers are not self-evident; and yet the entire project of reducing sin through law can only be justified if one assumes particular answers to each of these questions, for whichever vice is outlawed.

If my criticisms have merit, then George has not shown that outlawing vice helps men to make themselves moral. From a Christian perspective, one can agree with his perfectionist assumption that the law should provide an environment conducive to maximal righteousness and virtue; but that assumption need not lead to his conclusion that the law should outlaw certain evil acts in a way that limits overall human Choice. In fact, a preference for a virtue-encouraging environment might well lead us to the Choice Principle itself, for only in an environment of maximum Choice can maximum virtue be realized. If Choice is a necessary precondition to virtue, as George himself states, then it would seem that increasing total freedom of choice would increase total virtue, while reducing total freedom of choice would reduce total virtue.

3. IS THE PRESCRIPTION RECONCILABLE WITH GOD'S WILL FOR SOCIETY?

To be fair, George never explicitly addresses the question of God's will, since he is not writing from an explicitly or exclusively religious viewpoint. Instead, he attempts to answer the similar, but slightly different, question of whether his theory will lead to a better or more virtuous society. But the question of God's will is the precise question the committed Christian must ultimately confront, as George never does.

It is important to see that this is not necessarily the same question as question #2 above. In other words, just because George's legal prescription leads to better and more virtuous people, that doesn't mean God approves of the prescription. Although we assume God wants every person to be virtuous, we need not also assume that God approves of every means possible to bring about that end. God is not necessarily a utilitarian, at least not on every issue. For example, if God cared about nothing but maximizing human virtue (or maximizing virtuous human acts), so that this end justified any means necessary to accomplish it, perhaps God could have "hard-wired" human beings to be virtuous continually (or at least to choose virtuous acts continually). Even more to the point, God surely could have created the Garden of Eden *without* a Tree of the Knowledge of Good and Evil, thereby eliminating man's access to the particular wrongful choice that introduced sin into the world. In that case the Garden of Eden would certainly have exemplified the "good moral ecology" George advocates. But God did not choose to create such a good moral ecology. If God had wanted to eliminate human opportunities to choose the bad, he could have accomplished this completely and perfectly, far beyond the modest abilities of George's legislative agenda. Perhaps God's refusal to do this should give us pause.

Does God in fact want our temptations to be minimized? No biblical text of which I am aware seems to support this view. On the contrary, at least two biblical texts regarding temptation seem to imply that, while God does not tempt anyone to sin, such temptations can accomplish useful, godly results.[29] If God does not minimize the temptations we face, our attempts to generally minimize the temptations faced by others must not spring from an accurate imitation of him.

I have argued that one reasonable understanding of the New Testament is that God desires governments to prevent and punish only victimizing activities. In so doing, governments will maximize human opportunities for Choice, even if opportunities for bad (and good) choices are increased thereby. To use the non-religious terminology George employs, my argument for the Choice Principle might be characterized as a moral perfectionist argument that freedom to choose, even freedom to choose wrongly, is an instrumental good which produces virtue, and since Choice is essential to all virtue, it is an instrumental good that ought to be maximized by law.

But George disagrees that we should maximize the freedom to choose *wrongly*; he wishes to allow a right to free choice only when people are in fact using the freedom wisely, making good choices. He supposes that in order to prioritize Choice as the Choice Principle would, in the face of evidence that people are choosing wrongly, one must endorse a strong moral right to choose wrong, and Choice must somehow be viewed as an *intrinsic* good—something which is good or virtuous for its own sake—and not merely an instrumental good, valuable only to the extent it contributes to the realization of some intrinsic good. Upon this assumption, he proceeds to attack the notion of a strong moral right to choose wrong, claiming that any moral right to choose wrong is so weak that it cannot possibly provide a principled justification for governmental non-interference with a particular immoral choice.[30]

But when I argue that freedom is an instrumental good that ought to be maximized, I am not supposing a moral right to choose wrong. What I am supposing is that there is *no* moral right to *prohibit someone else's* wrongful choice as such. This is a very different claim (as George explicitly recognizes, see below) from the claim of a moral right to choose wrong. In other words, rather than asking, "What moral principle gives Joe the right to choose a sinful behavior?" I think we should be asking, "What moral principle gives us the right to take away, without Joe's consent, his opportunity to engage in a sinful behavior?"

We have already considered whether God wants our temptations to be minimized. But once we begin examining the morality of the *legislator's* behavior, rather than any supposed right of the one who is tempted, the question about minimizing temptations also changes. Rather than the question, "Does God want my temptations to be minimized?" the more relevant question in this context is: "Does God want us to minimize the temptations of others?"[31]

And this latter question is indeed worthy of the serious consideration of any Christian who considers adopting George's prescription for lawmaking.

As an approach to answering that question, let us consider an example involving video games. Suppose I want you someday voluntarily to limit your exposure to video games, for your own good, because I am convinced they are addictive and bad for your mental and social development. It *might* be a virtuous idea to immediately and forcefully restrict your access to video games—*if* you are my ten-year-old child.[32] But what if you are a forty-year-old stranger? Is it morally right for me to forcefully restrict your access to such "tempting" activities? What if I only want to restrict your access to the *most addictive* video games—will that justify the restriction? Surely our intuitions about the ways parents may legitimately treat their minor children have little bearing on how the government, or any of us individually, may legitimately treat a mentally healthy adult we have never met.

Recall that George seems to view people as "addicts" to various harmful vices—in much the same way heroin addicts are addicted to heroin. He also seemingly views each of us as having a moral duty to destroy each other's "heroin" whenever we get the chance. In this way, he assumes, the addicts will be unwillingly weaned away from their habit until they just don't want to engage in it anymore, at which point they will have "made themselves moral" and virtue will be increased. The heroin thieves will then be heroes, having played a useful role in the creation of this new virtue. Suppose for the moment that George's view of the addictive nature of vice is correct. We should ask ourselves, not whether it is morally right to abuse heroin, but whether it is morally right to steal and destroy other people's heroin, literally or figuratively, in the name of creating new virtue. Is it morally right for me to kidnap and tie up drug addicts against their will, in order to free them of their vice? Is it morally right to kidnap and "de-program" cult members against their will, for their own good? Whatever our answers might be if the addict were our fourteen-year-old child, the paternalism and force involved in these scenarios becomes much more morally repugnant when the addict is a mentally healthy adult we have never met.

As we consider exercising paternalism toward others, we would do well to recall that each of us is, in a sense, God's child, which means that God has a more legitimate right to exercise paternalistic force over us than any of us has to exercise the same force over our fellows. And yet God does not seem to exercise this "right." Specifically, he does not, as far as we know, forcefully remove from us any opportunities to sin.[33] How then may his children presume to know that he wants them to exercise such power over other people?

Again, in claiming that Christians have no moral right to forcefully limit others' access to vice as such, I am not claiming a moral right to choose wrong. Nor am I arguing that Choice has intrinsic rather than instrumental value. Instead, I am arguing that the instrumental value of Choice is so necessary to virtue that it ought to be protected despite evidence of its misuse. And I am arguing that Christians have no moral right to deprive others of Choice, even when those others make wrong choices that they have no right to make.

But George apparently believes we have a constant duty to minimize temptations. He first admits that even though people do not have the moral right to perform immoral acts, the government may be morally required to legalize some of these acts, or even to grant someone a private cause of action against other private parties who would interfere with the person's choice to perform a certain immoral act.[34] These claims are quite consistent with the Choice Principle. But George argues that this governmental moral duty to protect liberty is only occasional. It is not the necessary result of the wrongdoer's right to be left alone (which would presumably exist equally in every case of wrongdoing); rather, it only exists when there is some *other* moral consideration which outweighs the wrongness of the act itself. In other words, George believes that whenever we determine an act is truly immoral, morality demands that we prohibit it, unless some countervailing moral consideration (say, the impossibility of nondiscriminatory enforcement, which would render the prohibition fundamentally unfair) imposes a moral duty on us not to interfere with this particular type of act.

It is easy to see why there is always a background moral duty not to interfere with another's choice unless there is a good reason. But it is much less clear why the immorality of another's act should, by itself, provide such a good reason to interfere. George admits that it might sometimes be morally wrong to interfere with an action even if the action itself is morally wrong.[35] But George believes this is because the moral wrongness of the act merely provides one rational motive for interfering—one moral reason to interfere—which may sometimes be outweighed by moral (or other prudential) reasons *not* to interfere. George's lawmaker must not assume a general right to choose wrong; rather, for each particular vice, he must weigh the moral (and other) costs and benefits of interfering with the individual's choice. Sometimes the costs of legislating will outweigh the benefits, so liberty will be protected. In other cases, he concludes, the moral good realized by interfering will outweigh the resulting moral evil or other costs, and in such cases legislation, even if it reduces overall Choice, would be justified.[36]

Perhaps, indeed, there is no general moral right to choose wrong; but one need not conclude from this that government should sometimes be allowed to limit *overall Choice*. Of course, the lawmaker does not act immorally every time he bans conduct that happens to be morally wrong. But one might rationally assert that the lawmaker *does* act immorally (i.e., contrary to God's will) whenever he bans conduct *solely because* the conduct is morally wrong (i.e., contrary to God's will). And further, one might logically endorse this view while simultaneously claiming that there is no moral right to choose wrong. In other words, it is possible that the wrongness of an act does *not* by itself, as George supposes, automatically defeat the background assumption that it would be morally wrong to interfere with another's choice. The bare fact that an act is wrong, by itself, does not necessarily provide the government (or anyone else) any sort of rebuttable presumption that interference with that act would be morally *permissible*, much less morally required. Why should the moral status of another's act, by itself, affect the moral status of my interference with it—unless I am constantly under a (weak) moral duty to keep others from doing wrong acts?

So perhaps we have reached the true foundation of George's argument: the assertion that people (and governments) are constantly under some sort of rebuttable moral duty to forcefully prevent others from committing immoral acts. But one might doubt this assertion. I can understand that I am under a constant moral duty to keep *myself* from doing wrong—whether by outward act or inward thought—but why should I assume I am also under a moral duty to keep *others* from doing wrong *deeds*? (Even George would admit, I think, that no one is under a moral duty to keep others from having wrong *thoughts* or *desires*. Is this exception merely pragmatic?)

Of course it would be morally permissible (or perhaps even morally required) for me to keep a murderer from murdering if I can. But that is not because murder is *wrong* (although it is); rather, it is because murder *reduces overall Choice*. For the same reason, I should interfere to forcefully knock someone out of the way of a dangerous rock slide if I can, even though neither rock slides nor unknowingly walking under one is morally wrong. Forcefully prohibiting others' wrong deeds which do *not* lessen the autonomy of myself or third parties is a different matter.

It is difficult to choose relevant illustrations because it is difficult to say for sure what George would think all the countervailing moral reasons *not* to interfere might be in particular cases. But there are several examples that I find compelling. Prostitution, for instance, is an act that George thinks is morally wrong and should be outlawed ("interfered with") on that basis.[37] But does the bare fact that prostitution is wrong give one the moral right to interfere with another who is doing it? George apparently thinks so; in fact, with regard to prostitution at least, he claims that the wrongness of prostitution, by itself, outweighs any reasons *not* to interfere. But I am not so sure. Would I (individually) be morally entitled to (if I could) somehow shock prostitutes with a mild, very uncomfortable electric current every time they engage in this activity, in order to effectively prevent them from doing it? Or if I knew someone who frequented a brothel, would I be morally justified in forcefully eliminating his access to it—say, by convincing the brothel to relocate to a distant city against his wishes? I suspect that most people who believe prostitution is wrong would still feel inclined to think of me more as a busybody than a moral giant if I did such things. Why is this? Perhaps it is because there is no general moral duty to interfere forcefully with the immoral choices of others, while there *is* a general moral duty to refrain from limiting others' choices. For forceful interference with the choices of others to be morally permissible, their chosen acts must be more than simply morally wrong; their chosen acts must reduce overall Choice. This would explain why it might be morally permissible for me (as an individual) to interfere forcefully with a murderer's choice to murder, but not with a prostitute's choice to engage in consensual prostitution, or a drunkard's choice to drink alcohol.

Christianity supports this understanding of our duties. If there is a conflict between George's prescription and Christianity, perhaps it can be summarized as follows. George asserts that "where an attempt to enforce a moral duty would be self-defeating, one has a *conclusive* reason not to make the attempt. Consider the duty to repent of one's wrongdoing or the duty of someone who has been wronged to forgive the sincerely repentant wrongdoer. Given the nature of such duties, one cannot be coerced to fulfill them. . . . Moreover, any attempt to require repentance or forgiveness (by law or otherwise) is likely to do moral harm by, for example, encouraging the evils of hypocrisy and personal inauthenticity."[38] The committed Christian can easily agree with all this. But Christianity teaches that the goal of all law (and everything else) should be to achieve the result of more people being in a better relationship with God—which is a matter of the *heart*, not mere outward actions. The heart, as George admits, cannot be coerced. The only reason for making a *law*, however, is to coerce someone, to forcefully modify someone's outward actions. Therefore, to the Christian, perhaps *every* attempt to use the law to "enforce a moral duty" (even indirectly) will be "self-defeating," *by definition*. In Christ, the only "moral duty" is the moral duty of a right heart (and of course, right acts will flow therefrom).[39] The goal in every case is not merely that fewer people commit a given wrongful external behavior, but that more people grow closer to God, which is a very different matter.

Two analogies will help illustrate the point. Assume that a wife wants her husband to quit golf because it is addictive to him and is taking all his free time from his family. Mary, a friend of the wife, knows this. Suppose that Mary has connections at the country club such that she could secretly cancel the husband's membership without his knowledge, and in a way that he could not undo—he would simply believe the club had kicked him out. Assume also that he has no other place to play golf, so that without a membership, he would essentially be "forced" to give up the game and stay home with his family. The question is, will the wife get what she really wants if Mary secretly cancels the husband's country club membership? The nobler we assume the wife's character to be, the more natural it is to imagine her gently asking Mary to butt out. Perhaps what the wife really wants is the same thing God wants in his relationship with us: a partner that *voluntarily* gives up whatever may be destroying the relationship.

Or assume a man and a woman are beginning to date each other. If the man wants the woman to love him, does he get what he wants by getting a friend of his to somehow pull strings to make sure she never sees another man? Perhaps his friend could somehow secretly restrict her access to ten of the most attractive and eligible bachelors he knows, so that she will never meet them. Will the lovesick young man be well-advised to order his friend to put this scheme into action? This all sounds like the plot of a very ordinary farce; this is the type of plan that is sure to backfire on any man who adopts it. The Bible teaches that God is "lovesick," so to speak, for human beings. He longs for a loving, two-way relationship with each of us. It does not help God or further his will for us to keep our fellow human beings from seeing or experiencing God's rivals. But this is exactly what George and other legal moralists propose, in the name of helping people to make themselves moral. God has not called us to deny other people access to temptations. He has promised not to allow people to be tempted beyond what they can bear (1 Cor. 10:13). That should be enough for all of us.

Christian lawmaking must also be practical, and as a practical matter, Christians must recognize that one person's temptation is another person's salvation—that often an opportunity that leads some people to sin is productive of much good in others. We have observed this earlier in passing, but the point is especially important as we consider God's will explicitly. Are there not some temptations that Christians ought to allow, because they are potentially productive of good as well as evil? For example, if I can easily purchase good books, I might be tempted to read good books all the time instead of developing relationships, taking care of my family, praying, helping the less fortunate, or spreading the gospel. In other words, the availability of good books might tempt me to sinfully neglect weightier matters, and the temptation might be so powerful that I usually succumb to it. It would not, however, be justifiable for someone to ban good books on that basis, even if there are hundreds or thousands of people like me. George recognizes this point and works around it through a list of prudential considerations that can defeat a moral impulse to outlaw a particular wrongful act. Thus he, too, believes that there are some temptations (such as good books) that even good policymakers ought to allow, on the ground that the temptations are potentially productive of good as well as evil. But his point is: not *every* opportunity is potentially productive of good as well as evil. Putting it another way, his point is that some opportunities never produce good in anyone, and ought to be outlawed on that basis.

But is this in fact true? Is there some particular tempting opportunity to sin that has *never* resulted in good? Even prostitution and pornography, two vices George would outlaw, sometimes produce good in people, if for no other reason than the fact that a course of bad behavior sometimes leads to feelings of guilt and a realization of sin. If this is true, then no sin could be outlawed under George's prescription, because they would all fit under the prudential consideration of acts that are potentially productive of good as well as evil.

Perhaps George would respond that as long as prostitution leads to more bad than good (leads more people to be bad than good?), it is morally right to outlaw it. But besides sounding awfully utilitarian about moral absolutes, that response misses the point of this criticism. Mightn't *good books also* lead more people away from God than toward God? If so (and if George is correct about our general duty to minimize temptations), why is there *any* countervailing prudential consideration that outweighs, *for the Christian*, the moral impulse to ban them? What is more important than preventing people from being led away from God? (Certainly not the opportunity for the masses to read *Pride and Prejudice*.) For the Christian, then, prudential considerations must be jettisoned, once we start to believe we have a general duty to minimize temptations and the wrongdoing of others. There is no logical stopping point.

Professor George has noble values and goals which are naturally appealing to Christians. He prioritizes virtue, and he views law as an instrument to be used in preventing some bad choices, in order to bring about more virtue. Unfortunately, however, the plain truth seems to be that virtue cannot be engineered into man, or his environment, so easily. Even if the law is able to prevent some sinful behaviors, law and government will never be able to do what is most necessary to engender virtue: they will never be able to produce godly hearts. (Recall that this was precisely Paul's point about the law in Galatians 3-5.) Without this power, it may well be that the most that government force will be able to accomplish for God is the expansion of opportunities for human hearts to willingly choose the good. And that would mean nothing less than the priority of Choice.

NOTES

1. Robert P. George, *Making Men Moral* (New York: Oxford University Press, 1993).

2. George, *Making*, 1 (emphasis in original).

3. In the words of James Madison: "It is vain to say that enlightened statesmen will be able to adjust these clashing interests and render them all subservient to the public good. Enlightened statesmen will not always be at the helm." *The Federalist* No. 10 (James Madison) (Clinton Rossiter ed., Mentor paperback, 1961), 80.

4. Regarding the need for such preset limits on majoritarian democracy, see generally Friedrich A. von Hayek, *The Constitution of Liberty* (Chicago: University of Chicago Press, 1960); John Rawls, *A Theory of Justice* (Cambridge, Mass.: Harvard University Press, 1971). Of course, these preset limits may themselves be based upon more fundamental and widely shared notions of morality or justice.

5. In fact, George himself points out that in light of all his prudential considerations, including the consideration that there are multiple paths to the good, "it becomes clear that legislators concerned to uphold morality cannot prohibit all that much." George, *Making*, 40.

6. George, *Making*, 41–42.

7. George, *Making*, 32 (quoting with approval Thomas Aquinas, *Summa Theologiae*, I-II, q. 95, a.1 and a.3, and ibid., q. 96, a. 2).

8. Patrick Devlin, "The Enforcement of Morals," Maccabaean Lecture in Jurisprudence, *Proceedings of the British Academy*, 45 (1959), 129–51; reprinted under the title "Morals and the Criminal Law," in ibid., *The Enforcement of Morals* (London: Oxford University Press, 1965), 1–25.

9. George, *Making*, 71.

10. George, *Making*, 71.

11. George, *Making*, 79–80.

12. George, *Making*, 40–41.

13. If not, George needs to explain the objective standard for knowing the true extent of danger, and for knowing how much that ought to count in our weighing of countervailing considerations.

14. See *Plessy v. Ferguson*, 163 U.S. 537, 550–51 (1896), the infamous U.S. Supreme Court opinion establishing the "separate but equal" doctrine, where the majority alludes to the "preservation of the public peace and good order" as a possible motive for a Louisiana statute requiring racial segregation on railroad cars.

15. George, *Making*, 31.

16. The quotation in parentheses is taken from George, *Making*, 31.

17. George, *Making*, 42.

18. George, *Making*, 198–99.

19. See George, *Making*, 209.

20. See, for example, George, *Making*, 27 (seeming to endorse legal restrictions on the circulation of "pornography"); ibid., 42–43 ("Wise legislators whose goal is to encourage true moral goodness . . . seek to secure and maintain a moral ecology that is inhospitable . . . to . . . pornography. . . .").

21. Perhaps it goes without saying, but I believe it is easier to agree on and substantiate how a law or private act would influence overall freedom of choice, than to agree on and substantiate things like the *magnitude of the wrongness* of a particular

vice, or the "*value*" of any given piece of speech in contributing to "communication and cooperation."

22. George, *Making*, 176–80, 192.

23. Of course, I do not mean by this to suggest that George is not a committed Christian. But he does not premise his argument upon particular religious presuppositions. And as I have tried to show, this is precisely the problem with his assertion that values like temperance are more socially desirable than values like freedom.

24. George, *Making*, 1.

25. George, *Making*, 46.

26. George, *Making*, 44.

27. See, for example, Augustine, *City of God*, bk. 14, ch. 13; Augustine, *The Problem of Free Choice* 1.2.5–1.4.10; ibid., 1.15.31–1.16.35; Aquinas, *Summa*, II-I, q. 24, a. 1–4; Thomas à Kempis, *The Imitation of Christ*, bk. 1, ch. 13, sec. 5; Immanuel Kant, *Religion Within the Limits of Reason Alone*, Bk. 1, General Observation, pars. 3–5. See also Matt. 5:21–22, 27–28.

28. George, *Making*, 25 (emphasis omitted).

29. See James 1; Job 1–2, 42.

30. George, *Making*, 115, 124, 128.

31. Note that this is not the same question as, "Does God want *me* to tempt others?" I think the answer to *that* question is clearly no, and I feel relatively certain that most Christians would agree with me. But even though God does not want me to tempt others, it does not follow that he wants me to forcibly limit their opportunities to choose virtue and vice. Again, if we may judge God's will by his actions toward us, it would appear that God wants us to do neither. God tempts no one; but he does allow us a full range of temptations from which to choose.

32. It is interesting to note that George supports his brand of legal moralism partly on the ground that *parents* need morals legislation to help them restrict *their children's* access to temptation. E.g., George, *Making*, 27, 45–46. When we talk about forcibly limiting people's access to temptation, the argument naturally sounds more plausible when those people are minors. But how does this need to protect children justify a sweeping legal prohibition applying to adults as well? We usually (and justifiably) think of minors as needing special legal protections because they do not have full capacity for Choice. But in the face of certain temptations, George apparently believes *none of us*, even adults, have full capacity for Choice—at least, for using Choice rightly. See ibid. at 9–10, 227. This, I suppose, is why he (like Aquinas) believes the government should treat adults somewhat like parents treat their teenaged children. It is a separate question, of course, why we should suspect that government officials will be more "mature" (immune to temptation) and more likely than the average adult citizen to accurately define right and wrong in concrete cases.

33. Scripture does assure us, however, that he will provide a "way out" of every temptation, "so that [we] may be able to endure it." 1 Cor. 10:13.

34. George, *Making*, 121.

35. George, *Making*, 115–22.

36. George, *Making*, 44–45.

37. But as we have already noted, Aquinas, seemingly the inspiration for so much of George's theory, specifically disclaimed any wish to outlaw prostitution. Aquinas apparently believed outlawing prostitution would lead to more overall lust. See Chapter 2. It is worth considering whether Aquinas's insight might be applicable not only to prostitution, but to a host of other vices as well. At any rate, it illustrates the practical difficulties implicit in applying George's prudential considerations; for if lawmakers who are in as much agreement as George and Aquinas could come to such different conclusions regarding the practicality of outlawing prostitution, what chance is there for the rest of us to reach significant consensus on which vices to outlaw pursuant to George's prescription?

38. George, *Making*, 125 n. 21 (emphasis in original).

39. As Paul said, "For in Christ Jesus neither circumcision nor uncircumcision counts for anything; the only thing that counts is faith working through love. . . . Live by the Spirit, I say, and do not gratify the desires of the flesh. . . . If you are led by the Spirit, you are not subject to the law." Gal. 5:6, 16, 18.

Part IV

IMPLICATIONS

Chapter Nine

Selected Applications

So far, our study of God's will has led us to the Choice Principle, a rule of thumb we have fashioned to help us decide which of the myriad calls for legislation are legitimate topics of government concern, from a Christian perspective. We have also examined various arguments against the Choice Principle and have discarded each in turn. But to this point, we have analyzed the Choice Principle (and its competition) in the abstract, without spending much time applying it to real-world policy debates.

I attempt in this chapter to point the way, in a very limited fashion, to possible applications of the Choice Principle. Admittedly this is an incomplete effort, but I hope these few examples will provide a foundation upon which others can build, while more fully explaining both the meaning and the utility of the Choice Principle as I have framed it.

FORCE AND FRAUD

I begin with a set of real-world situations in which I expect the vast majority of Christians (and Non-Christians as well) will agree with the outcomes dictated by the Choice Principle. I will categorize these as cases of "force and fraud." When we claim that our criminal laws prohibit acts of "force" and "fraud," it is difficult to spell out all that we mean by those terms, and I will not attempt to define them very precisely here.[1] But generally, by "force" I mean *physical* force, such as that used in the act of firing a gun, swinging a baseball bat, shoving someone, or putting an object in one's pocket; I mean to suggest situations in which a person intentionally uses physical force, or the threat of it, and thereby deprives another of life, liberty, or property rightfully belonging to him. By "fraud" I generally mean to suggest situations in which a person accomplishes the same result by means of intentional deceit. Our criminal laws do indeed prohibit acts of force and fraud. As we will see, the Choice Principle would not only permit such laws, but would affirmatively require them.

We might say there are two kinds of force: the forceful act, in which physical force is actually used, and the coercive threat, in which physical force is merely threatened. Let us consider each separately, using a specific wrongful act to illustrate each kind of force.

Forceful Acts: The Case of Murder

Almost everyone supports laws against murder, notwithstanding the fact that such laws deprive us all of the freedom to choose to murder others. Perhaps this is simply because very few of us strongly desire to murder anyone, so that murder laws are deemed to be cost-free. But even if few people desire the freedom to murder others, the real explanation for the popularity of murder laws probably lies not in our apathy toward killing others, but in the massive benefits we believe such laws provide. For most of us would be terrified of daily life in a society in which people might murder us with impunity. Because I so highly value all the *other* choices of life, choices which would be denied me if I were murdered, I am willing to give up whatever benefit I might realize at some future point from being able to choose to murder others. We support murder laws because we believe they protect more Choice, and more valuable Choice, than they take away.

But how would these laws fare under the Choice Principle? The Choice Principle says, "Criminal laws are legitimate only if they cause a net increase in overall human Choice, and forbid only those individual choices that would directly harm others." Laws forbidding murder certainly restrict the choices of would-be murderers. However, the choice to murder is a choice that would harm others, and restricting that particular choice greatly enhances the range of choices available to the potential victims of such acts, and helps to secure our freedom of choice with respect to our own bodies and lives. Laws that restrict the freedom to commit murder are justified by their protection of the freedom to live. One might argue, I suppose, that this proposition is not self-evident—that we cannot say for sure that the choice to murder others is inherently less valuable than the choice to live and make other choices. But actual human experience, at least in Western cultures, suggests the opposite. People *do* in fact value the second kind of choice much more highly than the first. It would seem to be one of history's clearest lessons that the great majority of people, if given a choice, would prefer protection against murder to some sort of no holds barred, might-makes-right free-for-all. The right to live surely outweighs the right to deny life to others, so that we should have no trouble affirming that murder laws cause a net increase in overall human Choice.

Thus, the Choice Principle would indicate that Christians should support murder laws—not because murder is sinful (which it certainly is), but because murder victimizes others and deprives people of a choice more important than the choice to commit murder: namely, the choice to live.

Coercive Threats: The Case of Armed Robbery

Coercive threats are another example of the use of force. A coercive threat occurs when someone threatens to use physical force to cause something bad to happen to me, my loved ones, or my property, if I do not do his bidding. The purpose of the threatener is to induce me to obey him. A clear example of a coercive threat would be a robber that points a gun at my head and says, "Your money or your life." He is trying to induce me to hand him my money, threatening an immediate use of physical force against me if I refuse.

Again, almost everyone supports laws against this sort of behavior, even though these laws also keep us from being able to make such threats ourselves. Indeed, we would not feel free at all without such laws, which is why we all support them. The Choice Principle would reinforce our intuitions here as well. Laws against this kind of extortion certainly restrict the liberty of would-be robbers, but they are justified because they enhance the weightier liberties of potential victims to be secure in their property and persons, while penalizing only those who would directly harm others and reduce their range of Choice.

Fraud: The Case of Forgery

"Fraud" denotes a situation in which another person has intentionally and actively deceived me into doing something I would not otherwise have done, with the result that I am deprived of life, liberty, or property that is rightfully mine. An example of fraud would be when a person agrees to sell a Rembrandt painting to me, but delivers a clever forgery instead, representing it as the Rembrandt. Perhaps he also forges a letter purporting to be from a noted art expert, attesting to the painting's authenticity and value. I pay the seller an exorbitant price, far in excess of the true value of the painting I received, just because I (reasonably) believed his intentional lie. Although many forms of deception are perfectly legal (even if immoral), our laws criminalize *this* sort of deception. I suspect that most of us support such laws, despite the fact that we are thereby disallowed from practicing certain (perhaps lucrative) deceptions upon our fellows. For one thing, as a practical matter, fraud laws help make contracts possible. If the law did not forbid fraud, the costs of contracting would go up as we tried independently to verify every important fact and shift the risk of misinformation to others. These costs would almost certainly prevent a great number of contracts from ever being made. We want to be able to make contracts, and we want to feel a certain degree of security that strangers will not deceive us.

What does the Choice Principle have to say about fraud laws? Laws forbidding fraud certainly limit the freedom of the would-be deceiver, but fraud directly victimizes others by essentially denying them what is rightfully theirs without their true consent. In light of Romans 12 and 13, we could say that fraud is the sort of "wrongdoing" which would tempt a victim to take revenge on the wrongdoer (even though no physical force was used). But Paul counsels Christians to leave room for the vengeance of God, manifested through his agent the government—which enacts fraud laws serving just this purpose. And fraud laws are justified, under the Choice Principle, by their protection of the freedoms of potential victims of fraud, including the freedom to keep one's own property without having it stolen. Obtaining money by deceit is little different in substance from outright theft at gunpoint. To be sure, we should not regard as "theft" every contract we make without being fully informed of all relevant facts. Perfect information is not a prerequisite for all true Choice, and we all have made free choices in ignorance. But one who defrauds me is not merely failing to educate me. He is actively lying to me in order to persuade me to act when I otherwise would not. This is how he victimizes me, and this is why his act deprives me of true Choice. There may be hard cases and gray areas at the margins, but garden-variety fraud is essentially indistinguishable from garden-variety theft. For all these reasons, I think, fraud is (and should be) viewed as a victimizing activity that limits a freedom more important than the freedom to commit fraud. Hence, the Choice Principle would require that fraud be outlawed.

We have now shown that while the Choice Principle *forbids* certain kinds of laws, it *commands* other kinds of laws. Each of these "force and fraud" examples is designed to show the kind of laws the Choice Principle *commands*. It is not as if the Choice Principle dictates a world of anarchy. When force and fraud are banned, we have already gone a long way toward establishing an orderly, peaceful society.

Probably, these conclusions fit comfortably with most people's preexisting political attitudes. We all want to criminalize acts of force and fraud that victimize innocent people. But what about other types of laws? What does the Choice Principle suggest about laws prohibiting "victimless" crime, or laws that may actually reduce overall Choice in the society in the name of promoting some officially endorsed conception of well-being or virtue?

SUICIDE, ASSISTED SUICIDE, AND EUTHANASIA

Strictly speaking, suicide and assisted suicide might often qualify as forms of euthanasia (defined as the causing of a person's death in order to end that person's suffering); but to be as clear as possible, let us distinguish among three different scenarios. "Suicide" obviously refers to the intentional killing of oneself. For this discussion, "assisted suicide" will denote a suicide accomplished with the help of another, at the explicit request of the person who is trying to die. "Euthanasia" will refer to the intentional ending of another's life *without* explicit consent or aid from the dying person (and without their opposition either), where the actor is motivated by: (1) a concern for the comfort and dignity of the dying person, or (2) what it is believed the dying person would want if that person could express a preference. Let us examine each of these three acts to see how the Choice Principle would have the law respond to them.

Suicide

Suicide is the intentional killing of oneself, usually to end one's own physical or emotional suffering. Of course, laws will never be able to punish anyone who *successfully* commits suicide, since the wrongdoer would be dead. But criminalizing suicide might be a conceivable way of punishing, for example, those who unsuccessfully *attempt* suicide ("attempted suicide" now becomes a crime as well) or those who help others commit suicide (the "accomplice" or "accessory" to suicide, or someone who engaged in a "conspiracy to commit suicide"). Since we will analyze accomplices and conspirators later when we discuss the scenario of "assisted suicide," let us focus for the moment on those who attempt suicide—that is, those who try unsuccessfully to kill themselves. Should their attempt be a crime?

In applying the Choice Principle to any proposed law, we must remember that the Principle is not designed to tell us whether the outlawed act is sinful; nor does the sinfulness of the act affect the outcome of our analysis. I believe Scripture indicates that suicide is a sinful act, but if we are prioritizing Choice in our laws, the sinfulness of suicide will be irrelevant to our legislation. The question before us is not whether people should try suicide, but what our *laws* should do to them if they have already tried suicide. With this in mind, consider what the Choice Principle says about laws banning attempted suicide.

The New Testament does not speak of suicide laws at all. In light of the absence of biblical authority for this specific type of law, the Choice Principle would say, "Laws criminalizing suicide or attempted suicide are legitimate only if they cause a net increase in overall human Choice, and forbid only those individual choices that would directly harm others." Suicide laws certainly restrict the choices of those who might otherwise try to commit suicide—at the margins, at least, we suspect that the law would cause some people to be dissuaded from the attempt (because of the risk of failure, the additional social stigma of having a criminal record, or whatever). So the restriction will impose some costs in terms of freedom of choice, and therefore will be justified only if: (1) the law *protects* someone's freedom of choice enough to justify those costs, and (2) attempting suicide is an act that directly harms others. Do suicide laws satisfy these two tests?

I think not. Let us consider the first test: whether the law against attempting suicide protects anyone's freedom of choice in a meaningful way. The law would certainly discourage suicide attempts, but how does that add to anyone's freedom of choice? It will not do to claim that discouraging suicide adds to the freedoms of the friends and family and community who would have been adversely affected by a certain person's suicide. It is simply not true that when someone dies, someone else will always suffer some significant adverse effect as a result. Suicide laws would apply to everyone who tries to commit suicide, even to the person who has no home, family, or friends, and pays no taxes. It would be driving the concept of "effects" into the ground to claim that this person's death must necessarily adversely affect someone else, who can only be assured full liberty if this person lives. And this is why suicide laws would also fail the second of the two tests above. Attempting suicide is simply not one of those acts, like robbery or fraud, that will always impose direct harms on others.

Even in cases where attempting suicide *does* hurt others in some way, killing oneself (or trying to do so) does not limit the Choice of those others in the direct and meaningful way that murder, robbery, or fraud does. While it may be true in some sense that no man is an island, that every little thing we do affects others somehow, it is also true that even in close-knit communities and families, there is a meaningful difference between being dependent and independent, between being interfered with and being left alone. And there is a huge difference, one that most of us intuitively appreciate, between being forced not to harm other community members and being forced to help them. Criminalizing theft forces each of us to leave other people alone; criminalizing suicide (or its attempt) forces each of us *not* to leave other people alone.

It forces each of us to be around when others need us, to give them choices they would not have if we died or left. This law goes beyond preventing the direct limitation of their range of Choice.

So if suicide laws protect anyone's freedom of choice, it must be that of the person who tried to die. The argument would be that this person will have a much fuller range of Choice available to her if she lives than if she commits suicide. And yet, this sort of paternalistic attitude toward the chooser is the very opposite of freedom of choice. A true respect and protection for freedom of choice would allow the chooser voluntarily to limit her own range of future choices—say, through a business contract, a common way of limiting future choices. We would not call the law that outlawed all business contracts a "freedom-enhancing" law, even though contracting parties would be under fewer obligations (and therefore "freer"?) if they had never signed any contracts. We all understand in that context that freedom includes the freedom to tie our own hands voluntarily, to take risks, to commit ourselves to limits on freedom that we may even regret down the road. But that's what Choice is about.

Surely freedom of choice includes the freedom to do what one chooses with his own body, as long as no one else is thereby disallowed a similar choice (we would not want to allow a person to try to kill himself by means of dynamite on a crowded train). According to the Choice Principle, then, the typical suicide (or attempted suicide) should be legal, for there is no justification to outlaw it. And in fact, suicide and attempted suicide are legal in most or all states today, although usually a state reserves the power to forcibly examine and treat those who have attempted suicide, under the state's civil statutes regarding involuntary commitment of the mentally ill.[2]

Assisted Suicide

This is the intentional aiding of another who wants his own life to end, where the one being aided has explicitly asked for the aid. The aider may be merely an *accessory before the fact* (as when the aider knowingly prepares some device which the sufferer then uses in a solitary moment to kill himself) or he may be the *principal in the first degree* (as when the aider actually kills the sufferer at the sufferer's explicit command). We may further subdivide the latter group of assistants into *active principals* (who cause death that would not happen in the natural course of events, as when an assistant injects into the sufferer a lethal dose of morphine) and *passive principals* (who cause death indirectly by ending some life-prolonging treatment, as when an assistant turns off a ventilator and the sufferer dies as a result). In any case, what counts as "assisted suicide" under our definition are only those acts that are done *at the victim's clear and explicit request*.[3]

According to the Choice Principle, we should support a criminal law only if it forbids acts causing direct harm to others and its restrictions of particular choices are justified by its protection of Choice overall. A law against assisted suicide would restrict the freedom of those who would otherwise assist suicide at the victim's explicit request. It would also restrict the Choice of the victim herself, by limiting her options for aid. But do such restrictions protect more Choice than they restrict? Again, I think not. Assisting suicide, and being assisted at one's own request, do not significantly and directly limit the Choice of others, as robbery does. If suicide itself does not reduce overall human Choice, as I have argued, then assisting suicide doesn't either, as long as the assistance always must be at the clear and explicit request of the victim.

Thus, it is especially troubling to note the law's inconsistency in this area. While it is generally legal in this country to commit suicide, attempt suicide, or ask someone to help you commit suicide, it is generally *illegal* to help someone *else* do this act that they are legally entitled to do, even if they explicitly begged for your help and even if your only motive is genuine pity.[4] Some states even regard such assistance as first-degree murder.[5] One might argue that this double standard not only flies in the face of rationality, but actually discriminates within the class of persons considering suicide by allowing suicide generally, but foreclosing the suicide option to those who happen to have the sorts of illnesses which debilitate victims to the point that they lack the physical ability to end their lives without outside help. One might make this argument; but apparently one would lose in the U.S. Supreme Court.[6]

Note that the Choice Principle does *not* require the legalization of "assisted suicide" (so-called) when there is *no explicit request* by the victim, or when the victim's request cannot be considered legally valid because of youth or some mental incompetence. In situations like this, the dying person could easily be understood as a victim, having his Choice directly limited by the "assistant." Perhaps even some extreme (and documented) emotional trauma of the victim should be sufficient to defeat an otherwise clear and explicit victim request (although I think we should be quite careful here that the exception doesn't swallow the rule—after all, if one wishes to commit suicide, the chances are good that he is experiencing what most of us would call "extreme emotional trauma"). The point is, in those cases where the victim's request was undeniably explicit and knowing, the law should not criminalize the provision of assistance to him, as it currently does almost everywhere in the United States.[7] To do so is to reduce Choice overall and to punish an act that did not directly limit anyone's Choice. The acts of committing or assisting suicide may be sinful, but if the Choice Principle is valid, Christians should not outlaw them.

Unrequested Euthanasia

This is the intentional killing of another, in order to end his suffering, under circumstances where the sufferer has not requested the killing.

Here, it seems to me, we have a completely different case from suicide or assisting suicide, and one that is much more akin, possibly, to abortion of a fetus with serious genetic defects (if we assume the fetus has personhood—see the abortion discussion in Chapter 10). Let us assume that everyone agrees the suffering person is a living human being—that is, everyone agrees he had not yet "died" in any sense before the killer acted. Notwithstanding the good intentions of the killer, the killer has denied the sufferer an extremely important choice: the choice whether to live or die, a choice which should belong to the sufferer alone if we are trying to maximize individual Choice. Had the victim clearly and knowingly expressed a desire to die, either at the moment before death or sometime in the past through some kind of "living will" document, we would have a different case; but as things stand, the best the killer can do is to *guess* what the victim would want. No matter how close the relationship between killer and victim, we would have serious doubts about allowing the killer's skill at mind reading to determine the fate of the victim. I believe the Choice Principle would require a law against unrequested euthanasia in order to fully protect the Choice of the victim. Although such a law would restrict the Choice of merciful assistants, it would protect the Choice of victims in a much more profound way, assuring them the opportunity to decide for themselves whether to continue their lives. The law would thus be protecting overall Choice, and it would be limited in its application to those whose acts have directly deprived others of Choice.

HOMOSEXUAL SODOMY

There is probably no current issue that ignites the Christian Right like homosexuality. They note with dismay the increasing tolerance within our culture of homosexuality as merely one alternative on a long menu of acceptable lifestyle choices. Many leaders of the Christian Right view a pro-rights stance in this area as necessarily grounded in moral relativism. Christians favoring the legalization of homosexual practices and homosexual marriage are viewed as having endorsed homosexuality as a permissible alternative lifestyle, selling out to the forces of impurity, humanism, and secularism in our culture.

For our discussion of homosexuality, let us consider the practice of sodomy, which is one homosexual behavior the law has historically addressed.[8] To most people, the word "sodomy" may indicate homosexual anal sex, but many of the state statutes outlawing "sodomy" have defined that term more broadly—in some cases to include all oral or anal sex between consenting adults, even between married heterosexuals acting in the privacy of their own bedrooms. Historically, these laws formed part of a web of legislation aimed at forbidding, not homosexual behavior as such, but all non-procreative sexual activities, which were seen as contrary to nature.[9]

In June of 2003, in the case of *Lawrence v. Texas*, the U.S. Supreme Court struck down a Texas law forbidding sodomy between persons of the same gender.[10] The decision was grounded in the Court's holding that the U.S. Constitution forbids governments from regulating the sexual conduct of consenting adults, whether homosexual or heterosexual, who are acting without compensation in the privacy of their own homes.[11] At the time of the decision, thirteen states had such regulations in place: nine banned specified sexual acts even for heterosexuals, without regard to the participants' genders, while four others—including Texas—banned specified sexual acts only if committed with another person of the same gender.[12]

The *Lawrence* decision, then, effectively rendered the laws of these thirteen states unconstitutional, but did not strike down any of the laws of the other thirty-seven states. Nevertheless, many evangelicals were outraged. Rev. Lou Sheldon, president of the Traditional Values Coalition, lamented that "in this court, you do not have friends of the Judeo-Christian standard" and promised that "people of faith are not going to lie down and allow their faith to be trampled because a politically correct court has run amok."[13] Rev. Flip Benham, head of Operation Rescue, led a demonstration to declare the U.S. Supreme Court in contempt of the Court of Jesus Christ and to publicly burn a copy of the *Lawrence* decision.[14] The president of the Family Research Council, Ken Connor, denounced the "classic judicial activism arrogance" illustrated by *Lawrence*.[15] Tom Minnery of Focus on the Family characterized the Court as "pillaging its way through the moral norms of our country."[16] And Rev. Jerry Falwell told the *New York Times* that the day the *Lawrence* decision was announced was "probably as bad a day as the court has had on social issues since Roe v. Wade."[17]

But should Christians indeed be upset by the Supreme Court's decision in *Lawrence*? For the purposes of argument, let us narrow the scope of the discussion by focusing on those sodomy laws that forbid only same-sex contact between consenting adults in private, without compensation. What does the Choice Principle prescribe as to these sorts of sodomy laws?

Again, recall that the Choice Principle has nothing whatever to say about whether homosexuality is sinful, whether homosexual acts are sinful, whether people should be homosexuals, or whether, as an empirical matter, people in fact have any choice about their sexual preferences or desires; the only issue before us is how the *law* should treat those who commit homosexual acts (the law cannot police, of course, a person's sexual "orientation," or inner desires that never result in behavior). For the committed Christian, this in turn boils down to the question, "What does God want our laws to say about homosexual behaviors?"

A sodomy law certainly is a criminal law that restricts the choices of the consenting adults involved. Therefore, it would be justified only if: (1) the law protects someone else's freedom of choice enough to justify the burdens on Choice, and (2) sodomy is an act that directly harms others. Do sodomy laws satisfy these two criteria? I do not see how. Any other human beings affected by the partners' sodomy are affected only very indirectly (and probably unintentionally). Sodomy does not deprive non-participants of Choice in any meaningful sense. And sodomy between consenting adults does not, in itself, directly harm anyone else. Therefore, the Choice Principle would require that we legalize sodomy. Anti-sodomy laws exist, if at all, because of some other concern besides the protection of human Choice, and therefore the Choice Principle would counsel us to reject them.

Note that this answer is the same even if we assume that "sodomy" includes (as it often does in the law) *heterosexual* sex acts as well. In other words, it is not the *discriminatory* elements of this law that violate the Choice Principle; rather, it is the law's reduction of overall human Choice. What would save this law, under the Choice Principle, is if it only applied in cases where one or more participants did not consent or were minors or mentally deficient (and therefore part of a class that is generally *incapable* of "knowing" consent). But states criminalized these acts already, through other laws—for instance, laws against rape, "statutory rape," and child molestation. Those laws could be justified under the Choice Principle, but laws forbidding any particular form of private sex act between consenting adults clearly restricts overall Choice rather than expanding it.

Again, this stance need not indicate some new "sin tolerance" or moral laxity. The law is not a moral code, nor is it society's (or God's) final statement as to what is right and wrong.

ALCOHOL, NICOTINE, AND OTHER DRUGS

For this discussion, let us define "drug" as a chemical which tends to be habit forming and has some immediate and significant metabolic effect, often causing a marked change in consciousness, when taken into the bloodstream. This definition seems to capture our meaning when using the word in everyday conversation. By this definition, there are a number of "drugs" floating around in our society. Some are currently illegal altogether (for example, heroin or cocaine), some are legal but available only by doctor's prescription (morphine or codeine), some are legally obtainable over the counter to anyone older than some minimum age (alcohol or nicotine), and some are legally obtainable regardless of the buyer's age (caffeine or various cold and allergy formulations). But they all have a significant metabolic effect in the bloodstream, they often cause a marked change in consciousness, and they all tend to be habit forming.

In considering drug laws, the first thing one notices is their apparent inconsistency. Are the legal distinctions between the various drugs justifiable because of some natural difference between the drugs themselves? Are the legal ones less addictive, or more helpful, or what? Along these lines, it is particularly enlightening to compare pairs of very similar drugs that the law treats differently (say, alcohol and marijuana, or heroin and morphine), to see if there are substantial differences in physiological or societal effects that would justify the disparate legal treatment they receive. We may determine that the Choice Principle requires us to treat them alike.

What would the Choice Principle require of our drug laws? Granted, drug abuse is a harmful, even sinful, act. But drug laws prohibit much more than abuse; and besides, the sinfulness of drug abuse is irrelevant to our analysis of the propriety of the law. What matters under the Choice Principle is that a drug law is a criminal law restricting the choices of the adults who want to use drugs in private. (We are not considering whether the law should restrict minors, who have a reduced capacity for free Choice and consequently might need special rules for their own protection.) Therefore, the law would be justified only if: (1) the law protects someone's freedom of choice enough to justify the costs to Choice, and (2) drug use is an act that directly harms others. Are drug laws justified under this test?

It seems doubtful. The short of it is that drug use, by itself, is an act that *may*, but *need not*, harm others, and the harm is almost never direct. It is true that often many lives are affected, tragically, by an individual's decision to use (for example) heroin, and other people's range of acceptable choices might be limited thereby; but those effects are merely incidental and tangential to the drug abuse, and in some cases of drug abuse they are completely absent.[18] The heroin addict who abuses the drug alone, in private, may or may not use up his $2,000 savings on his addiction, money he might otherwise have used to feed and clothe his wife and children, but he is still a far cry from a burglar who sneaks into the house at night and steals $2,000 from the wife. I am not arguing that the effect of drug abuse on non-participants is not widespread or important; I believe that, in the aggregate, it is both. I am instead arguing that the individual effect on others is of a lesser and more indirect and uncertain order than the effect of robbing them. I am also arguing that the private drug abuser's effect on others is of a lesser order than the effect on the user of a law forbidding his use.

Moreover, the harmful effects of heroin (or at least marijuana) abuse are really not so different from, and not nearly so widespread as, the harmful effects of *alcohol* abuse. And alcohol is currently legal. The argument that justifies outlawing marijuana, as libertarians have been saying for years, will also justify outlawing alcohol. Are we prepared to outlaw alcohol too, entering another Prohibition Era? Are we prepared to imprison as a thief the husband who spends the family savings on liquor? What if he spends the food money on a new boat or a wide-screen television set—will we imprison him then? The "theft," the harm to others, is the same.

Christians who are not prepared to outlaw alcohol should take the drug legalization argument seriously. With all its real-world societal repercussions, whatever they might be, legalization may also hold the promise of alleviating some of our current societal problems. I have tried to exclude from this discussion practical considerations of cost savings, violence and addiction levels, and the like, but I will at least point out that a wide body of scholarship suggests (though the point is far from uncontested) that the world will actually be a safer, healthier, less criminal, and more pleasant place after legalization than before.[19] It is probably impossible for anyone on either side of the drug criminalization argument to predict with complete accuracy what the world would look like after legalization. My purpose here, however, is not to show all the societal effects of drug legalization; I merely wish to illustrate an application of the Choice Principle. If we follow God's will in making our laws, we have done our job; we ought to trust that he will take care of the societal results. And it seems to me that under any reasonable analysis, the Choice Principle would require a widespread legalization of drugs of all types, but criminal penalties for those who harm others—whether the actor is sober or voluntarily under the influence of drugs.

REDISTRIBUTIVE TAXATION

Governments do more than define and punish crimes. In the United States today, at any rate, our governments all play the role of benefactor of certain groups in our society. Our governments are major spending forces in our economy, and they are spending on us—or at least some of us. We have come to expect it. In fact, we expect it to proliferate. It is not uncommon any more for a legislature to pass a law granting a group of people newly created legal rights to receive government benefits if they meet certain criteria defined in the statute. Such programs are called "entitlements." Some entitlement programs (for example, Medicaid) target recipients based at least in part on their financial need; such programs are called "means-tested entitlements." Other entitlements, the "non-means-tested" variety (for example, Medicare), set up criteria that ignore the potential recipient's financial need, granting the aid on some other basis (like age, disability, or occupation).

At first, the Choice Principle might not seem relevant to spending laws that create entitlements. After all, the Choice Principle only applies to criminal laws, and a spending law does not criminalize private behavior. It is no crime to refuse benefits one is legally entitled to receive. But these spending laws cannot properly be viewed in isolation, as if the resources they distribute fall like manna from heaven. The only way to properly understand these laws is to view them in connection with the taxation schemes that fund them.

When the government distributes money or other resources, it obviously must get the resources from somewhere. To provide this funding, it has two choices: raise taxes, or borrow money and then raise taxes to repay the borrowing.[20] Either way, the government must ultimately resort to taxation in order to pay for its beneficent programs. But taxation, unlike spending, is always quite coercive, limiting the Choice of those who must pay. And tax laws have a criminal aspect as well: willful failure to pay taxes is usually a crime.[21] The Choice Principle might well have something to say about laws that criminalize the refusal to provide financial support to some entitlement program.

First, let us stipulate that forcible taxation itself is not contrary to God's will; in fact, as we have seen, the practice is specifically approved in the Scriptures. The New Testament clearly teaches two things about taxes: first, taxation as such is not forbidden to government; and second, if the government imposes a tax, whatever its purpose, a Christian is to pay it.[22] This, however, does not answer the question of whether all taxes, regardless of purpose, are equally justifiable for a Christian lawmaker to impose. And until we see evidence to the contrary, it is natural to suspect that some taxes would *not* be justifiable, on the grounds of their immoral purposes. For example, how could we justify a law forcing citizens to pay into a fund to finance the complete destruction of all copies of the Bible? Or to finance a pogrom against Christians? Or, for that matter, against Syrians?

We are left with the conclusion that, from God's point of view, taxation itself is permissible for governments, but only for permissible purposes. And this conclusion, in turn, raises the question whether particular entitlement programs, schemes of forcible resource redistribution, qualify as "permissible purposes" for which a Christian may force someone to surrender property to the government.

Entitlement programs are in fact systems of forcible resource redistribution within a society. The spending side of the program cannot be divorced from the revenue gathering side. Taxes are raised for the purpose of financing government spending programs of one sort or another. For some entitlements, such as Social Security or Medicare, the connection between the tax and the spending is quite explicit and even legally binding on the government: payroll taxes designated for Social Security, for example, can only be spent on providing Social Security benefits.[23] For other entitlements, like student grant programs, the connection between tax and spending is less explicit. But it is always true that if there is spending, there will sooner or later be taxes, in an amount sufficient to pay for the spending. This is the way it must be, for people do not voluntarily contribute very much money to the government, and spending always has to be funded by someone. And if entitlement programs are best viewed as forced redistributions from one group of citizens to another, with criminal penalties imposed for refusal to submit one's property for redistribution, then it becomes easy to see how the Choice Principle could apply to laws creating entitlements.

To make our discussion more concrete, let us consider the Social Security entitlement. This entitlement is the most costly in U.S. history; it is also probably the most popular. Currently, 20-25 percent of total federal spending is allocated to paying Social Security benefits, for which one qualifies based on either advanced age or disability (wealth and income are irrelevant). Money to fund the program is collected via a payroll tax legally restricted to this purpose. Willful failure to pay the required payroll tax is, of course, a federal crime. Thus, the entitlement scheme as a whole imposes criminal penalties which restrict the Choice of adults who do not wish to distribute their property to the people the law has classified as beneficiaries. The New Testament does not explicitly approve forcible property redistribution laws. Therefore, according to the Choice Principle, the Social Security laws would be justified only if: (1) these laws protect someone's freedom of choice enough to justify restricting the Choice of those taxed, and (2) refusing to distribute property to the elderly or disabled is an act that directly harms others. Is the Social Security entitlement justified under this test?

Refusing to give property to someone cannot reasonably be viewed as a victimizing act, an activity that directly harms everyone who does not receive the gift. It is difficult to argue that someone directly harms me whenever he refuses to make a gift to me of some of his resources. If that were the case, then everyone in the world would be directly harming me, constantly, by a simple refusal to act. This nullifies the whole idea of direct harm. Of course, I am better off if others give me property and worse off if they do not; but being directly harmed is more than simply being worse off than I can imagine being. I am not directly harmed whenever someone refuses to give me whatever I want; in the same way, I do not directly harm the elderly or disabled whenever I don't give them everything I own. They may have been victimized (or not), but not by me.

It is likewise difficult to say that the Social Security entitlement protects more Choice than it limits. The law expands the Choice of beneficiaries, perhaps, but the Choice of contributors is limited by exactly the same amount (or more, since part of the tax goes to fund the program itself), in exactly the same way. It is no answer to say that the recipients are more needy than the contributors. The Social Security redistribution must occur even if that condition is not met, because Social Security is not a means-tested entitlement.[24] And even as to those entitlements that *are* means-tested, who is to say that the choice of how to spend $1,000 is less significant to a rich person who is taxed than to a poor person who receives? The nature of the choice involved is the same; the only difference is perhaps in the particular choice that is made—that is, how the money is ultimately spent. In sum, the Social Security entitlement is justified, if at all, on some basis other than the enhancement of individual Choice, and therefore the Choice Principle would counsel us to oppose it.

This is not an argument for greed or cold-heartedness; it is simply an argument *against* theft, even in the name of the poor (or elderly, or whatever the group *du jour*). We should be careful to distinguish between charity and coercive redistribution. The Bible commands charity; it does not command, or even condone, forcible redistribution, which is just a particular variety of theft. Robin Hood, in the end, was a thief. It is noble of me to give my own property to others; but it is immoral of me to take someone else's property, against his will, and give most of it to a third party, keeping a bit for myself to cover the expenses of my theft. No amount of third party need will make that act morally permissible. And this is what redistributive taxation is.

Of course, taxation itself may be justified, but only if the tax has a legitimate, biblically endorsed purpose. We have seen in Chapter 5 that *some* uses of force are biblically permitted to the government but disallowed to individuals (for example, imprisonment of thieves—or taxation itself). But that surely does not show that *all* uses of force are morally permissible for the government. The Choice Principle is our way of distinguishing between permissible and impermissible uses of government force. It may be proper to use government force to compel innocent people to contribute to the government so that the government can continue, as God's agent, to protect their lives and property and their range of Choice; it is a Christian's duty to pay duly imposed taxes even if they are being used for other purposes; and it is certainly proper, even morally required, to give up one's own property to help those in need; but all that is not to say that it would be proper for a Christian, or the government, to force innocent people to give property to other people in need (much less to those who are not in need). Governments that aim to prioritize Choice will not undertake that sort of coercion, even when it is disguised as charity.

PROSTITUTION

Let us define "prostitution" as a seller's provision of physical sexual contact between the seller and a buyer in exchange for compensation from the buyer. By this definition, prostitution has been practiced from the earliest days of recorded history, and is sometimes called "the world's oldest profession." In most Western civilizations, at any rate, prostitution as defined above has historically been permitted by law, although sometimes heavily regulated.

In ancient Greece and Rome, prostitution was a legal but highly regulated activity which was generally regarded as instrumentally useful to the state.[25] In the Christian era, as we noted in Chapter 2, both Augustine (ca. 400) and Aquinas (ca. 1270) favored the continuing legality of prostitution.[26] Reformation thought, however, tended to favor prohibiting the act, and where the Reformers' influence was felt the practice was sometimes criminalized.[27] But in English common law, prostitution was legal,[28] and in our country, "from colonial times through most of the nineteenth century, prostitution was not a distinct criminal offense . . . . In general, legal toleration was the rule, and [even other laws, such as those prohibiting vagrancy, disorderly conduct, indecent exposure, and the like] were enforced against prostitutes only sporadically."[29] The states began to criminalize prostitution itself during the Progressive Era, partly as a result of the activism of feminist "purity leagues," which were also the main moving force behind Prohibition.[30]

Today, the United States is one of the few countries in the developed world in which prostitution as such is a crime.[31] In our country, every state except Nevada has statutorily criminalized prostitution; in Nevada, where the criminalization decision is left to each county, fifteen of the state's seventeen counties have opted to legalize the practice.[32] In the other states, there is some evidence that enforcing the prostitution laws requires a great deal of a community's law enforcement resources, particularly in the biggest cities.[33] And there are serious practical problems associated with the legal definition of "prostitution" itself. Often in our society, unmarried couples seem to work out a "one-night stand" type of exchange of dinner and entertainment for sex. Isn't that "prostitution" according to our definition above? And if a woman decides to begin a sexual relationship (even a marriage) with a man because he is rich, gives her gifts, and promises to "take care" of her, is she a prostitute? She would meet the definition, and yet these are seemingly not the types of offenders the laws' drafters had in mind.

Whatever the practical difficulties associated with prostitution laws, our task is to examine these laws in light of God's will. But the question is not what God thinks about the practice of prostitution. Prostitution (at least as we commonly think of it) is surely a sinful practice; but our question, again, is related to the morality of *the law*, not the practice of prostitution itself. Does God want us to outlaw prostitution, or not?

The Choice Principle provides a possible answer. What would it mean to prioritize Choice in this context? A law prohibiting prostitution is a criminal law that restricts the choices of the adults who wish voluntarily to enter and fulfill such a contract in private. Therefore, according to the Choice Principle, the law would be justified only if: (1) the law protects someone's freedom of choice enough to justify the restrictions on Choice, and (2) prostitution is an act that directly harms others. Are prostitution laws justified under this test?

The analysis by now should be familiar. Prostitution may sometimes cause ancillary problems for other, nonconsenting parties, such as the wife of the "john" who contracts a venereal disease from him because of his contact with a prostitute; but these harms must surely be regarded as indirect and speculative—they will not occur in every single instance of prostitution, the way a thief harms someone else every single time he steals. Prostitution is not an act that directly harms others or limits their range of Choice. And outlawing the practice reduces the Choice of would-be prostitutes (and their would-be clients) without providing any compensating protection of anyone else's Choice (nonparticipants are just as free *without* the law). Therefore, the Choice Principle would counsel legalization of prostitution, as a step toward providing a government more in keeping with God's will—a government that, as God's agent of wrath, punishes only those who would victimize others and cause the victim to desire revenge.[34]

CONCLUDING REMARKS

Of course there are many other situations to which the Choice Principle could be applied, but space does not permit their consideration here. The purpose of this chapter, again, is to present a few examples illustrating how the Choice Principle might be rationally applied.

People are bound to disagree about what the Choice Principle might require, even in the few situations I have described above. This disagreement, however, does not defeat my central premise that the Choice Principle might be a wise and biblical approach for Christians and Non-Christians alike in deciding these cases—unless, of course, one concludes that the Principle is too vague to be applied at all. However, I suspect that in most cases, the dictates of the Choice Principle will be quite clear, although following them consistently may lead us into unfamiliar territory.

Some readers may be tempted to recoil at the strange kind of world they believe the Choice Principle would create, a world they assume would be characterized by widespread suffering or sin. But who would argue that the world is unencumbered by such problems already? Applying the Choice Principle as we make laws might well *reduce* suffering and sin in our society, relative to the current levels. How far have we already sunk? How widespread, or unfair, is the suffering now? Much depends on one's point of view, which in turn may greatly depend on which side of the law one currently finds oneself on, most of the time.

And we must remember that the ultimate question is not whether the Choice Principle leads to a perfect world, or even whether we think it would lead to a safer or more prosperous or more equal world, but whether it would lead to a government more in keeping with the purpose for which God ordained governments. Predictions of future calamity are often greatly exaggerated, if not completely speculative. People of faith should be the last ones to fear the unknown and unknowable future. For protection from a drug-crazed, sex-crazed, selfish, and convenience-driven society, we must ultimately place our trust in God, not government.

And even if the Choice Principle would require our society to sacrifice some of the "order" to which we have grown accustomed, who is to say that God would disapprove? Perhaps our view of God's preferences has been distorted by our own legal and social traditions. We should at least admit the possibility that God may think our criminal laws currently place too much emphasis on "order" and not enough on liberty and Choice. God is a God of order, of course, but also of liberty and human Choice. From his perspective, our current system of criminal law, with its numerous rules about private victimless behavior, may look much like a classroom of first graders making behavior rules for the kindergarten class next door. As we saw in Chapter 6, Jesus died to free God's children from behavior regulations (Gal. 5:1)—not to assure that we would never have to follow any rules of behavior, but to show us the futility of making such rules for the purpose of bringing ourselves or others closer to God.

In adopting the Choice Principle, we would avoid the trap of legislating such rules for others; we would strike a balance between order and freedom while respecting both. Who can say that from God's point of view, the gain in individual liberty would not be worth the cost to "order"? Certainly not those who, without bearing ill will toward anyone else, happen to have preferences for activities currently forbidden by our laws. We Christians, beneficiaries of God's grace, should think seriously about how God wants us, and our governments, to treat those people.

NOTES

1. For some of the relevant considerations in precisely defining "force" and "fraud," see Robert Nozick, "Coercion," in *Philosophy, Science, and Method: Essays*

in Honor of Ernest Nagel, ed. Morgenbesser, Suppes, and White (New York: St. Martin's Press, 1969), 440.

2. Daniel E. Hall, *Survey of Criminal Law*, 2d ed. (Albany, N.Y.: Delmar Publishers, 1997), 110–11.

3. I find it difficult to see the justification for any legal or moral distinction between active and passive principals in the assisted suicide context, so I have analyzed them together for purposes of this discussion. I think I would likewise want to treat accomplices and principals alike. But if I am wrong in these conclusions, it would be easy to analyze each kind of actor separately under the Choice Principle.

4. Hall, *Survey*, 111; Thomas J. Gardner and Terry M. Anderson, *Criminal Law*, 8th ed. (Belmont, Calif.: Wadsworth, 2003), 287–88. But see The Oregon Death With Dignity Act, Or. Rev. Stat. 127.800 *et seq.*, which specifies some circumstances under which physicians assisting suicide may escape criminal liability in Oregon. This statute is the first of its kind in the United States. After U.S. Attorney General John Ashcroft issued a directive stating that Oregon physicians who complied with this law would be violating federal statutes regulating controlled substances, a federal district court struck down this directive as exceeding Ashcroft's authority under the federal statute. *Oregon v. Ashcroft*, 192 F. Supp. 2d 1077 (D. Or. 2002). The decision was upheld on appeal. *Oregon v. Ashcroft*, 368 F.3d 1118 (9th Cir. 2004). The U.S. Supreme Court has now agreed to hear this case, *Gonzales v. Oregon*, 125 S. Ct. 1299 (2005), but at the time this book went to press no opinion had been announced.

5. Hall, *Survey*, 111; Gardner and Anderson, *Criminal Law*, 287–88; Frank Schmalleger, *Criminal Law Today* (Upper Saddle River, N.J.: Prentice-Hall, 1999), 272; see also, for example, *Gilbert v. State*, 487 So.2d 1185 (Fla. Dist. Ct. App. 1986), *cert. denied*, 494 So.2d 1150 (Fla. 1986) (upholding life sentence for first degree murder imposed on 75-year-old man who was a "respected citizen" with no prior criminal record, upon evidence that he had shot his wife at her explicit request as a means to end her suffering brought on by Alzheimer's disease and osteoporosis); *State v. Forrest*, 362 S.E.2d 252 (N.C. 1987) (upholding life sentence for first degree murder, upon evidence that on Christmas Eve, defendant had shot and killed his bedridden father, who had been determined by physicians to be suffering from "terminal" condition and was classified as "No Code," in order to end father's suffering and to fulfill promise earlier made to father not to let him suffer).

6. See *Vacco v. Quill*, 521 U.S. 793 (1997).

7. It may be, as some have suggested, that there would be insurmountable practical problems in assuring that such requests were knowing and explicit. See *Washington v. Glucksberg*, 521 U.S. 702, 730–35 (1997). I express no opinion about that here. My only point is that if we can be sure that a person has clearly, explicitly, and knowingly requested aid in killing himself, the Choice Principle would suggest that it should be no crime to comply with that request, at least if the assistant has no more sinister motive than to earn money or to help a person in need.

8. Some of the issues surrounding sodomy laws, particularly discriminatory enforcement problems, were discussed earlier in Chapter 7.

9. See *Lawrence v. Texas*, 539 U.S. 558, 568–69 (2003); Gary D. Allison, "Sanctioning Sodomy: The Supreme Court Liberates Gay Sex and Limits State Power to

Vindicate the Moral Sentiments of the People," Tulsa L. Rev. 39 (2003): 102–3; see generally John D'Emilio and Estelle B. Freedman, *Intimate Matters: A History of Sexuality in America*, 2d ed. (Chicago: University of Chicago Press, 1998).

The understanding of all non-procreative sexual activity as being "contrary to nature" is reflected in the terminology that was most often employed in the earliest statutes to describe what was forbidden. The statutes in the American states, following English law, defined the forbidden actions with wording such as "the infamous and detestable crime against nature" or "unnatural and lascivious acts," often with no further definition at all. William N. Eskridge, Jr., "Hardwick and Historiography," U. Ill. L. Rev. 1999 (1999): 643–47, 655–59.

10. *Lawrence*, 539 U.S. at 578–79.

11. *Lawrence*, 539 U.S. at 566–67, 571–72, 573–74, 578–79.

12. *Lawrence*, 539 U.S. at 573; Evan Thomas, "The War Over Gay Marriage," *Newsweek*, 7 July 2003, 40.

13. Thomas, "Gay Marriage," 42.

14. Jeffrey Rosen, "How to Reignite the Culture Wars," *New York Times Magazine*, 7 Sept. 2003, 48.

15. Ken Connor, as reported in Neil A. Lewis, "The Supreme Court: The Opposition," *New York Times*, 27 June 2003, sec. A, p. 19, col. 5.

16. Tom Minnery, as reported in Lewis, "The Supreme Court," sec. A, p. 19, col. 5.

17. Jerry Falwell, as reported in Lewis, "The Supreme Court," sec. A, p. 19, col. 5.

18. For purposes of this discussion, I am ignoring the harm the addict does to taxpayers who may have to fund government programs to provide him various forms of aid. This sort of harm is entirely contingent on the preexistence of the government programs, which may themselves be immoral violations of the Choice Principle. See the discussion of "Redistributive Taxation" later in this chapter.

19. See, for example, Timothy Lynch, ed., *After Prohibition: An Adult Approach to Drug Policies in the 21st Century* (Washington: Cato Institute, 2000); James P. Gray, *Why Our Drug Laws Have Failed and What We Can Do About It* (Philadelphia: Temple University Press, 2001); David Schultz, "Rethinking Drug Criminalization Policies," Tex. Tech L. Rev. 25 (1993): 151; Kurt L. Schmoke, "An Argument in Favor of Decriminalization," Hofstra L. Rev. 18 (1990): 501; James Ostrowski, "The Moral and Practical Case for Drug Legalization," Hofstra L. Rev. 18 (1990): 607; Michael Z. Letwin, "Report From the Front Line: The Bennett Plan, Street-Level Drug Enforcement in New York City and the Legalization Debate," Hofstra L. Rev. 18 (1990): 795; Steven B. Duke, Drug Prohibition: An Unnatural Disaster, Conn. L. Rev. 27 (1995): 571; Steven B. Duke and Albert C. Gross, *America's Longest War: Rethinking Our Tragic Crusade Against Drugs* (New York: Putnam, 1992); Eric Grant Luna, "Our Vietnam: The Prohibition Apocalypse," DePaul L. Rev. 46 (1997): 483; Steven Wisotsky, "Exposing the War on Cocaine: The Futility and Destructiveness of Prohibition," Wis. L. Rev. 1983 (1983): 1305; David R. Henderson, "A Humane Economist's Case for Drug Legalization," U.C. Davis L. Rev. 24 (1991): 655.

20. I suppose a third option would be for the government to sell goods or services in the market, receiving money or other resources in a voluntary exchange with someone

and then distributing those resources to someone else. But only a very small proportion of governmental revenues comes from these sorts of exchanges. In any event, the resources gained from such governmental operations (such as Amtrak, the U.S. Post Office, government-owned museums, and federal and state parklands) are usually kept within the program that generated them, to defray the expenses of operating the program.

21. See, for example, 26 U.S.C. 7203 (2000), making it a federal crime to fail willfully to pay income tax or file an income tax return.

22. See, for example, Luke 20:20–26; Rom. 13:6–7. See also the discussion of taxation in Chapter 5 and the few additional thoughts on taxation in Chapter 6, note 29 and accompanying text.

23. To be sure, the government may *borrow* money (as it regularly does) from the surplus Social Security payroll taxes collected, and then use that money to pay general expenses of the government; but the government must make a legally binding promise (usually in the form of government securities) to repay the amount borrowed with interest.

24. In fact, that condition is not *currently* met, by a long shot. Currently, to qualify for full Social Security benefits based on age, one must be at least 65 years old. And in the United States, the wealthiest age group in the population, as measured by median household net assets, is the group of people who are 65 years of age or above. See U.S. Census Bureau, "Table 1: Median Value of Assets for Households, By Type of Asset Owned and Selected Characteristics, 2000," *Asset Ownership of Households, 2000*, <http://www.census.gov/hhes/www/wealth/1998_2000/wlth001.html> (9 Dec. 2005).

25. David A.J. Richards, "Commercial Sex and the Rights of the Person: A Moral Argument for the Decriminalization of Prostitution," U. Pa. L. Rev. 127 (1979): 1195, 1208–9; Susan E. Thompson, Note, "Prostitution: A Choice Ignored," Women's Rts. L. Rep. 21 (2000): 217, 219–20.

26. See Chapter 2, note 24 and accompanying text; see also Richards, "Commercial Sex," 1210–11.

27. Richards, "Commercial Sex," 1212.

28. John M. Scheb and John M. Scheb, II, *Criminal Law*, 3d ed. (Belmont, Calif.: Wadsworth, 2003), 204.

29. Ann M. Lucas, "Race, Class, Gender, And Deviancy: The Criminalization of Prostitution," Berkeley Women's L.J. 10 (1995): 47, 50. But it should be noted that some of the colonies, and some of the states—particularly in their early history—criminalized other, broader offenses like adultery and fornication, which would include just about all of the activity we now generally consider "prostitution." See Sue Titus Reid, *Criminal Law*, 5th ed. (New York: McGraw-Hill, 2001), 300. Lucas suggests that these laws were not widely enforced against prostitutes.

30. Lucas, "Race," 51; Richards, "Commercial Sex," 1213.

31. Richards, "Commercial Sex," 1202–3.

32. Gardner and Anderson, *Criminal Law*, 414.

33. See, for example, Julie Pearl, Note, "The Highest Paying Customers: America's Cities and the Costs of Prostitution Control," Hastings L.J. 38 (1987): 769;

Michael Conant, "Federalism, the Mann Act, and the Imperative to Decriminalize Prostitution," Cornell J.L. & Pub. Pol'y 5 (1996): 99; Thompson, "Prostitution," 225.

34. We are not here considering a law that forbids *only* prostitution involving a *married* person, as a violation of the marriage contract and a victimization of the non-adulterous spouse. But at first blush, such a law would certainly seem to present a more compelling case of validity under the Choice Principle than would a law against all prostitution. For that matter, laws generally criminalizing "adultery" could similarly be understood as Choice-protecting, on the same basis. But our judgments here might depend on whether we decide to enforce marriage contracts the way we enforce other legally binding contracts and to view the contracting parties as having property rights in the expected performance of the other party under the contract.

Chapter Ten

The Choice Principle and the Pro-choice Principle

As a final application of the Choice Principle, let us consider abortion laws. For many evangelicals and other Christian moral absolutists, this is not just an important political issue; it is the only political issue that matters. No matter what else God may want, these people feel, surely his top priority is ending our merciless slaughter of babies. Such people may find themselves unable to vote for any candidate (even candidates for local offices like mayor or sheriff) who supports abortion rights or the legalization of abortion. They are unable to support any nominee for the U.S. Supreme Court until they are convinced the nominee would vote to overturn *Roe v. Wade*.[1] They believe any political agenda or judicial philosophy that includes ending the killings must be preferable, from a Christian perspective, to one that does not.

The Choice Principle posits that God wants governments to ban victimizing activities that reduce overall Choice, but otherwise to leave people to their own devices. It is not immediately apparent what this would mean for abortion law. Despite the similarity of nomenclature between "the Choice Principle" and the "pro-choice" movement, adherence to the Choice Principle may not dictate a pro-choice position on the question of abortion rights. What would it mean to affirm the value of human Choice in the context of abortions? The pro-choice argument, entailing widespread legalization of abortion, may affirm the value of Choice. Or it may, instead, be a form of legal intolerance and Choice-reduction, merely masquerading as an affirmation of individual freedom by cloaking itself in the rhetoric of Choice.

THE CRUCIAL ISSUE

Abortion laws are criminal laws which penalize women and physicians for the crime of abortion. Despite *Roe v. Wade* and other court cases declaring the constitutional right to an abortion, the right has never been held to be unlimited. States are still allowed to outlaw some abortions during some stages of pregnancy, and so our question about what abortion laws to make has some relevance even if we take the U.S. Supreme Court's current stance on abortion rights as a given. But then again, why should we? The precise question we are raising in this chapter is what the law *ought* to say, not what the U.S. Constitution or some court will allow it to say. For the moment, then, let us ignore whatever the constitution may currently require (or be interpreted to require), and simply ask what legal policies the Choice Principle would suggest in the realm of abortion.

Once again, recall that the Choice Principle has nothing to say about whether abortion is sinful or whether people should have abortions. The only issue before us is how the *law* should treat those who have abortions. For the committed Christian, this in turn boils down to the question, "What does God want our laws to say about abortion?" This is the question the Choice Principle tries to answer.

The Bible does not speak at all of abortion laws, or the practice of abortion itself for that matter. In light of this absence of biblical authority for abortion laws, the Choice Principle would say, "Laws criminalizing abortion are permissible only if such laws cause a net increase in overall human Choice, and forbid only those individual choices that would directly harm others." Abortion laws certainly restrict the choices of pregnant women and abortion providers to voluntarily undergo or perform abortions. But does the choice to terminate a pregnancy directly harm others? And do abortion laws foster some greater quality or quantity of human Choice than they prohibit?

In my view, the answers to both these questions absolutely depend on one's answer to a single prior question: When does a human being first attain moral status as a human being? Or, to reword the question: When does "personhood" begin? However we word it, that is the crucial issue in the debate over abortion laws. We cannot speak of "human Choice" unless we know who counts as "human"; and we cannot speak of "direct harm to others" unless we know who to include in the category of "others." In most contexts, of course, almost everyone agrees on what these terms mean and who is included in them. But when it comes to the abortion debate, we disagree widely. Everything hinges on whether terms like "persons" or "humans" or "others" include any *unborn* human beings.

THE BIBLICAL VIEW

To figure out if the unborn should count as "persons" or "human beings," it seems desirable to discover what guidance (if any) the Bible might provide as to how God views the unborn. The Bible suggests that an indicator of personhood is the soul (or "spirit"). Every living "human being" has one.[2] Further, the New Testament view seems to be that souls never literally "die" or cease to exist; after the body dies, the soul continues to live in some form of "afterlife" for eternity. There is a very real sense, then, in which we can say that souls have no end. But the Bible never suggests that souls have no *beginning*. In fact, the suggestion from Scripture seems to be the opposite: souls begin to exist at the point life begins in a human body. The Bible suggests that the soul is in a saved or lost condition before God by virtue of the choices it made while in the particular human body it inhabited, while that body lived on earth. As far as we know, there are no souls to save that have never inhabited living human bodies. And we have no indication that there is a pool of souls gathered in heaven awaiting the creation of human bodies to inhabit. (If there is such a gathering of pre-embodied souls, our souls certainly seem to have no awareness or memory of their time there, as Jesus seemed to have of the time he spent in heaven before he walked the earth.) It seems, rather, that each human soul begins to exist at a discrete point in time, which is apparently the time when the life of the body begins.

But what, exactly, is the point when the body begins its life, when a human soul comes into existence? Although many evangelicals seem to assume the Christian faith dictates that this point is fertilization, I am not sure there is biblical authority for this assumption. The Bible clearly condemns murder, and it unquestionably tells us that human life, whatever that might be, is valuable. But the Bible seems to provide no guidance at all on the narrow question of when human life begins. In other words, it seems to provide very little indication as to whether an unfertilized egg, a fertilized egg, a first-trimester embryo, or a viable fetus (respectively) has a soul, or would be considered "a human being" in God's sight.[3] Further, I find little evidence *in Scripture* to buttress the typical evangelical assumptions that deliberately destroying a sperm or an unfertilized egg is no sin, but destroying an embryo one week after fertilization is tantamount to murder. This is not to say that abortion is not sinful; it is just to say that the Bible alone does not tell us. The Bible tells us that *taking life* is sinful. Determining whether *abortion* is sinful will depend on a determination of when "life" begins for moral purposes, which must in turn depend on evidence *outside the Bible*.

I am familiar with at least some of the Scriptures often advanced to "prove" that life begins, or the soul joins the body, at the moment of fertilization or "conception."[4] But as far as I can tell, none of them in fact say that. For example, one oft-quoted passage reads: "Indeed, I was born guilty, a sinner when my mother conceived me" (Ps. 51:5). That passage falls far short of asserting, as a theological matter, that David had a soul at the moment of conception and no earlier. The most important reason is that it is no part of

David's purpose in the Psalm to weigh in on that issue. The passage is a poetic (and moving) confession of guilt before God, not a theological explication of the human soul-body relationship. For another thing, if we do read it literally, as a theological assertion about the origins of the soul, it will also show that this soul in the womb was sinful already—which is bound to present huge theological problems for Christian traditions which disavow the notion of original sin inherited by infants (or is it possible to sin even within the womb?). Moreover, if this passage shows that the soul is present at conception, what are we to make of passages like Jer. 1:5, where the poet has God saying: "*Before* I formed you in the womb I knew you" (emphasis added)? Or Eph. 1:3–6, which says (non-poetically) that God "chose us in Christ *before the foundation of the world*" (emphasis added)? If the passage from Psalm 51 shows that human souls are alive in the womb, don't Jeremiah 1 and Ephesians 1 both indicate that each of our souls were alive *before* conception—in fact "before the foundation of the world"? Where were our souls back then? What were they doing? Why don't we remember? And more to the point, would that indicate that *contraception* is also murder? Again, the problem is that we are reading too literally, trying to interpret a confessional poem as if it were a theological treatise. The fact is, no biblical authors ever tried to answer the question of precisely when life or the soul begin. So we are barking up the wrong tree to try to find our answer to such questions in the Bible.

The Torah and the Unborn

As we contemplate God's view of the unborn, one passage worthy of extended study is Exod. 21:22–23, which says: "When people who are fighting injure a pregnant woman so that there is a miscarriage, and yet no further harm follows, the one responsible shall be fined what the woman's husband demands, paying as much as the judges determine. If any harm follows, then you shall give life for life . . . ." I have sometimes heard this passage used to demonstrate that God views the unborn as full-fledged human beings. After due consideration, I am persuaded that this passage tells us little, if anything, about how God views the unborn.[5] But if it does tell us anything, it demonstrates just the opposite: that God does *not* view the unborn as full-fledged human beings. Under the rule announced in this passage, a violent act forcing miscarriage (and fetal "death") is punishable by mere monetary fine, as if the unborn child were not a person, but rather property belonging to the husband (like a sheep or an ox, as in Exod. 21:33–34 and 22:14); but "if any harm follows," that is, harm to the *woman* (not the child, since it is already dead), the attacker will be punished according to the punishment for harming a *person*—that is, life for life, eye for eye, tooth for tooth.

To see this point even more clearly, consider a literal word-for-word translation of the Hebrew text at verse 22: "And when men fight, and they strike a pregnant woman, and her child goes forth, and there is no injury; surely he shall be fined . . ."[6] The phrase "there is no injury" suggests that the miscarriage itself was not considered an "injury" (to a person), but merely a loss of property.[7] Quite contrary to our modern notions, in ancient Hebrew law the unborn child was treated as neither a part of the mother's body nor a separate human being, but rather a separate entity having property status.

It should also be noted that the Hebrew text says "her child goes forth" rather than "she miscarries." Logically, a child who "goes forth" from its mother prematurely may be delivered either alive or dead. In fact, the Hebrew word (*yatsa*) translated "to go forth" was used in the Old Testament for both normal births, on the one hand, and miscarriages or stillbirths, on the other (although there are no passages in the Old Testament where the term is clearly used in reference to a premature birth).[8] It might be argued that, since the terms of this law do not distinguish between premature live birth and stillbirth, this law might encompass both. In other words, one might argue that this law applies not only (or even primarily) to miscarriages, but to live birth scenarios, in which the attacker causes a woman to prematurely deliver a child that lives. In that case, the phrase "her child goes forth" would be interpreted as "she delivers prematurely," and thus the "no injury" language could be understood to apply to the *child* as well as the woman. Perhaps the rule then could be read to say that an attacker who causes a healthy premature birth and does not injure the mother should be fined; but if as a result of the attack the mother dies *or* the child is stillborn (if there is "injury"), then the attacker must be put to death.

There are good reasons, however, to think the rule imposing a fine whenever there is "no injury" was not anticipating situations of live birth. In the first place, whenever premature labor was induced by violent attack in the ancient world, live healthy births must have been a very exceptional result. Laws, especially ancient laws, are not written for exceptional cases. In the second place, in these rare situations where the woman was attacked but unharmed and her baby was born prematurely but alive and healthy, why would the rule require *restitution* (restitution for *what*)? Why should a fine be levied if the only "harm" is an earlier-than-expected birth? In the ancient world, that sort of "harm" would be cause for celebration, not restitution. It makes little sense, then, to read the rule as applying to cases of live birth.

Probably what the rule denotes here are situations where a male attacker tries to hurt another man but instead accidentally strikes an intervening pregnant woman (perhaps the intended victim's spouse or relative) so that she miscarries, delivering a stillborn child. The rule says that in such a case, the attacker is to pay a sum of money, fixed by the husband and collected by the courts on his behalf, as restitution for the loss of the unborn child (regardless of the woman's stage of pregnancy); but the rule also says that if the *woman herself* has been physically harmed by the attack (i.e., if "any harm follows"), the attacker must also suffer the criminal penalties for battery or murder of a person, as if he had intended to attack the woman in the first place. In modern criminal law, we would call this an application of the doctrine of transferred intent. The point of the rule seems to be that any harm to the woman will be viewed as having been caused intentionally, not accidentally, because the man intended in the beginning to harm *someone*. The fact that he incompetently hurt the wrong person should not insulate him from the severe punishment he would otherwise receive.

So it would seem the central meaning of this passage from Exodus is that Mosaic law applies the transferred intent doctrine in cases of personal assault resulting in unanticipated personal injury or property damage. While the passage may or may not tell us, in addition, how God views the unborn, and may or may not be relevant to the current abortion debate, one thing it surely does *not* tell us is that God views unborn children as being fully human.[9]

The Biblical Witness and the Early Church

Although many evangelicals seem to assume that abortion is murder and contraception is not, the Bible does not make any distinction among unfertilized ova, zygotes, embryos, and fetuses. Furthermore, the Bible is silent regarding the act of abortion, despite the fact that abortion was widely practiced in the ancient world. In Romans 13 Paul even gives his vote of confidence to a government that did not ban abortion, characterizing that government as a generally reliable agent of God to punish those who wrong others.[10] That in itself does not prove that abortion is not murder—that same Roman government also allowed the widespread practice of infanticide by exposure, without comment by Paul—but it is far from showing that abortion is murder and contraception is not. At a minimum, Paul's endorsement calls into serious question the contention that conscientious Christians can never support any candidate or government that favors the legalization of abortion. Paul certainly seems to have supported such a government.

It is clear, however, that the early Church, whatever it may have thought about the propriety of abortion laws, did not embrace the practice of abortion. Outside the pages of the Bible, early Christian teaching seems to have regarded the private act of abortion as a great sin.[11] Most often the teachings characterize abortion as murder.[12]

On the other hand, these teachings may have been erroneous. Some widely respected early Christian teachers seem to have viewed even contraception as sinful murder.[13] And some early Christian teachers opposed abortion (and contraception as well) for reasons beyond the personhood of the unborn, such as abortion's interference with procreation or its utility in concealing sexual sin.[14] Some early Christian teachers even held capital punishment to be forbidden murder.[15] For reasons discussed in Chapters 3 and 5, that position would seem to find as little support in the New Testament as the proposition that imprisonment of murderers by the government is tantamount to sinful private kidnapping. In sum, there are several reasons to think that "early Christian teachings" should not be viewed as conclusive on the questions of whether certain acts (like abortion) are sinful, or which acts constitute murder in particular. Besides, evangelicals have always claimed to prioritize the Bible over the teachings of men, and the Bible is silent about abortion.

In any event, neither the Bible nor the teachings of the early Church seem to define authoritatively the precise beginning point of personhood. If this is true, the Christian will be forced to rely on other evidence to decide this crucial question—evidence from biology and medicine, from history, from anthropology, from sociology, and probably from other disciplines too. This is not to say that these other disciplines can answer the question for us. The question of when human personhood begins is at its heart a philosophical and theological one, a moral one, for it hinges on what we mean by "personhood." The experts in the natural and social sciences can claim no special expertise in answering the moral question of what constitutes "personhood"; they can merely provide evidence (such as information about heartbeat, brain activity, attitudes toward the unborn in early Christian communities, and so on) which we may find useful in order to answer the question intelligently ourselves. The point is, though, that Christians wrestling with this question must necessarily rely on evidence outside the Bible. Therefore, the evangelical answer to the question of when personhood begins need *not* logically depend, as so many on both sides seem to assume, on religious beliefs.

THE CHOICE PRINCIPLE AND ABORTION LAWS

Most Americans today (although not all people in all places and times) would agree that human life or "personhood" begins *no later than* the time of birth. But Americans disagree about whether it begins at some earlier time. The answer to this question, as we have seen, turns out to be crucial in deciding what to do about abortion laws, and it is the principal point of disagreement between the pro-life and pro-choice camps (their rhetoric to the contrary notwithstanding).[16] Indeed, the question of when human life begins also seems to be the key to answering the theological question whether abortion is sinful, for the understanding of abortion as sinful (and ordinary contraception as permissible) must rest on the assumption that a woman's choice to have a (safe) abortion *harms others*. But if an unborn child is not a discrete, living human being with its own soul, then abortion is not murder; it is simply elective surgery. If performed safely, it harms no one. If the unborn child is nothing more (morally speaking) than a collection of living cells, which are presumptively part of the mother's body and no one else's, the unborn child would then have the moral standing of an appendix, and an abortion would be no more sinful than an appendectomy, or some sort of cosmetic surgery.

Recall, however, that according to the Choice Principle, the sinfulness (or not) of abortion is not directly relevant to our decision about the law. For purposes of the Choice Principle, we are trying to decide when personhood begins, not in order to decide whether abortion is sinful, but in order to decide who counts as a person and whose opportunities for Choice we must protect in the law. If personhood never begins before a baby completely exits its mother's body, then an unborn child is not a person, and we need not protect its range of Choice. It is nothing more than living tissue, a part of the mother's body—like an unfertilized egg. It might have the *potential to become* something more, but as yet, like an unfertilized egg, it has not. It does not have its own moral status. In that case, the Choice Principle would dictate that the law freely allow voluntary abortions, at any time during pregnancy, because criminalizing abortion would restrict more Choice than it promotes and would forbid an individual choice that does not directly harm others. Abortion would be properly viewed as victimless elective surgery, and the Choice Principle would not allow the state to interfere with a woman's choice whether to have the procedure. Restricting the choices of the pregnant woman and her doctor would not be justified by the need to protect any overriding outside Choice interests, for there are none involved of significant enough weight. The Choice of other human beings would not be directly affected by the individual choice to have an abortion.

On the other hand, if one determines that human life begins at some point before birth, then the Choice Principle would clearly dictate that the law must prohibit all abortions occurring after that point. Such abortions would have the effect of killing a person without that person's consent. In those cases, the choices of the pregnant woman and her doctor to undergo/perform an abortion would be clearly outweighed by the overriding, greater Choice interest of the unborn human being to live. Under those circumstances, the Choice Principle would require abortion laws for exactly the same reason that it requires murder laws. An abortion would be exactly the same act, from a moral or ethical standpoint, as intentionally smothering a one-year-old baby—an act that we surely agree should be outlawed. And just as no excuse would be sufficient to allow a mother to intentionally kill her one-year-old, no justification would be sufficient to allow a voluntary abortion—not rape, not incest, and not some grave danger to the health of the mother.[17]

ABORTION RIGHTS AND *ROE V. WADE*

Any treatment of abortion laws that does not discuss *Roe v. Wade* seems to be somewhat incomplete, so here I, too, will include a few thoughts on that landmark case and the constitutional right to an abortion. In *Roe*, the first court opinion in the United States to declare a legal right to an abortion, the U.S. Supreme Court held that: (1) states could not limit or regulate abortions in any way during the first trimester of pregnancy, except to require that they be performed by a physician licensed to practice medicine in the state; (2) during the second trimester (i.e., from the beginning of the second trimester until the point of viability, which in 1973 was approximately the end of the second trimester), states could not outlaw abortions completely but could regulate abortions in ways reasonably related to protecting maternal health; and (3) during the third trimester (i.e., after the point of viability), states could outlaw abortions completely if they wished, except those that were deemed by the mother's physician to be medically necessary to protect her life or health.[18] The practical effect of the holding in *Roe* was to declare the abortion laws of all fifty states to be unconstitutional.

Even if one agrees with this outcome as a matter of constitutional interpretation, one can certainly attack the Court's rationale on a number of grounds. One of the most glaring flaws in the opinion, in my view, is the Court's insistence that "we need not resolve the difficult question of when life begins" in order to issue the opinion in this case.[19] To take the Court at its word, we must assume the majority believed that human life *might* begin at the very moment of conception (or at least that their reasoning would not be any different if they *did* admit this possibility). If they really believed this might be true, it becomes very difficult to understand where the Court would derive the authority for overruling the laws of all fifty states—a move we would not typically make, I trust, unless we were *certain* that the states' laws were *wrong*. Judicial uncertainty about the point of life's beginning cannot logically serve as a justification for striking down the states' decisions on the matter. Lawmakers and judges *must* decide when, as a philosophical or moral matter, human life begins, for resolving "the difficult [moral] question of when life begins" is logically prerequisite to resolving the difficult *legal* questions surrounding abortion. I find it difficult to understand how a judge could conscientiously forbid a state from outlawing the destruction of an embryo or fetus without determining that the state is wrong in judging the embryo or fetus to be a human life.

The explanation that "it's debatable, so we must let the mother decide" will not do. We typically do not let those accused of murder decide for themselves what constitutes human life, even in "debatable" cases; the state does that. For example, in cases where someone attacks a pregnant woman and she miscarries, the state decides for itself the moral and legal status of the unborn. Some states (ignoring the *attacker's* definition of "life") punish the offender for "homicide," at least if the fetus has reached the point of viability.[20] Other states would punish the offender for "homicide" only if the fetus is "born alive" before it dies—that is, the attack causes the mother to deliver prematurely (at whatever stage of pregnancy or fetal development) a fetus that is completely expelled from her body, shows some clear indicia of life such as breathing or heartbeat, and then dies.[21] In every case, though, it is the *state*, not the attacker, that is privileged to decide when legally protected life or personhood begins.

The states also impose their own definitions of "life" to decide when life legally *ends*. Suppose, for example, that after being violently attacked, a man is comatose and is being kept alive by a respirator. His doctors consider him to be "brain dead"—that is, all brain activity has ceased—and in their best medical judgment, this condition is irreversible. Apparently, all states today would consider him for legal purposes to be dead, even if his heart and lungs continue to function.[22] This determination of death is important, for it means that the state could immediately begin a murder (not battery or attempted murder) prosecution against the attacker who put him in this condition.[23] And by the same token, doctors and family members could *not* be charged with murder for agreeing, after the determination of death, to remove life support devices or harvest his vital organs for transplant.[24] Importantly, each state defines for itself, in these "debatable" cases, when life has ended; no state allows the *attacker* (the doctor, the family, or the thug who initially attacked the victim) the right to decide whether his victim is "alive" or "dead," either before or after the attack. To do so would be ludicrous.

Further suppose that, in some bizarre brain death case, a judge nullified state law by declaring that the attacker had the right to decide for himself whether the brain dead man was "alive" even after brain function had ceased. This is not, it seems to me, what we want judges to do. But more to the point, it would be fair to presume that in order to strike down state law, the judge must have been relying on more than the fact that the point of death, and the meaning of life and personhood, are hotly debated in our society; rather, the judge himself must have drawn a conclusion about when life ends. Specifically, he must have determined that the state law was wrong and that the brain dead man was in fact "alive"—otherwise how could the judge justify forbidding the state from defining the end of life for itself and its people? Similarly with the state's definition of the *beginning* of life: if the time of life's beginning is so debatable, why is that a reason to allow the *attacker* to decide? Isn't it, rather, a reason to allow the *state* to decide (without input from the attacker) when human life begins? Unless, of course, the judge has already decided that the state has clearly gotten it *wrong*.

One response might be that the unborn child's life affects the pregnant woman's body in ways that the lives of victims in other homicide cases do not affect the bodies of their attackers. This may be why the Supreme Court held in *Roe* that the mother and no one else (not other attackers, and not even the father) has the constitutional right to choose whether to terminate her pregnancy. The reasoning goes like this: Everyone understands that we would *ordinarily* not allow attackers to choose how to define "life" for legal purposes. Indeed, if a pregnant woman assaulted another pregnant woman and intentionally caused the victim to miscarry her fetus, we would not allow the pregnant attacker to decide whether the fetus miscarried by her victim was a living person. But, the argument goes, it is different when a pregnant woman attacks the embryo or fetus inside her own body, because the attacker's rights of bodily integrity are implicated by the victim's continued existence. Therefore, we try to accord the "attacker" in abortion cases some choice in how the state can legally define "life."

The problem with this explanation is, again, that we *never* treat attackers this way in any other similar situation in homicide law. There are in fact other situations that would seem to be analogous to abortion, in which an attacker's bodily integrity or health is threatened by the living existence of the victim, thus provoking the attacker to kill the victim. Specifically, we can speak of the law of self-defense, which excuses even homicide when, but for the homicide, the victim would have been reasonably likely to kill the attacker. The homicide in self-defense is excused because the attacker's life was threatened as long as the victim was alive. However, the "self-defense" defense only applies when the homicide victim had *wrongfully* attacked or threatened the attacker. I cannot legally kill an *innocent* person in "self-defense," even if some disaster or thug has threatened me (or a thousand other innocent people) with immediate death if I do not.[25] Similarly, I am not allowed to kill an innocent person for food, even if I and others (and even the innocent person himself) will otherwise starve to death.[26] Intentionally killing an innocent person (like a baby) is, to my knowledge, never justifiable under the law, for any reason—and certainly not (as the rule from *Roe v. Wade* would have it) in every case in which the attacker's life or health is endangered by the innocent person's existence. An unborn child would certainly meet the test for being "innocent," so if it is a "person," abortion would certainly constitute an "intentional killing" of that person, which no threat to the mother could ever justify.

Thus, when deciding the constitutionality (or wisdom) of abortion laws, the central question is the same one we have been considering all along: what counts as a "person"? Or, in other words, when does human life begin? The majority in *Roe* said that this question is irrelevant; but in announcing a nationwide right to abortion, which extends to the very point of birth in all cases where existence of the fetus threatens the mother's health, perhaps they really answered the question, after all.

If the Court (as it essentially said) indeed admitted the possibility that human life might begin at conception, its decision boils down to the following judgment: Perhaps a large group of children are being killed every year, but since we're not sure ourselves, no state is allowed to protect them. This is a strange decision indeed. Whenever the Court is uncertain in other contexts, the default rule is "leave it to the legislature," not "create an individual constitutional right." We are entitled, then, to doubt their claim of uncertainty. If the Court forbids states from prosecuting those who request and perform abortions, perhaps the Court has actually decided that those people are *not* murderers. In fact, there is no way logically to establish any nationwide abortion right, as the Court did, without deciding when life begins. While denying that it had made that determination, the Court prohibited states from outlawing certain "medically necessary" abortions *at any time* during pregnancy, right up to the moment of birth. If the Court had not determined that life begins no earlier than birth, how could it have forced states to legalize what might be the murder of an innocent child, any time it is necessary to prevent risk to the mother's health?

PRO-LIFE VS. PRO-CHOICE

It is interesting to note that many on the "pro-life" side of the abortion debate embrace that label because they see the abortion controversy through the lens of their larger assumptions about American history and the degradation of American culture. They allude to an increasing cultural apathy, or lack of respect, toward human life in all forms, and claim that the abortion rights movement is just another manifestation of that attitude. As further evidence, the pro-life camp specifically alleges that our society increasingly tolerates and even justifies the acts of suicide, assisted suicide, and euthanasia (examined earlier in Chapter 9). It should now be apparent that their analysis ignores several crucial differences among these different acts, differences which might well lead us to treat the acts in three or four different ways under the law without any logical inconsistency. In any event, we should be reluctant to cavalierly combine them all under the heading "acts stemming from a disrespect for life." The pro-choice camp, on the other hand, often makes the same mistake of generalization in reverse, accusing those in the pro-life camp of repeatedly disrespecting individual Choice—a claim that only makes sense if one ignores the Choice interests of the unborn.

The national debate over abortion, which has percolated near a boiling point since 1973 at the latest, is in fact a debate over when personhood begins for human beings. It is a shame that neither side seems to frame the issue in those terms, for if they did we might make real progress toward some national consensus on abortion laws. Instead, each side frames the issue differently, and inaccurately, in order to appeal to values it believes no one can reasonably deny. In their rush to demonize each other and to market their own point of view, both sides miss opportunities to foster and engage in the moral debate we most need: the debate about when personhood begins.

The very nomenclature of the two camps contributes to the misunderstanding. The "pro-choice" name implies that anyone who wishes to outlaw abortion is Anti-Choice or is apathetic about human Choice. But of course if the unborn count as human beings, it is the pro-choice camp itself which is ignoring the value of human Choice—specifically, the choice the unborn would presumably make to live (and the undisputable fact that they have clearly *not* made a choice to die). Similarly, one sometimes hears the argument from the pro-choice camp that abortion rights are a subset of "women's rights"—but of course, if the unborn count as human beings, then a concern for "women's rights" would seem to dictate that we *prohibit* abortion, since a huge number of its victims (approximately half) are female.

On the other hand, the "pro-life" label implies that anyone wishing to legalize abortion is Anti-Life, or at least apathetic toward protecting human life. The pro-life camp pretends that their opponents systematically devalue the sanctity of human life, citing examples of the supposed cultural acceptance of such practices as assisted suicide—a practice that (even assuming life begins at conception) is about as far removed from abortion as charity is from theft. But of course, if the unborn are not yet living human beings, the pro-life rhetoric falls apart completely, and it is the pro-choice side which seems to place greater value on human life—that is, on the human lives that actually exist. The pro-choice side has simply embraced the notion that human life never begins at any point prior to the time the baby fully exits the mother's body. Or perhaps they believe that no one can know for sure, and until such time as we can, our moral uncertainty should counsel legal toleration. On either assumption, they are actually trying their best to protect, respect, and affirm human life, by removing any unnecessary obstructions to the full, free, and healthy life of all living human beings.

Again, the central point of disagreement between the two camps is not a disagreement about the value of human life, or about the value of human Choice, but about *when human life begins*. Once having decided that human life begins at conception, it is almost impossible to be pro-choice; after deciding that human life begins at birth, it is almost impossible to be pro-life.

Deciding that human life begins sometime between conception and birth would seem to dictate a pro-choice stance for the period of pregnancy prior to that point and a pro-life stance for the period thereafter. And deciding that it is impossible to know when human life begins would seem to dictate inaction. On the part of *legislators and voters*, such inaction might logically be manifested as legalization and a "leave it to the individuals involved" position; but the uncertainty of *judges* would seem to require a "leave it to the legislatures" position. Judicial inaction is judicial restraint, not judicial activism in the service of some new constitutional right.

CONCLUSIONS ABOUT ABORTION LAWS

As we have applied the Choice Principle to the abortion debate, it has become clear that the dictates of the Principle depend on when personhood begins. We must answer this prior question in order to know what laws we should make. Our answer will also likely determine whether we believe abortion is sinful. There are, of course, many reasons, and contrasting rationales, for adopting a particular view of when personhood (or the soul, or "human-ness") begins. To explore these fully would likely require another book. My purpose here is not to advocate a particular view of when life begins, but rather to assert that: (1) This is the crucial question that must be answered, and the *only* one we should be debating when it comes to either the *morality* or *legality* of abortion; (2) It must be answered rationally, by reference to *evidence*; and (3) That evidence will only be found *outside* the biblical text.

Given all this, it should not surprise us when rational Christians of goodwill, even evangelical Christians, draw varying conclusions about: (1) whether abortion is sinful, or (2) whether it should be legalized, or (3) whether it should be deemed a constitutional right. (We should recognize that these are three distinct questions.) And since God has not spoken directly on the subject of abortion, it would seemingly behoove us to be extremely reluctant to bind our own point of view about abortion or abortion laws on our brothers and sisters in the faith, or to assume that all true Christians must believe as we do.

NOTES

1. 410 U.S. 113 (1973).
2. Recall James 2:26: "For just as *the body without the spirit is dead*, so faith without works is also dead" (emphasis added). The implication is clear: living human beings have spirits.

3. No less an authority than Augustine reached the same conclusion almost 1,600 years ago. In considering the question of when the human soul comes into existence, he wrote: "Who is it that makes from seeds various kinds of things appropriate to their origins, except He who made the very seeds without seeds? When a thing naturally obscure surpasses our limited intelligence, and there is no assistance from a clear passage of sacred Scripture, human conjecture is rash in presuming to define any opinion on it. . . . I [have] found nothing certain about the origin of the soul in the canonical Scriptures." Augustine, *Epistula* 190, in *The Fathers of the Church*, Wilfred Parsons trans., vol. 30 (New York: Fathers of the Church, Inc., 1955), 281.

4. See, for example, Job 10:8–12; Ps. 139:13–16; Luke 1:39–45.

5. My thinking on this passage has been greatly influenced by Russell Fuller, "Exodus 21:22–23: The Miscarriage Interpretation and the Personhood of the Fetus," *Journal of the Evangelical Theological Society* 37, no. 2 (June 1994): 169–84.

6. Jay Green, ed. and trans., *The Interlinear Hebrew-Greek-English Bible*, vol. 1 (Wilmington, Del.: Associated Publishers & Authors, 1976), 197–98.

7. See Bruce M. Metzger and Michael D. Coogan, eds., *The Oxford Companion to the Bible* (New York: Oxford University Press, 1993), 4, s.v. "abortion."

8. See Fuller, "Miscarriage Interpretation," 182. Old Testament passages using the term to refer to a normal birth include Jer. 1:5 and Job 1:21. But Num. 12:12 uses this same term to refer to a miscarriage or stillbirth.

9. If pressed, I would actually go further than this: In my view, this passage from Exodus does not say anything one way or the other about the personhood of the unborn. Alternative interpretations are extremely problematic because of passages like the immediately preceding verses at Exod. 21:20–21, which provide *no penalty at all* in cases where an owner beats a slave so violently that the slave dies two days later. This law is explicitly grounded in the rationale that the slave is the property of the owner. If Exod. 21:22–25 shows that the unborn have "personhood" in God's sight because those who kill them are punished by death—*or* if it shows that the unborn do *not* have "personhood" in God's sight because those who kill them are *not* punished by death—then the conclusion is inescapable from Exod. 21:20–21 that slaves do not have personhood in God's sight, because those who kill them are clearly not punished by death. I find this interpretation extremely disturbing, and on balance less plausible than the conclusion that the Mosaic law's punishments tell us only about legal status under the Mosaic law, not necessarily about God's views of personhood or moral value. See Fuller, "Miscarriage Interpretation."

10. See the discussion of Romans 13 and the Roman law governing abortions in Chapter 5, notes 14–15 and accompanying text.

11. See, for example, *Didache* 2.1–2.

12. See Tertullian, *The Soul* 25, 27; Athenagoras, *A Plea for the Christians* 35.

13. See St. John Chrysostom, *Homily 24 on the Epistle to the Romans*; Hippolytus, *Refutation of All Heresies* 9.7; Jerome, *Letters* 22.13.

14. See Augustine, *On Marriage and Concupiscence* 1.17 (interference with procreation); Jerome, *Letters* 22.13 (utility in concealing sexual sin).

15. See Lactantius, *Divine Institutes* 6.20.

16. See the discussion of the pro-life and pro-choice positions later in this chapter.

17. Thus, those who want to outlaw abortion "except in cases of rape or incest" or "except in cases where the mother's health is endangered by the pregnancy" must explain how it is that the personhood of an innocent child can be affected by what has happened in the past to someone else. In other words, how is it that a particular fetus can be the moral equivalent of a one-year-old if its mother was *not* raped, but the moral equivalent of an appendix if its mother *was* raped? Is the child of a rape victim somehow less than human? See also below, notes 25 and 26 and accompanying text.

18. *Roe*, 410 U.S. at 164–65.

19. *Roe*, 410 U.S. at 159.

20. See, for example, *State v. Merrill*, 450 N.W.2d 318 (Minn. 1990), *cert. denied*, 496 U.S. 931 (1990) (upholding state statute imposing the criminal penalty for murder on attacker whose battery of a pregnant woman caused her to miscarry her one-month-old embryo); *Commonwealth v. Cass*, 467 N.E.2d 1324 (Mass. 1984) (construing the meaning of "person" in certain state homicide laws to include any viable fetus). Of course, when a state issues a murder conviction for anyone who intentionally attacks (or hires someone to attack) an unborn child, causing miscarriage, but also allows a complete defense in many cases upon proof that the attacker (or instigator) is the mother of the unborn child, the logical inconsistency is patent.

21. See, for example, *Commonwealth v. Booth*, 766 A.2d 843 (Pa. 2001) (declining to depart from the common law "born alive" rule in interpreting the meaning of "person" in state homicide statute); *State v. Oliver*, 563 A.2d 1002 (Vt. 1989) (same).

22. Samantha Weyrauch, Note, "Acceptance of Whole-Brain Death Criteria for Determination of Death: A Comparative Analysis of the United States and Japan," UCLA Pac. Basin L.J. 17 (1999): 91, 104–5.

23. See, for example, *State v. Guess*, 715 A.2d 643, 650–52 (Conn. 1998); *State v. Meints*, 322 N.W.2d 809, 813–14 (Neb. 1982).

24. See, for example, *State v. Velarde*, 734 P.2d 449, 454–56 (Utah 1986) (removing life support devices not deemed proximate cause of death); *People v. Eulo*, 472 N.E.2d 286, 294–97 (N.Y. 1984) (harvesting vital organs before removing life support devices not deemed proximate cause of death).

25. See *U.S. v. Holmes*, 26 F. Cas. 360 (C.C.E.D. Pa. 1842) (No. 15,383) (murder conviction for seaman in shipwreck who threw certain passengers overboard to save his own lifeboat which was filled with greater number of passengers).

26. See *Regina v. Dudley and Stephens*, 14 Q.B.D. 273 (1884).

Chapter Eleven

Conclusions

In this book I have tried to suggest to moral absolutists an alternative to legal moralism. The alternative is the Choice Principle, a variety of legal toleration. My argument for legal toleration has accorded primacy to the New Testament while also considering the arguments of several influential Christian thinkers of the past. I have tried to show that the Choice Principle protects a space for government—an institution we know is ordained by God as part of his plan for us—while also protecting a space for private freedom of choice, another divine concern. I have also tried to show how the Principle would counsel us to decide some individual cases, how it could stand in support of some laws and in opposition to others.

But we certainly have not settled all the questions about how the Choice Principle would be applied. In particular, I realize I have not yet elaborated a very thorough framework for deciding in a given case whether a government law or act "enhances total Choice" or "reduces total Choice," or whether the "harm" imposed on others by a forbidden private act is "direct" or merely "indirect." Providing this framework would, in my view, require a more extended treatment than I can provide in this book, and could perhaps form the topic of an entire book by itself. I must leave that project for another day. Suffice it to say, however, that I believe the line between "Choice-enhancing" and "Choice-reducing," and between "direct" and "indirect" harms, can be drawn in a rational way by a rational set of up-front rules. For now, I will be quite content if this book causes Christians to consider, as they evaluate laws, what value God might place on human autonomy; this in itself would be a giant step forward. Then, if we conclude that Choice should be a priority in our laws, we can debate which laws are Choice-maximizing and which are not. I predict, however, that there would be fewer "hard cases" and disagreements about classification than we might at first suspect.

By now, we have considered legal toleration from a number of different perspectives. It probably appears more attractive from some angles than from others. Still, on the whole, it seems to be a rational way of understanding God's will for our government. Let us remind ourselves where we have been, and where we have ended up, in this study of God's will.

In a sense, this book seeks to answer one question: What, in God's view, is government for? We have turned to the Bible for our answer, but not, I realize, to both Testaments equally. That selectivity may puzzle some. To many Christians, no doubt, the Old Testament seems like a fruitful source of information about God's will for governments, because it speaks of "governments" and "nations" quite a bit (often, it must be noted, in the form of poetry). But as noted in Chapter 3, the Old Testament is probably not the best place to find an answer to our question about God's will for government today. The Old Testament writings on the subject of government, where they are not specific to the Jewish state, are mostly miscellaneous proverbs or prophecies, advising nations generally to fear the Lord and to do justice to the poor and downtrodden, with no further guidance as to how to structure their laws or their forms of government. There are of course more specific provisions particularly related to Israel's law and government; but God's relationship with ancient Israel was an undeniably unique one even in its day, as both Testaments affirm time and again. Even though God loved Gentiles, he did not see fit to establish a covenant, or rule an earthly government, or write civil laws, for any nation besides the Jews. Moreover, when the New Covenant was made, the Old Covenant and its Hebrew-specific provisions were set aside (Col. 2:14; Gal. 3:23–29; Rom. 7:1–6; Hebrews 8). Since the coming of the New Covenant, God simply has not indicated any intention of forming this sort of relationship with any other nation or state, including the United States of America. The Old Testament, then, will not likely provide the key to our thorniest questions about God's will for government today.

The New Testament writings do, however, hint at an answer to our questions, an answer that apparently conveys something of God's will for all nations and governments of the world until Jesus returns. It is found most explicitly in Romans 12 and 13. In these chapters, as we have seen, Paul warns Christians not to take vengeance upon those that wrong them, but to allow God to do this through his earthly agent of vengeance, the government, which God has established for *just this purpose*, and to which each Christian should therefore pay taxes and show honor. Paul suggests here that the purpose of government, from God's perspective, is to punish those who harm its citizens, thereby maintaining peace and order. The tasks of promoting virtue more generally, or punishing sin generally, are apparently outside the government's realm of concern. As Jesus himself said, "My kingdom is not of this world"

(John 18:36, KJV). Jesus was always careful to distinguish between the kingdom of Caesar and the kingdom of God.

This is a lot to ponder, and I am still thinking through these issues. I am certainly not claiming to have fully grasped God's will for governments. In this book, I have tried to demonstrate that the Choice Principle is a *legitimate possibility*, both as a theological and a practical matter. I believe it represents a coherent alternative to the dogmatic view that God wants Christians to vote for laws that will overtly praise God, force righteousness, or forbid certain sins because they are sins. I have further tried to show that legal toleration is a reasonable alternative for Christians and Non-Christians alike, and presents some unique opportunities for building coalition and understanding between groups that have been polarized and incomprehensible to one another.

However, lest I be accused of dogmatism myself, let me remind the reader that it is *not* my intent to prove absolutely that: (1) God has a will for government policy, and (2) his will is the Choice Principle. I have presented (I think) a rational argument why this *might well be* the case, but one does not have to believe the Choice Principle is *certainly* God's will, in order to admit that the Choice Principle *might be* God's will. Perhaps God's will is unknowable on these political issues, or perhaps we can conclude that he cares not at all about them. Very well—but let us never contend that God's will is clearly for his people to outlaw prostitution simply because prostitution is a sin. Let us never contend that God's will is clearly for his people to outlaw heroin possession simply because heroin abuse is a sin. For that matter, let us never contend that God's will is clearly for his people to outlaw murder simply because murder is a sin. God may want one or more of these things outlawed, or none of them—or it may make no more difference to him than who wins the Super Bowl next year. I am reluctant to say with certainty that I know God's will in this area, and I wish other Christians would be too.

Nevertheless, I have (with fear and trembling) proposed a possible understanding of God's will that is evangelical and grounded in moral absolutism, and yet very different from the understandings advanced by the most vocal evangelicals today. If my conclusion is plausible (as I believe it is) and sincere (as I know it is), then perhaps all of us should be less dogmatic in the political realm. God may not care what our laws are, and even if he does want one or more sinful acts to be outlawed, it is not unreasonable or hypocritical to believe that it is *not* because the act itself is sinful. Christians, even evangelical Christians, may conscientiously, consistently, and rationally oppose any efforts to legislate God's moral code upon mankind, without embracing moral relativism in any form. What the Choice Principle suggests is the same thing Roger Williams suggested so long ago: legal toleration that is born of an uncompromising moral absolutism. And *that*, I believe, is a countercultural idea. It is an idea that most Christians, and Non-Christians too, still seem to have trouble understanding.

Lately, a lot of Christians have been writing books about the intersection of Christianity and public policy. In particular, authors like Richard John Neuhaus, Stephen Carter, George Marsden, and others have drawn our attention (rightly) to a certain kind of unjustifiable discrimination in the public square against policy arguments founded on religious beliefs. My own policy arguments are often founded on my religious beliefs, and I share these authors' concerns. In fact, the Choice Principle is not an argument that Christianity has nothing to say about politics, or that Christians should not be making public policy. Quite the opposite.

But while I believe these authors are onto something important, I think this is only part of the story about why some Christian views get short shrift in the public square. Perhaps another reason Christians are being excluded or tuned out in the policy debate—in some cases, perhaps, the *only* reason—is that their specific proposals are viewed by most other people as unwise or immoral or both. Sometimes the discrimination has little to do with a distaste for religion or religious arguments *per se*. Consider an illustration. As the authors above would probably concede, the dominant secular voices in the public square, those who so often shout down the Christian voice, seem perfectly willing to hear and even applaud someone who argues that we should *repeal racially discriminatory laws*—even if that someone is a priest who explicitly proclaims that his argument is religiously motivated and biblically supported. The religious motives and evidence he brings to the debate will not be viewed as automatically out of bounds. The public square is still open, as always, to *acceptable* religious messages. What secularists will tune out, criticize, and marginalize is any viewpoint, religious or not, that currently seems hateful, dictatorial, unworkable, or foolish to most secularists on both sides of the political aisle—for example, the viewpoint that some races are naturally inferior to others and that our laws should discriminate accordingly. This argument will indeed be shouted down, not so much because its presuppositions are religious (though they may be), but because it is fueled by bigotry and ignorance.

In any case, the blending of religion and politics is tricky business. A few years ago, Stephen Carter wrote an insightful book called *God's Name in Vain*.[1] In this work, Professor Carter makes two central assertions: (1) religious arguments for or against public policy should not be considered by secularists to be out of bounds *per se*; and (2) religious people who become deeply embroiled in politics for religious reasons usually shouldn't, because they run such a great risk of tainting or diluting their religion.

The first assertion is, I think, mostly true, and is perfectly consistent with the Choice Principle. Sometimes political action by Christians leads to good results, and religious motives themselves should not defeat the legitimacy of an otherwise sound proposal. A proposal to treat the races equally under law should not be viewed as illegitimate just because its proponents happen to have religious motives, believing God hates bigotry. By the same token, the Choice Principle should not be viewed as illegitimate just because its proponents believe it represents God's will for governments.

On the other hand, perhaps attempts to use law to coerce the conscience or send a moral message *should* be viewed as illegitimate, by Non-Christians and Christians alike, no matter what the motive behind the proposal, and regardless of whether the proponent is a Christian, a Muslim, or Joseph Stalin. And perhaps the reason American secularists tend to discount religious arguments about law is that more often than not, they are attempts to use law to coerce the conscience or send a moral message. Maybe those particular laws *should* find a cold reception in the public square. But not because they may happen to be motivated by someone's religious beliefs.

Professor Carter's second assertion is certainly true. When Christians become politically active, the danger to Christianity is real. As Roger Williams said 350 years ago: Once God's people "have opened a gap in the hedge or wall of separation between the garden of the Church and the wilderness of the world, God has ever broke down the wall itself, removed the candlestick, and made his garden a wilderness, as at this day."[2] Nevertheless, we should realize that the admonition to be uninvolved is only proposed as a general rule of thumb, and hinges completely on a pragmatic assessment of the dangers political involvement poses to the long term health of the church and the individual Christian. And, as Professor Carter notes, there may sometimes be more important considerations than pragmatic ones. In light of the demands of good stewardship, there may be a limit to how politically silent we should be in our democracy; and while pragmatism may counsel us, as a general rule, to avoid religiously motivated political involvement altogether because of the danger it poses to our faith, conscience and the Spirit may compel us in particular cases, for particular causes, to accept the risk and involve ourselves anyway, trusting God to protect our souls and his church.

What "causes," what particular legal or public policy debates, would be that important? The Choice Principle suggests an answer, for unlike Professor Carter's argument, it embodies an explicitly theological stance. The Choice Principle stands for the proposition that *certain* public policies, the kind that restrict overall human Choice, are *immoral* and should be opposed by Christians. Christians all over the world feel compelled by faith to join in all sorts of political struggles, but not all of these struggles are equally meritorious. In fact, some Christians' policy agendas are surely wrong. If this is so, we ought to completely abstain from political involvement directed to *those* ends, at least. Some religiously motivated political activism, even if pragmatic and successful, may be immoral. And paradoxically, the morally permissible and important activism, the kind that is worth the risk to the faith, may well turn out to be activism supporting legal toleration of sin. After examining our restrictive laws from God's perspective, we may determine that we have made far too many of them.

But perhaps we are worried over nothing. Morals legislation (if not redistributive taxation and other kinds of Choice-limiting laws) may be on the wane. The trend in most states seems to be toward reducing, not increasing, the scope of the old-time "sin laws." And the political power of Jerry Falwell, Pat Robertson, Gary Bauer, and other leaders who have favored such legislation may be declining. Several former leaders of Christian political movements seem to be rethinking their degree of political involvement and retreating from the political fray. However, we should not mistake a lack of leadership in certain Christian political organizations for a declining interest in these issues at the grassroots level. Among the rank and file of the Christian Right, at any rate, I have a feeling the zeal to legislate in God's name is as strong as ever. And judging by the interest in Jim Wallis's new book *God's Politics*, the interest of the Christian Left in coercive redistribution, for God's glory, does not seem to have flagged in the least. But God, being God, may well have intentions and desires for law that would take us all quite by surprise. Or he may, surprisingly, have no particular desires for law at all. This is why each Christian must honestly and carefully investigate God's will for the Christian's political involvement. Whether or not the committed Christian belongs to any active or powerful Christian political organization, he must ultimately decide for himself whether God wants him to participate in politics, and if so, how.

These questions of "whether" and "how" are theological questions that deserve much more thought than many Christians, including evangelicals, have given them to this point. Even among those Christian leaders who have abandoned politics, we do not find much discussion of these two questions, particularly the second. Their abandonment of politics does not seem to stem so much from a revised understanding of God's will for governments as from a revised understanding of what might be called the "practicalities" of political involvement: that it is hard, slow work; that it often seems to require compromise of core convictions; that it sometimes sullies those whom it rewards with electoral success. So it should come as little surprise if, even after the implosion of groups like Moral Majority and the disarray of groups like Christian Coalition, many evangelicals (Left and Right) retain theological commitments to use the machinery of government to require obedience to divine commands of various sorts. The Christian Right would legally require obedience to commands like sobriety and sexual purity, while the Christian Left would legally require obedience to commands like charity and compassion; but in the end, both views are premised on the same sort of theology, a theology which assumes that God wants us to make laws forcing people to obey his divine commands. What I hope this book demonstrates is an alternative to that sort of theology.

But however we ultimately resolve these issues, we must remember our priorities: to seek first the kingdom of God and his righteousness. And we must keep in mind that the key to righteousness before God is not outward actions, but a heart that willingly accepts Jesus Christ. John Locke, a man so often ahead of his time, recognized this elemental truth long ago when he wrote:

> True and saving religion consists in the inward persuasion of the mind, without which nothing can be acceptable to God. And such is the nature of the understanding, that it cannot be compelled to the belief of any thing by outward force. . . . I may grow rich by an art that I take not delight in; I may be cured of some disease by remedies that I have not faith in; but I cannot be saved by a religion that I distrust, and by a worship that I abhor.[3]

These words are as true today as ever. And Christians who would use the law to condemn sin, or to promote righteousness, would do well to dwell on them. Whatever else laws may accomplish, they stand little chance of making men moral. The human heart cannot be forced to love. The Bible makes this much, at least, abundantly clear. And it is just as clear that coercing the hearts of others is no part of a Christian's business. Once again, Locke has it exactly right:

> The Gospel frequently declares, that the true disciples of Christ must suffer persecution; but that the church of Christ should persecute others, and force others by fire and sword to embrace her faith and doctrine, I could never yet find in any of the books of the New Testament.[4]

We evangelicals, who take the biblical text so seriously, should have been among the first to take these lessons to heart. But we have perhaps been slow to learn. We are indeed much like Peter. We are people of action, impetuous, zealous for God, sacrificial, anxious to make a difference in the world. But we are often arrogant and thoughtless as well. Too often, like Peter, we try to rebuke Jesus, to set his worldly agenda for him. Gently he reminds us: "You are a stumbling block to me; for you are setting your mind not on divine things but on human things" (Matt. 16:23).

By God's grace, Peter learned from his mistakes. In John 21 and Acts 2, we are told that Jesus forgave and restored Peter, and the Holy Spirit inspired him to be a great leader among the early Christians, spreading the truth about Jesus to the ends of the earth. Peter learned to stop swinging his sword for Jesus and start living his life for Jesus. And when Peter stopped playing defense and started playing offense—when he stopped trying to defend Jesus from the power of the world and began to realize that Jesus had already overcome the world—Jesus used Peter to turn the world upside down. My prayer for evangelicals, and for all Christians, is that we will awaken to Christ's transformative power, his power to remake the world around us from the inside out. If Peter could wake up, so can we.

NOTES

1. Stephen L. Carter, *God's Name in Vain: The Wrongs and Rights of Religion in Politics* (New York: Basic Books, 2000).
2. Roger Williams, *Mr. Cotton's Letter Lately Printed, Examined and Answered* (1644), in Perry Miller, *Roger Williams: His Contribution to the American Tradition* (Indianapolis: Bobbs-Merrill, 1953), 98.
3. John Locke, *A Letter Concerning Toleration*, Great Books in Philosophy Series (Amherst, N.Y.: Prometheus Books, 1990), 20, 41.
4. Locke, *Toleration*, 25.

Index